Niamh O'Connor is one of Ireland's best-known true crime authors. A crime reporter with the *Sunday World*, she has interviewed infamous murderers, gone undercover to expose an international prostitution ring and infiltrated a gang running a mortgage racket swindling the banks out of multi-millions, which led to intervention by the Criminal Assets Bureau.

Her first crime novel will be published by Transworld Ireland next year.

BLOOD TIES

The Real Stories behind Ireland's
Most Notorious Murders

Niamh O'Connor

TRANSWORLD IRELAND

Transworld Ireland
TRANSWORLD IRELAND
an imprint of The Random House Group Limited
20 Vauxhall Bridge Road, London SW1V 2SA
www.rbooks.co.uk

First published in 2009 by Transworld Ireland,
a division of Transworld Publishers Ltd.

A CIP catalogue record for this book
is available from the British Library.

ISBN 9781848270862

Addresses for Random House Group Ltd companies outside the UK
can be found at: www.randomhouse.co.uk
The Random House Group Ltd Reg. No. 954009

The Random House Group Limited supports The Forest Stewardship
Council (FSC), the leading international forest-certification organization.
All our titles that are printed on Greenpeace-approved
FSC-certified paper carry the FSC logo.
Our paper procurement policy can be found at
www.rbooks.co.uk/environment

Typeset in 11/14pt Sabon by
Falcon Oast Graphic Art Ltd.
Printed and bound in Great Britain by
CPI Cox & Wyman, Reading, RG1 8EX

2 4 6 8 10 9 7 5 3 1

For Brian and the boys
and mam and dad

Contents

Blood Sisters: The Story of Charlotte and Linda Mulhall and Ireland's Most Brutal Killing

Wife Killer: The Murder of Rachel O'Reilly

Lyin' Eyes: Sharon Collins and the Hitman-for-Hire Murder Plot

When the torso of a man turned up in the Royal Canal in 2005, I found it hard to believe that the victim had been slaughtered in a satanic murder ritual, as first suspected.

But even in gangland, where life is very cheap, the victims executed are rarely dismembered.

The truth, when it emerged that a mother and her two daughters – Kathleen, Charlotte and Linda Mulhall – were behind the crime, seemed the most unlikely scenario of all. The story told by the women was that the grisly events were the culmination of a drink- and drug-fuelled domestic incident. But it was the plot to cover up the crime that made this case extraordinary, and the fact that not one of the three women present on that gruesome night shouted, 'Stop!'

Niamh O'Connor
August 2009

Prologue

Dun Laoghaire, Dublin – Saturday, 4 September 1999

Seventeen-year-old Raonaid Murray had to squint in the dark but was pretty sure the street was empty. It was hard to tell as it was gone midnight, and pitch black between the street lamps. It was a good thing she was nearly home. The walk from Scott's Pub in Dun Laoghaire where she'd been drinking with friends to her home in Glenageary's Silchester Park took only fifteen minutes, and she had almost reached the lane linking it to Silchester Crescent. Only five hundred yards to go.

Platform ankle boots made it difficult to speed up, and with a handbag criss-crossed over her chest, Sally West boutique bag in one hand and black coat slung over her arm, she was laden down. She was heading home to offload her stuff so she could go on to the Paparazzi nightclub with her friends. Raonaid also wanted to change her clothes and to organize money. She'd promised the others she'd meet up with them later. Now that the Leaving Cert results were finally out, they were all celebrating the end of their school years. In a matter of weeks it would be full-on study for Raonaid, cramming a two-year course into one. She was repeating in the Institute of Education on Leeson Street to get the points she needed. For now she was enjoying the freedom of letting loose for a bit.

She knew loads of people in the same boat, and they knew her. Raonaid had always stood out from the crowd. A nose stud gave her individuality among her peers; and in a top fee-paying girls' school like St Joseph's of Cluny, Killiney, popularity was everything. She was also a Goth, and her heavy black eyeliner, pale make-up and dark clothes always made an impression because they were such a contrast to her delicate blue eyes and long silky blonde hair.

The throughway was dark and narrow but she knew it like the back of her hand. She'd grown up here, played here, hung around with her friends here. Her sister, Sarah, was due to walk the same way home any minute now.

A sudden, agonizing pain brought her to the ground and left her paralysed with fear.

Someone was hovering over her with a knife. She curled to try to protect herself as they lunged three more times, then ran off. Terrified, she began to drag herself as far as she could – if she could just get home, she was so close . . .

Half an hour later, it was Sarah who found her. But it was too late. Raonaid was gone.

Six years passed before a man who was fixated with knives, who liked to hurt women and who was in Dun Laoghaire on the night Raonaid died emerged as a major suspect for her killing. He was a Kenyan immigrant and he too met a brutal end, also stabbed to death. His name was Farah Noor . . .

1

Murder

Farah Noor staggered over to the blood-red settee. The Kenyan had fine, wide-eyed features but years of booze-fuelled brawling had given him a down-and-out, smashed-up look. His ageing lover's blonde daughter sidled away to the far end of the couch, folding her arms across her chest. Linda Mulhall was stoned but monitoring Farah out of the side of her eye. He was the last person on the planet she wanted to be left in a room on her own with. She was only here in the squalid flat he shared with her mother, Kathleen, to celebrate her sister Charlie's twenty-second birthday.

The rapper Sean Paul was blaring so loud from the stereo, the sitting room-cum-kitchenette was practically throbbing. But even with all the Ecstasy and vodka inside her, Linda couldn't get in the party mood. Not with him around. He was wrecking her buzz. She hated him. The only reason she'd the music blasting was to drown out the sound of his voice. She trained her glassy, heavily eye-lined eyes on the door, willing Charlie and Kathleen to hurry back from the other room where they were

7

supposed to be spiking Farah's drink with a crushed E tab to calm him down. She couldn't bear to be alone with her ma's 38-year-old toy boy much longer. He was giving her the creeps.

Suddenly Farah was shunting up alongside her and running a clammy hand up her back. Linda's pencil-thin eyebrows soared up her forehead. 'Farah, get your hands off me,' she warned, elbowing him in the ribs. She strained away, pulling a face of disgust. He'd been drinking for twelve hours solid and his white, long-sleeved Ireland away jersey stank of perspiration.

She did her best to ignore him so he wouldn't see he'd unnerved her and start getting off on it. He was a sadist when he was drunk. She tapped her tender top lip to check if the angry swelling from a new piercing had gone down. The one above her left nostril had never given her any trouble.

But Farah was not taking no for an answer. He was rubbing her back again, this time pressing his face into her GHD-straightened hair and slurring into her ear, 'We two are creatures of the night.'

She shuddered. Everything he said was so weird. The smell of his breath was turning her stomach and she tried to shrug, then push him off. He just pawed her more. She bolted up but he reefed her back down, his wiry strength taking her by surprise – he was only five foot six.

Farah tightened his grip. 'You're the image of your mother,' he whispered in a dirty tone.

Linda let out a roar, 'Charlie!' Nothing. Maybe her sister couldn't hear her over the din. 'Ma!' Louder but still no sign. It was only a two-roomed flat. Where were they? She squirmed and struggled. What if they'd gone to the chipper? They'd been talking about it earlier. They hadn't left her alone with Farah, had they?

It was only a week since he'd hammered Kathleen for refusing to continue to collect his Social Welfare because he was working. He'd wrecked the flat, then battered her, waving one of his knives in her face.

'You fucking cunt,' Farah had raged, straddling the 49-year-old on the floor and trying to smother her with a pillow. 'Kathy, I am going to chop you up in little pieces, put you in the fridge and eat you piece by piece. No one will ever find you because I will say you fucked off.'

Kathleen managed to beat her way free and dial 999. Farah taunted her about two of her sons, both in prison.

Later, Kathleen maintained that she'd be dead before the year was out if she got back with Farah. Then she got back with him. But Linda was in no position to judge her for staying with a violent man, even a killer . . .

Linda was starting to freak out now. She'd suffered panic attacks since she was a kid and she was getting the same claustrophobic feeling that the walls were closing in. If Charlie or her ma didn't come soon, Farah was going to hurt her really badly. He was going to rape her.

She hadn't thought it was possible to hate him any more than she already did. He was the reason her parents' twenty-nine-year marriage had broken up. Because of him her father, John, had been kicked out of the family home in Kilclare Gardens in Tallaght, moving from pillar to post for the best part of a year. John had moved into Linda's home in Bawnlea Green for a month. When Farah moved into the Mulhalls's house, the family had split in two, with Linda's brothers, James, John and Andrew, and sister Marie siding with their father. Linda would have done the same if it wasn't for Charlie, who was the only one to stand by Kathleen when the others eventually managed to force her out of the house.

But Linda didn't want to fall out with her younger sister. Charlie was eight years Linda's junior but more like her big sister. If Linda needed a few quid, Charlie would do whatever she had to in order to get it. And with four kids and a drink and drug problem, Linda always needed money.

She hollered again at the top of her lungs. She was here only because Charlie had had a crap twenty-first. By today's standards it had been a dream. Farah and Kathleen had spent today fighting non-stop after they'd all met up in town and hung around the Liffey's Boardwalk, taking Ecstasy and drinking vodka and Coke. He'd even scared the shite out of some poor Chinese kid, chasing him down O'Connell Street, convinced he was his son. The young fella was only about five. Kathleen and Charlie knew all this. So why weren't they responding to Linda's screams?

Linda's emotions shifted gear again, this time to hysteria. She was already on blood pressure tablets. If she ended up in hospital, her father would find out she'd spent the day with her mother and Farah, and there'd be hell to pay. What if he kicked her out over it?

John had let her move back into the family home with

her four children after her last relationship broke up. Now there were nine of them living in the cramped three-bed semi; they'd even had to turn a shed out the back into her bedroom.

When Linda's hard-faced mother suddenly appeared in the doorway, she almost cried with joy. The sharp-nosed brunette was dressed much younger than her years to try to keep her lover interested. In Farah's country, women were covered up. Kathleen used the burka he'd given her as a tablecloth.

Kathleen shot a thin-mouthed look at Linda as she sized up the situation – her young lover wrapped around her daughter.

Linda's fear turned to anger and it was directed at her mother for putting her in this situation in the first place. 'What's he saying about "creatures of the night", Ma?' she challenged.

Kathleen flared up, turning on Farah. 'What do you mean? What are you saying to Linda?' she bawled. 'What do you mean about "creatures of the night"?'

Charlie appeared behind her mother. Her expression was blank but her Cleopatra eyes gave her an evil look. 'What the fuck are you saying to Linda, Farah?' she asked.

Linda finally managed to scramble to her feet but Farah locked his hands on her waist and kept saying her name.

'Linda, Linda, Linda,' he taunted. He was mauling her. 'You are so like your mammy. You are so like your mammy.'

Linda tried to drag herself free, getting as far as the kitchen end of the kitchen-cum-sitting room.

Charlie was primed and started to whack Farah. 'What the fuck are you doing? Get your hands off her. She's nothing like me ma.'

Linda started crying. Black mascara streaked down her face, leaving tracks in her heavy foundation. She screamed at Kathleen, 'He would sleep with your daughter just as soon as he would look at you.'

Charlie continued to try to pull him off Linda. 'Get your fucking hands off her now.'

Farah finally let go, held his hands up in surrender, then used the element of surprise to grab Kathleen instead. He shoved her towards the adjoining bedroom. Looking back at the sisters, he grinned and drew his index finger across his throat in a slitting motion.

Kathleen became inconsolable. She fell on to her knees as he kicked and punched and dragged her. He was yanking her hair so hard, she thought he was going to scalp her. She suffered from chronic airways disease and was wheezing badly. She needed her inhalers. She locked eyes on Charlie. 'Help!'

But even burly Charlotte couldn't stop him. Farah was crazed and battering Kathleen. Charlie tried to get between him and her mother and sustain blows herself. But Farah was a seasoned street fighter and she was no match for him. Nothing she did could stop him.

'Kill him!' Kathleen screeched. 'Just kill him for me! Kill him!'

Linda shot a look at her sister.

From the kitchen bench Charlie grabbed an orange-handled Stanley knife that a carpet fitter had left behind.

Flicking the button, she strode up behind Farah. She grabbed his head by the hair with one hand, reached across the front of his neck with the other and sliced.

Linda grew silent.

Kathleen screamed, 'Get him away from me.'

Farah stumbled through the bedroom doorway, clutching his oozing neck. The room was eight foot long and crammed with a small double bed, bunk beds, a dresser and wardrobe. Farah fell and whacked his head off the bunks.

He managed to pull himself back to his feet. He stared at the amount of blood in terror and called out, 'Katie, Katie.'

She was frozen to the spot.

Charlie paced in after him and slashed at his throat again.

Farah fell to his knees, blood pumping from his severed artery like a gushing tap. His arms started flailing.

'He's still alive, Linda, he's still alive,' Charlie warned, lunging with the blade.

Linda darted into the kitchen and pulled a hammer from a drawer. She followed her sister into the bedroom and as he struggled to get back up, she raised her hand and brought the weapon down on the top of his head with full force. She struck repeatedly as Charlie stabbed.

Linda pounded at his head; Charlie jabbed at every inch of his chest and, when he spun, at his back. They stopped out of exhaustion, gasping for breath like a pair of sprinters.

Farah was lying flat on his back in front of them, his

head under the bunk bed where he'd tried to scramble for shelter.

'He's dead,' Charlie said. They stood frozen to the spot for about a quarter of an hour before returning to the sitting room where Kathleen was sitting rigidly on the couch, staring straight ahead.

'Get him out!' Kathleen commanded.

2

Web of Deceit

Kenya – 1987

Downtown Mombasa is a heady mix of haggling markets and the modern, gridlocked roads associated with a busy port. On his wedding day in 1987, the young fisherman Sheilila Said Salim must have been feeling the divide between the old and new worlds more keenly than ever. He was nineteen years old and the only women he'd encountered up to now were dressed in head-to-foot black *buibuis*.

As a strict Muslim, Sheilila would have been expected to respond to the wailing cry of the muezzin – the official of a mosque who calls the faithful to prayer. Five times a day he would have knelt on his prayer mat facing Mecca, the holiest city of Islam where the prophet Mohammed was born. He would have prostrated himself and chanted from the Koran, reciting its sacred principles.

As he made his way down the palm-lined streets, he must have been feeling the heat as the prospect of even more discipline and restrictions on his life edged closer. The Manchester United-mad teenager was used to fishing in the Indian Ocean and most comfortable in a sarong.

But on this day, he would have dressed in his best suit to impress his in-laws, sending his body temperature up even higher. His entire life probably panned out in front of him: toiling day in, day out to support his new family. Perhaps his mouth grew dry. The stifling humidity of the city parches throats at the best of times. Did the pressure of duty colliding with his secret dream of building a life abroad make Sheilila begin to plot his escape?

His elders would have slapped him on the back and warned, '*Mke ni nguo, mgomba kupalilia*': a wife means clothes like a banana plant means weeding. Sheilila must have felt suddenly very far away from the only thing he wanted in life – to move to Western Europe, the land of promise. He'd watched the easy cash squandered by tourists. They arrived in Kenya in droves every year on safari, to visit the ancient Maasai Mara tribe and experience the wildebeest migration at a crocodile-infested crossing point of the swollen Mara river. Perhaps he was lured by the sight of the travellers' long, loose hair, considered extraordinarily provocative in Islamic regions and doubly so if blonde. Was he lured by the idea of countries where women travelled without male escorts, made eye contact with men and even shook their hands?

His betrothed was Husna Mohamed Said, a seventeen-year-old virgin. Her presence would not have been required when the contract of marriage was agreed between her father and her new husband's family. A dowry, usually of cattle, would have been paid to her people. The younger the bride, the more cattle. Her virginity would have been guaranteed. The ritual of female circumcision or genital mutilation is still a rite of passage for an estimated 60 per cent of Kenyan girls.

Only after the wedding would Husna have been shown in public. Sometimes this involves a party and the bride is allowed to celebrate with her female friends by dancing and removing her black veil – but no men would have been allowed to attend. She would have been forgiven for acting like a star in one of the Bollywood movies so popular with young women in Mombasa. It softened the blow of the often grim reality of an arranged marriage.

The most Husna could have hoped for was that Sheilila would treat her with respect and provide for her and any children. Everything, right down to her clothing – the traditional dazzling kanga – would be chosen for her by him. The bright cotton dress would even contain his own private message to her, something like '*Mahaba ni haba, akili ni mali*': love counts for little, intelligence is wealth. If she was unlucky enough to end up with a cruel husband, sexual violation would occur on a daily basis. On her wedding day, Husna could have had no idea that anything worse than this lay ahead.

Three years and two children later, Sheilila had become convinced he was the one enslaved and was secretly organizing his escape. Perhaps it was the draw of women of loose morals. Maybe it was the idea of being closer to one of the greatest football teams in the world. One thing is certain. Sheilila knew if he stayed in Mombasa, on an island connected to the Kenyan mainland by two causeways and a bridge, the chances were he would live and die a fisherman. He believed his only chance of fulfilling his potential was if he made it to Ireland, which had lax immigration laws at that time.

When his older brother, Mohemedi Abuu, left for Toronto in 1991, Sheilila began to make similar arrangements for himself. In 1993, he paid €1,600 to a human trafficker to be smuggled out of Africa, telling Husna, who was pregnant with their third child, that once established he would send for her and the children. In reality, he was leaving her for good.

Three years later, he arrived in Dublin airport without any papers or documentation. It was 30 December 1996. He told gardaí attached to the National Immigration Bureau that his name was Farah Swaleh Noor and that he was fleeing war-torn Somalia. He also claimed he was twenty-nine, two years younger than his actual birth date of 1965.

What must Dublin have seemed like seen through his eyes? Cold? Wet? Grimy? A million miles from the community-based tropical paradise he had left behind?

Maybe it was because of his father's Somali roots that he had always felt like an outsider in Kenya, whose people consider themselves superior to the neighbouring race. Farah's facial features were distinctively Somalian; perhaps he was always made to feel different in Kenya, the country of his birth. Husna would later admit he had very few friends there. But the only thing going through his mind as he queued in St Stephen's Green at the asylum section of the Immigration and Citizenship Division of the

Department of Justice two weeks later was that he wanted to stay.

He lied through his teeth on the official forms, claiming to have been born on 2 July 1967 in Mogadishu, Somalia, and to be of the Bajun tribe. He had no passport or ID because 'I had no time to get these documents before I had to flee from Somalia.' He claimed to have spent the preceding five years in a refugee camp in Kenya, 'the Wayoni camp in the Magonogo region of Kenya. There was Bajun refugees mainly staying at this camp. Bad conditions, no water, nowhere to sleep.' He added: 'Kenya is not a good country for a refugee. No food in camp. Giriyama people do not like Somali people. Kenyan police do not like Somali people.'

In his appeal for asylum, he wrote:

I went to my family house. The door was open, when go inside nobody was in. The only thing I saw was the dead body of my wife, she was having a bullet in her chest. Then I start panic and I was afraid then I didn't know what to do because the war was spread all over the country. Then I decided to take some few stuff. I start to walk towards Port Mogadishu when I arrive there I got a small boat to go back to Kismayo. When I reached Kismayo I saw a lot of people which they were leaving the country with a big boat. I rush there and I ask where's the boat going. One of them tell me is going to Kenya. We spend three days to Mombasa, Kenya. We registered with UNHCR then they take us to the camp. I stay in the camp for five years. We face many problems at the camp. There were no doctors, no food, no water and overcrowding. There were many refugees from my country and also there were Kenyan people. They don't like Somalia people to be in their country. Sometimes to come to camp night time and start to attack us and sometimes kill some refugees so I was afraid with that, also I was lucky to find agent.

Then the agent ask me if I have 2,000 US dollars he can arrange me a trip to go abroad, then I told him I don't have that amount but I have 1,600 US dollars. Then the agent agree with me. I was very happy to leave the camp it was a terrible life at the camp. Before the war I was having a good life but the war affect me very much. It may be you refuse my application, I don't know what to do because the war destroy my house and I don't know where's my family are they live or dead. No government to protect me. Even if it is reach 20 years Somalia it will be never like before. The war affect my country as well. No hospital, no water, no animal, no light, no road and no food. So I will be very happy if you allow me to stay in this country.

It would be over two years before his appeal was processed. In that time the man born Sheilila Said Salim would move from emergency hostels to B&Bs and poky flats in North Strand Road, North Circular Road and in the Rosepark Hotel in Dun Laoghaire.

But if he was happy now that he was on the road to achieving his ambition, he was not showing it. He was a fish out of water and he coped by drinking his way into oblivion. Farah became a regular in dingy pubs and amusement arcades around the hardest areas of Dublin's city centre and also in Dun Laoghaire. He was unmistakable, usually dressed in a Man United tracksuit, wearing a Man United sovereign ring on his middle finger, and known for his propensity for drunken violence. His benders lasted days on end and brought him to the attention of gardaí for public order offences. He also began preying on the only women willing to put up with his antiquated and sexist views – society's most vulnerable.

In August 1997, he seduced a sixteen-year-old mentally disabled Chinese girl who was playing pool in Dr Quirkey's amusement arcade on O'Connell Street. He told 'Mae' (not her real name) that he wanted her to have his babies. It would be a recurring chat-up line. But when she found out she was pregnant a month later, he informed her he wanted nothing to do with her. Her son is the half-Chinese boy Farah thought he saw and accosted on O'Connell Street on the day he died.

Mae told gardaí: 'Farah lived by himself in the flat down the road. When [child] was born Farah never saw him. I think he was six years old when Farah first saw him. Farah called to the house to see him. I don't know if he saw Farah on 20 March 2005. He didn't tell me that he saw him. He would know what Farah looks like and he knows that Farah is his dad.

'When I first met Farah we used to play pool together. Sometimes Farah would phone me to meet with him. I didn't have a phone number for him. He would phone me 'cos he had my number. The last time I saw him before

March 2005 was last year. I was walking near Jurys on Parnell Street when I heard someone call me and when I looked I see Farah. He stopped but he told me he goes to work. He told me he stayed in a hotel and that's where he lived. He didn't tell me the name of the hotel.'

The next person to feel the full force of his charms was also more girl than woman. In April 1998, Farah hit on a third-year secondary school student who was celebrating her sixteenth birthday. 'Sue' (not her real name) was walking through town when he approached and chatted her up. He told her he was twenty, even though he was actually thirty-three. They started going out and she was pregnant less than three months later. Their son was born in March 1999.

Farah moved in with her family, and back in the safety of the family unit he finally seemed to be getting his life together. Now that he had a structure and a role and peers in his new life, he grew disciplined and respectful. He went fishing and hiking with Sue's father. It seemed like he had adjusted to his new environment. But when the baby was about three months old, in July 1999, he started drinking heavily again and this time his personality plunged to new levels of depravity. If Sue would not defer to him as Husna once had, he was going to make her. He might have traded his African world for an Irish one, but he was not going to surrender what he saw as his cultural right to male superiority. Sue may have been living in south Dublin but she was about to learn exactly what it meant to be a Muslim wife in Mombasa, one married to a tyrant.

3

An Appetite for Violence

When Farah and Sue got a home from South Dublin County Council, it should have been an opportunity to start their lives together afresh. Sue was still only eighteen, with her whole life in front of her, and on 30 July 1999 Farah was granted official refugee status. He was now entitled to every benefit the Irish state had to offer and had the opportunity to work. He registered with Adecco Recruitment Agency in Tallaght.

But his drinking was dangerously out of control. He was getting through three to four bottles of vodka a day. And his paranoia levels were growing; he had taken to carrying a dagger and a Swiss Army knife everywhere.

Sue had no idea just how off the wall Farah's behaviour actually was. In fact, he was displaying all the characteristics of a paranoid schizophrenic – conducting two-way conversations with himself in the mirror, pretending to be different people. When he wanted to relieve stress and tension, he'd burn himself with cigarettes. His arms were covered in scars from slashes he made if someone he knew died.

A good day for Sue was one which he spent sleeping off the drink. During bad episodes, Farah would go ballistic and smash the house up, destroying all the furniture and possessions in a psychotic fit of rage. He controlled every aspect of her life. She wasn't allowed to go to the shop without asking first. Farah was monitoring her phone calls and texts and keeping her locked in the house. She was still so young and inexperienced that she didn't know what to do. But worse was yet to come.

After a night out socializing, Farah became convinced that one of Sue's friends was a lesbian and had been making a pass at her. During a stand-up screaming match in the pub, he called the mother of his child vile names in front of everyone. She didn't go home with him that night, buoyed up by the false courage given to her by her pals. But when she went home the following day Farah was waiting for her in the hall and he battered her.

As the beatings became more and more frequent, they began leading to terrifying rape ordeals. Farah stripped her, tied her up, and took sick and degrading photographs of her in sexual positions. How much their son witnessed or absorbed is unknown.

On two of her braver days when she left him, Sue complained to gardaí at Tallaght Garda station, revealing he'd threatened 'he'd cut me up like a chicken'. She detailed how he was also mentally torturing her by bragging how he'd worked as a butcher in England. He was obsessed with knives, she said. The terrified teenager would steal and dump them when he lay in one of his drunken stupors, absolutely convinced he was going to carry out his promise to kill her.

Then, in 2001, 'Melissa' began lodging with Farah and

Sue and their now two-year-old son. At first, the new housemate was just shocked by what she witnessed – Sue directly under Farah's control at all times. She thought Sue was vulnerable and naïve in the extreme to put up with it. Sue couldn't do anything without Farah's permission and he was constantly checking on her.

Melissa's shock soon changed to horror when she witnessed the beatings. Sue would lie curled up on the ground to protect herself while Farah kicked her, sometimes even while she clutched the baby.

'He had no scruples whatsoever,' Melissa later said. 'He would do this in front of everyone, both in public and back at the house. The main motivation was jealousy and possessiveness . . . There was never any reason for him to be this way but he would never believe her. It was like he was looking for an excuse to beat her.' He was an 'unstable control freak', she said.

It was a relief for Sue to have someone her own age whom she could confide in; who could reassure her that she was not to blame for Farah's psychotic behaviour. When Farah went to work with Sydney Cooper on the Ballymount Road and later with DFDS Transport Ltd in Naas, Sue would pour her heart out, crying inconsolably. She even showed Melissa the negatives of the sexually explicit photographs of her tied up and blindfolded, revealing how she had been beaten in front of their child for trying to destroy them.

With every boost of confidence Melissa gave Sue, more awful stories poured out. A chance newspaper article on the unsolved Raonaid Murray murder case triggered

Melissa's own story of personal grief. They had been friends and in the same class all the way through secondary school from 1993.

Raonaid had been murdered in cold blood as she made her way home from the pub just after midnight in September 1999, stabbed four times in a laneway off Silchester Crescent. Melissa was still getting over the tragedy. She and Raonaid had socialized together outside school and had met in Scruples and had a few drinks together on the Saturday just before the murder.

Sue listened open-mouthed to Melissa's story. She didn't know Raonaid but she knew all about the murder because she'd been in Dun Laoghaire herself that night – with Farah. On Friday, 3 September 1999, Sue and a group of her friends had spent the afternoon drinking cans on Sandycove beach with Farah. He was living in Dun Laoghaire at the time, in the Rosepark Hotel.

At 5pm that night, she, Farah and a friend headed back to the hotel with their five-month-old son. Sue went into the communal bathroom to have a shower. Farah followed and wanted sex. Sue refused; her friend was with their baby in a room opposite and the bathroom was shared with other residents. Farah became violent and threw her into the bath and tried to force himself on top of her. She screamed and he punched her in the face and body, calling her a 'slut'. She managed to get out of the bath and grab her clothes and make it to the bedroom.

Her friend was waiting at the door with the baby and helped a hysterical Sue to flee the hotel and jump on a 46A bus that was passing. Farah chased the bus shouting,

'Sorry!' Sue travelled into the city centre with the baby and caught a bus back to her parents' home, arriving there before 9pm.

Farah phoned that night, very drunk. He apologized and said it would never happen again. He told her he was drinking in Dun Laoghaire town but she told him it was over and hung up.

She didn't talk to him again for a few days, but when she did meet up with him he was in good form. He told her he'd been questioned about Raonaid's murder and boasted with a big grin that he was a suspect. He said he'd spent the night drinking in a pub in the middle of Dun Laoghaire with two men. He also said he'd lost his dagger.

Melissa moved out only three weeks after moving in and appealed to Sue to do the same. But the teenager was too frightened, worried she had nowhere to go and that he'd find her and hurt her or their child.

Two weeks after being left alone again and at Farah's mercy, Sue made a hysterical call to Melissa in the middle of the night, begging for help. Melissa went to the house with a man and discovered it had been smashed up. Sue was on her hands and knees cleaning broken mirrors and glasses from the living-room floor. The Kenyan was in a state of high agitation and demanding more drink. When he calmed down he laughed and joked as if nothing had happened. He collapsed in a drunken stupor but Sue was too terrified to leave him, fearing even worse repercussions.

Melissa rang Sue's parents the next day and warned them that their daughter would be killed if they didn't get her away from the domineering African. Her father collected her and she never went back. That was in February 2001. Sue took out a barring order and won full custody of their child in April 2001, although Farah still had visiting rights.

For the next nine months, he continued to make her life a living hell. In May 2001, Sue and Melissa were followed to a southside pub by Farah. He arrived and started shouting and smashing glasses. He screamed at Melissa that she'd split up his family and when she tried to ring her boyfriend he pushed his face into hers to stop her. The girls ran but he followed, threatening to kill them. Melissa's father happened to be in the pub and he called Farah to one side. He warned him to leave them alone and Farah appeared to listen to the man and submitted, apologizing profusely.

He continued to stalk Sue, following her on the bus and making abusive calls, turning up outside her parents' house and threatening to kill her. He also threatened to kill Melissa in hate-filled phone calls. He followed the girls into Dame Street, where they were meeting a South African male friend. When the man saw Farah he confronted and punched him. A brawl ensued. Both men were arrested.

During an incident in the Penny Black pub in Tallaght, Farah shouted at Melissa that she was responsible for her friend's murder in Dun Laoghaire.

Nothing, it seemed, could get Farah out of his ex-girlfriend's life and she was terrified of what would happen to their son. Farah still saw him every second

Sunday. Cigarette burns had starting appearing on the two-and-a-half-year-old's body. In the end, the person who finally got Farah out of their lives was a Tallaght woman old enough to be Sue's mother. Farah had finally met his match – and her name was Kathleen Mulhall.

4

Alone Again

Kathleen Mulhall sat stony-faced with the stereo off and the TV on in the sitting room of her one-bedroomed flat. With her make-up on, she had the stern look of an ageing prima ballerina but with none of the grace and a lot more shook. Her partner of more than three years lay dead on the adjoining bedroom floor, murdered by her own daughters. But she was staying put. Linda and Charlie could sort it out without her. It was of their own doing. She would have no hand, act or part in it. Thanks to them, she was on her own again.

'How are we going to get him out, Ma?' Charlie interrupted. She was the most considerate of Kathleen's children.

It didn't matter any more. Kathleen was finished with all of them. 'Cut him up,' she replied, still staring at the telly.

Her mood had flicked like a switch since the murder. Her blood started to boil. Charlie and Linda were laughing and skitting, helping themselves to more of her drink and chain-smoking her cigarettes. They were blaming Farah for what had happened. He was a psychopath; a monster; they had to do it, to save her. As far as Kathleen was concerned, he had treated her better than her husband, John, and made her feel a million dollars. In her mind, John was every bit as much to blame for what had gone on tonight as he was for everything else that had gone wrong for her. She'd given him the best years of her life and six children. What had she got back for her trouble?

Her eldest daughter, Linda, was seriously troubled because of what her father had done to her in the past – a drug addict, an alcoholic, a bulimic who regularly self-harmed and now, to top it off, a killer. Kathleen's eldest and favourite son, James, was serving three years in prison for dangerous driving causing death, and had been in trouble all his life, with several convictions for assault causing harm. Another son, John, was also in prison, for an incident involving a stolen car. He was only twenty-eight but had notched up twenty previous convictions and a bad heroin habit. And her 22-year-old daughter, Charlie, was due up in court for soliciting on Lad Lane and had just ripped Farah's throat open from ear to ear as if she was slicing bread.

Kathleen's other two children, 21-year-old Marie and 17-year-old Andrew, were dead to her, having already cut her out of their lives completely.

Bar Charlie, not one of them had any idea how hard her life had been rearing kids in Tallaght in the eighties, in the pre-Square days when the suburb had no amenities and it fell to her to try to stretch John's paltry wages from fitting windows between all of them. As far as she was concerned, her relationship with him was already dead and buried when she met Farah in Cocos nightclub in Tallaght in the summer of 2001. She would never forgive John for having an affair with her sister.

When Farah focused his attentions on her in the club and chatted her up, he made her feel like the only woman in the world. It was one of the best nights of her life. She fell for him in a big way. The idea that a man eleven years younger wanted to pull her gave her confidence a real boost for the first time in years. He made her feel young again.

Her daughter Marie, a mechanic, already knew Farah and introduced them. Farah was a friend of Marie's boyfriend, Robert. Linda was going out with Robert's brother, Trevor, at the time. Now Kathleen hoped she and her daughters were all going to be part of the same social circle and she could redeem some of her lost years by enjoying herself. But Marie was having none of it and moved out in protest to look after her father. She was closest to him. And Linda had split up with Trevor. Nothing had gone according to Kathleen's plan.

At first she did manage to force John out of the family home, moving Farah into his bed. As far as she was concerned, John deserved no better after the life he had given her. But it seemed everyone, including her neighbours, begrudged her any last chance of happiness. Her son John had a fist-fight with Farah after a row over heroin, and Farah jumped out a window to escape. In the end, the constant warring and her own family's harassment forced them on after less than a year. She rued that move now. She should have dug her heels in and stayed put. It was a modest end-of-terrace house in a tough council estate plagued with social problems. Few of the neighbours had doorbells. Most had vicious dogs behind their garden gates. But it was complete luxury in comparison to any of the ten-odd addresses she'd had in the last three and a half years.

Kathleen was the first to admit she and Farah had had their problems. But so what if Farah had been possessive and locked her up so she wouldn't talk to other men? After years of feeling worthless and unwanted, it was a welcome change. True, he had hit her but what was new there? She'd taken a barring order out against John when they'd split. And yes, Farah put her down and called her 'the Boss', told his friends she was 'on her last legs' and flirted with other women. But John hadn't been faithful to her either. He'd almost left her after one affair in the nineties.

The way she saw it, the relationship was doomed the minute John forced her out of her home and into grimy flats, B&Bs and Social Welfare emergency accommodation.

Their first move was to Cork in the summer of 2002. Farah had lived there before and wanted to go back. His English wasn't great and he didn't understand the accent but he had African friends there who spoke Swahili. They'd nicknamed him 'America' after hearing him on the phone to his wife, Husna, in Mombasa.

'I'm in America,' Farah had lied, adding, 'I'm not coming home.'

At first it looked like they might have some chance. He

had got a job on the Clarion Hotel building site and was signing on. He would cycle to work on his black mountain bike from their flat on the Lower Glanmire Road. At night they'd go drinking and to regular parties held by Farah's friends.

Charlie and Linda had moved down too. Charlie was going out with another African man and Linda was living with her new boyfriend, Wayne Kinsella. They would meet a few nights a week, usually in McCurtain Street.

But before long, the constant pressure of rent arrears and problems with landlords and neighbouring tenants meant Kathleen and Farah were permanently on the move. Farah drank more than ever, and took out his anger on her. She'd suffered broken ribs, fractured hands, head injuries, cuts and cigarette burns. She reckoned she was hospitalized at least three times but she always told the medics she'd been mugged because she loved Farah. She'd even pretended she was pregnant for him. He thought it would make other women jealous. She'd had her tubes tied in the Mater in 1992 but she'd have done anything to keep him.

It wasn't just her who felt the brunt of his rage. He'd threatened to cut off one landlord's head with his knife when he called to collect rent. Farah also randomly fought anyone he viewed as racist, whether in the pub or on the street. He was paranoid people thought he was in Al Qaeda.

They moved back to Dublin in September 2004 and into the flat in Ballybough in December. Kathleen exerted more pressure on John to sell the home and give her her share of the proceeds. But life was harder than ever. Kathleen had to go on the game to earn money for Farah. He said it was for his family back in Africa. He said they were starving. Charlotte already knew the dos and don'ts and made it easy, keeping a lookout for her. Kathleen would have done anything to keep Farah in her life.

But now that he was gone, she was going to make her husband take the responsibility he had fudged. Kathleen considered him partly to blame for what had happened to Farah. She was going to make John pay for his part in all of this. She lifted the phone and dialled his number.

5

Linda and Charlotte

Linda and Charlie stared down at the lower half of Farah's body, lying spreadeagled on the bedroom floor. His head and shoulders were under the bottom bunk. Blood had seeped out in a five-foot radius around his body and continued to ooze from his twenty-two knife wounds. The hammer and Stanley knife lay alongside, right where the women had dropped them after the attack.

Charlie was the first to react. She knelt on his left side, clutched at his chest and yanked. Farah's head sprang out from under the bed.

Linda winced. His eyes were closed but his jaw hung open. The gaping slash across his neck was four inches long and grotesque. His crinkly hair had matted together in a crust of congealed blood, masking the pulverizing injuries he'd sustained in the hammer attack.

Charlie didn't react at all. 'You take that leg,' she instructed, unfazed.

Linda reached down to grab Farah's right foot and Charlie seized his left. They dragged the dead weight the six-foot distance into the tiny ensuite, leaving a trail of smeared blood.

The bathroom was filthy and not long or wide enough for a standard-sized bath. The tiles around the shower on the back wall were covered in slimy scum and the grout between them was speckled with climbing black mould. Between them, the sisters somehow hoisted, shunted and partially propped the body up and into the shower tray, leaning him against the wall. Farah's head fell forward, his lifeless legs dangling gruesomely over the edge. Linda threw a towel over his face. She didn't want him looking at them.

Charlie scoffed and began reefing his trousers off. Her mother had told her to cut him up. That was what she was going to do. It was their only hope of getting the body out of the flat without being seen.

Linda sat on the toilet seat on her right, a foot and a half away from the shower. Her head was in her hands and she was looking at Farah's feet, inches from her own, through splayed fingers. Her vision blurred as tears started to flow. The usual rites and rituals afforded to the dead are part and parcel of what it means to be human – to feel empathy, to value life and to honour those who have passed on.

The prospect of desecrating Farah Noor's remains, in his shredded, blood-soaked Ireland jersey, white underpants and grey socks, was a shocking affront to her own humanity. But Linda was not crying for Farah. She was not crying for what they had done or were about to do. In her mind, he deserved everything he'd got. Linda was crying because she knew if they were caught, she would go to prison for a very long time.

The bad choices she had made in her life came back to haunt her. She had left school early, become a teenage mother and gone on to have three more children and a serious drink and drugs problem by the age of thirty. Her relationship with her kids' father, Mark Farrelly, had broken down in 2000. Mark was a builder's labourer from Drimnagh with road traffic and public order convictions and they had lived together in Bawnlea in Tallaght. Shortly after the separation, she had started a disastrous affair with a man just released from prison for manslaughter, Wayne Kinsella, who was supplying her with drugs.

Even by the low standards Linda Mulhall had known in her short life, Wayne Kinsella marked an unprecedented plunge to rock bottom. Linda met Wayne through her brothers, who had befriended him in prison. He was a killer convicted of manslaughter who mugged pensioners, battering one to death as the old man laid flowers at his wife's grave in Glasnevin. Thomas Forman, a retired auctioneer, was targeted by Kinsella purely because he was easy prey. The heavily tattooed junkie was a drug peddler without a cell of mercy in his body. He killed 86-year-old Thomas Gerard Forman, and in a separate crime terrorized a young mother and her toddler.

Forman was kneeling to pray as he had done every single Saturday for the previous twenty-one years since his beloved wife, Ellen Mary, passed away. Also buried in the plot was their baby son, whom the couple had lost tragically as an infant. No sooner had Thomas laid the flowers on the grave than Kinsella struck. He wanted the frail old man's money for drink and drugs.

'I needed money for a few pints,' the cowardly thug later told gardaí.

In his statement, Kinsella claimed he went to the cemetery to search for his grandfather's grave but couldn't find it. He saw Mr Forman with flowers in his hand and demanded money.

'I pushed him and he fell back. I didn't mean it. He hit his head off the side of the grave and I heard him make a moan.'

Kinsella claimed he then rooted through the dying pensioner's pockets for a handkerchief 'to stop the blood'. In fact, he was rifling his wallet.

Kinsella described running to the flower shop and waiting until the girl phoned for an ambulance. He then fled and decided to 'cool his nerves' by drinking pints in a nearby pub.

People in the tightly knit Dublin suburb of Phibsboro were shocked by Tommy's death. He was regarded as a Good Samaritan, an 'old fashioned gentleman'. At the time the then-Taoiseach, Bertie Ahern, who lived in the area, said his death showed how society had 'reached new lows of depravity'.

Kinsella apologized to the Forman family but his hollow words were described in court as 'less than frank' and 'self-serving'.

The court was told how he had smoked hash and taken acid since the age of twelve. He needed easy cash to subsidize his drug habit. He had been jailed just a month previously for four-and-a-half years for robbing three bus drivers at knife point and was brought from prison to the trial. He was jailed in 1990 for four years for robbing an elderly woman who later became ill and died.

In court he sat handcuffed while a young pregnant woman talked to him from the bench behind. She put her arm around his shoulder. He kissed her and smiled at her. Even while being tried for a sick crime, the vile charmer was trying to woo the jury.

As he sat, he bounced his heels casually in a pair of Nike trainers with the laces untied, while admiring a two-inch scar on his left hand and a tattoo of a heart on his wrist.

As lawyers described how Thomas Forman went to his wife's grave every Saturday, Kinsella leaned forward from the bench, heels tapping. As they outlined how the pensioner died from a large blood clot on his brain, Kinsella shook his head and lowered it.

The State Pathologist found that Mr Forman's injuries were consistent with 'a single blow from another party'. Kinsella looked bored and stared at his hands. As the court heard details of the rest of the injuries inflicted on a frail, elderly man, Kinsella tuned out, summoned his solicitor and pointed angrily at someone in court. His father and brother were sitting in the back row of the public gallery and Kinsella was not impressed. His father looked haggard and remained impassive as the defence counsel described Kinsella as the black sheep in a family of eleven. (Since then, Kinsella's younger brother Lee, a drug addict, has been shot dead at his home in Finglas, murdered over some petty grudge or minor debt. The recovering junkie was executed at his sitting-room window in May 2006 in front of his horrified girlfriend and nine-year-old son.)

Having heard the litany of Kinsella's cowardly crimes, a judge gave the thug eight years and directed he get professional help behind bars. 'Unless this man is psychiatrically and psychologically treated while in custody, he will remain a danger to society,' he said.

It was to prove a prophetic statement. What Kinsella would do to Linda's children marked a new level of depravity and cruelty.

A short time after his release, Wayne Kinsella met Linda Mulhall and moved into her Tallaght home with her and her children.

He continued to regard everyone as fair game.

In May 2003, he forced a woman called June Byrne and her two-year-old son out of a car. He told her: 'If you get the police I'll kill you and burn your house down with your children in it.'

In August 2003, he flipped again and attacked three of the helpless Mulhall children while Linda was out. He put her two sons and a daughter – then aged ten, nine and eight – in different rooms and took time beating them separately.

He told the eldest of the three: 'Whenever I look at you, I want to hit you.' He had beaten the boy so violently on another occasion, he was left cut and bleeding, with over twenty different injuries to his body. Now Kinsella made the boy strip down to his underpants and lie face down on the bed as he beat him with a belt.

He then ripped flex from a lampshade and continued to whip the child.

He went into the next room, where he beat the younger brother in a similar manner. He also lifted him up and threw him down on the ground, smashing the boy's face off the wall before leaving the room.

Now he went into the third room and beat the little girl senseless before returning to the eldest boy to resume his torture. By now he was panting from the exertion. Throughout the attacks, he repeatedly told the children, 'You made Ma lose the baby,' a reference to a miscarriage Linda had suffered with his child. He threatened to kill them if they told their mother what he had done to them.

The gardaí were tipped off that the children might be in danger and arrived at the house. Kinsella put Linda's two sons in a box and made them stay there until the guards had gone. The gardaí took the eight-year-old girl with them into protection and retrieved the other children a few days later.

The episode was catastrophic and the children were taken from Linda and placed in care. As usual, Linda chose the wrong road. Instead of helping gardaí in the cruelty case they were preparing against Wayne Kinsella, she moved to Cork with him. Kathleen and Farah were already living there and Charlie had moved down too with her new boyfriend. While living in Cork, Wayne was suspected of a series of robberies and gardaí believe Linda was helping him. Later in the year the couple moved to

Manchester. Without her kids, her drug addiction went off the rails. Wayne was making her sleep with his friends to pay for heroin. He was now her pimp. And he was also beating Linda senseless whenever the mood took him.

Finally, she agreed to help gardaí in their case against him. In May 2004, she got her children back but she had nowhere to go. She moved them into a homeless hostel near the Coombe, but they were evicted for antisocial behaviour. Her father, John, bailed her out after she attempted suicide and allowed her to move back in with him in Kilclare Gardens, warning her to get her act together.

Wayne Kinsella would plead guilty to three counts of cruelty against Linda's children in July 2004 for incidents between 31 August and 1 October 2003. The court heard that Linda had been pregnant with his child and had miscarried at three months, shortly before the attacks.

Judge Michael White described him as 'a man with a predilection to violence' and sentenced him to four years for beating the eldest boy and three years to run concurrently for each of the two other children. He said the children were completely at his mercy and Linda Mulhall had not been affording them proper care. Kinsella said: 'It was totally out of character for me.'

A short time later, Kinsella was back before the same judge and given a consecutive four-year sentence for intimidating June Byrne, a mother of five, and hijacking her car. The victim told the judge she had lived in fear of Kinsella and could only relax knowing he was locked up.

Kinsella had now amassed twenty-five convictions.

Judge White said he had a violent history he needed to deal with and he suspended the four-year sentence on condition he underwent an anger management course in prison. He was bound over to keep the peace for four years after the date of release from his seven-year sentence.

It would take his imprisonment to completely break off Linda's warped reliance on him. In the claustrophobic confines of her mother's flat on 20 March 2005, the thought that now she'd squandered her last chance to get her life back on track must have made her sick to her stomach. Instead of getting herself clean and making it up to her kids, she'd made the single biggest mistake of her life.

The day had started full of promise. Linda was supposed to have been spending it with her eleven-year-old son, who was back in her care. When Charlie mooted the idea of going on a bender that morning, Linda had wanted to bring her son with them. Charlie went ballistic at the idea and Linda caved in. She never needed much persuading when drink and drugs were on offer. At least when she was wasted, her own problems – her issues with her father and the feelings of guilt about the life she had given her kids – subsided into oblivion. Drugs made anything possible – and anyone.

She could picture her son's face. He had barely looked up when she'd told him she was going to visit his granny in town and would see him later. He was used to surviving without his mam.

From her pew on the toilet lid, Linda became inconsolable. The noise Charlie was making with the knife was impossible to ignore. The drink and drugs were also starting to wear off. She looked at Charlie accusingly. She was the reason she was here. She was the reason Farah was dead. If it had been anyone other than Charlie asking her to go out, she'd have said no. She'd be with her son.

But Linda could never say no to Charlie. Once again, as Linda watched Charlie engage in her macabre task while she sat there doing nothing, she knew she was leaving it to her little sister to bail her out. It wasn't Charlie's fault – she was here. Linda blamed her mother.

Charlie had switched grim instruments, and was trying to sever Farah's right leg above the knee. The serrated bread knife sawed fine through the flesh and the bone was exposed but the knee joint was proving tricky to separate. She used the tip of the Stanley to try to pick the cartilage clear but it was taking for ever. The blood made everything slippery and a few times she nicked herself and cursed.

The heavy-set sister sat back on her hunkers, exhausted. In many ways her life was even more out of control than Linda's but because she had no children it was containable. Charlotte had been charged fourteen times for different offences ranging from soliciting and assault to damaging property, theft and being drunk in a public place. She had turned to prostitution in her teens and was a regular near Baggot Street Bridge. Like Linda, she also self-harmed by cutting herself and was a hardened drinker and drug user who sometimes drank outdoors and in the Hell Fire Club, a place at the foot of the Dublin mountains which draws those with an interest in the occult. Like Linda, she had squandered her own chance to break out of the poverty cycle. In late 2004, she was awarded €42,000 compensation for a road traffic accident. She bought her father a new motorbike, gave her mother more than €5,000 and Farah €1,500 and a mobile phone. She also looked after her brothers and sisters.

Linda watched her knuckling down to what had to be done, and suddenly remembered exactly why she was here. She loved Charlie more than anyone else in the world bar her kids.

'Here, you take a rest,' she told her sister, pushing down on the floor beside her and reaching for the hammer.

Charlie switched places.

Linda started bashing at the knee. She belted it thirty-odd times, then, exhausted, sat back.

'Happy birthday,' she reminded her sister, and the two of them burst out laughing. The tension was like a pressure cooker and gallows humour a welcome relief.

Charlie took over again.

Linda tackled the river of blood seeping into the hall and headed for the hot press. She registered her mother on the couch in the sitting room, glued to the TV screen. Useless bitch, Linda thought. She returned with towels and started mopping around her sister. Each towel became sodden after a single swipe and she went to the sink, wrung them out and soaked them in fresh water.

The shower tray was overflowing with the blood from Farah's torso, causing a new mini flood on the floor. She wrung out a towel and fired it into the sink to wash it. She used the wet towels to shore up the flow running into the hall, then turned her attentions to the tray. Linda picked at the plug and dry-retched as a wad of hair and bone chips came away in her hand.

Charlie looked up and cracked another joke. Now they were working as a team, they began to make some real progress. Every forty-five minutes or so, Charlie would rest while Linda took over the cutting. They limited their fag breaks. If you went outside and came back in from the fresh air, the smell really hit you and it was getting worse. The confined space was filling up with lumps of flesh and bone and Charlie started dumping them down the toilet and flushing as she worked.

When both Farah's legs were dismembered, they pulled him on to the floor and Linda became the butcher, tossing the body parts into the shower tray as she cut.

They removed the arms halfway between the elbow and shoulder. Next his thighs from below the hip. Next his torso.

With his stomach and entrails exposed, the smell became unbearable for Linda. The stomach had suffered multiple puncture wounds in the attack. She covered her nose and mouth and gagged. It was like the smell that hits you in a butcher's shop mixed with raw sewage, but multiplied by one million. They pulled Farah's Ireland jersey back down to try to contain the smell.

She cut through the midriff to the spine, leaving the ribs connected to the head.

They were nearly done. Linda was getting giddy. She pulled down Farah's underpants. She grabbed the top of his penis and sliced through it above the testicles. She tossed it with the other human remains. 'Now you will never rape my ma again,' she said.

Charlie laughed.

All that was left was to detach the head. Linda left the towel over his face and started hammering at his neck. She reached for the bread knife and began sawing, steadying the torso with her knee. It took about ten minutes and when it came off, she dropped it on the floor in disgust.

'I need a drink,' she told Charlie, and the pair of them headed back into the kitchen for more vodka.

The dismemberment of the man they had known as Farah Noor had taken over four hours.

6

Clean-up

John Mulhall was a long-faced man with a narrow
moustache and a flat nose that made him look like a
former boxer. His receding hair was shaved and his neck
looked even more bullish because of the round-necked
jumpers he wore without shirts. His hard exterior melted
like butter when it came to his children. He would have
done anything to try to help them get their lives back on
track. He had made mistakes himself in his youth that had
landed him in trouble with the law and he carried a lot of
guilt for their problems. But, unlike Kathleen, he was willing to face up to his own culpability.

It was 1am on Monday, 21 March, when he pressed the
buzzer to his ex-wife's flat in Richmond Cottages and he
was in no mood for niceties. He'd worked as a glazier
with City Glass in Donore Avenue on and off for the last
twenty-five years and he needed a night's sleep. He had
sworn never to cross this doorstep but he'd said a lot of
things he had to go back on when it came to bailing out
his kids. He'd collected Charlotte here on New Year's Eve,
2004. He still didn't know what was going on but
Kathleen's clipped phone conversation had scared him
enough to make him realize it was serious. Both Linda

and Charlotte were heavy drug users; he dreaded he was about to find one of them had overdosed or worse.

His estranged wife answered the door. He pushed past – he wanted nothing to do with her – but Kathleen looked so haggard he couldn't help but do a double take. She'd aged about ten years since he'd last seen her. Instantly, he knew something was seriously wrong from the foul, invasive smell climbing up his nostrils from the bin bags behind the door, tightly wrapped with strips of brown duct tape.

His eyes absorbed the squalid sitting room. It was a complete kip, filthy and crammed with a red couch, two single seats and a table and chairs vying for space with the mountain of different-shaped bin bags.

John held his breath. The smell was rank.

Linda and Charlotte appeared from the bedroom at the kitchen end of the room, and locked eyes with him. John was shocked by the state of them. Their clothes were soaking wet, there were wet towels in heaps all over the place, and strange spatters on the walls.

'Farah's dead. The girls killed him,' Kathleen hissed.

John didn't believe her but Linda and Charlotte were crying. The penny dropped . . . why he'd been summoned here . . . why he'd been sucked into their sordid little secret: his van outside. His stomach lurched.

'You're on your own,' he said, pulling the flat door open, storming back out into the communal hall and slamming the front door behind him. After getting sick on the pavement, he jumped into his 97D Berlingo work van and took off, full throttle.

Linda looked at Charlotte, horrified at the sound of the tyres screeching away. Their father was the one they could always rely on to bail them out, but not this time. The cocktail of drugs and drink and adrenalin sustaining her for the last few hours instantly drained away. She felt about as pumped as a flat tyre. Her hands were red raw from all the cleaning and scrubbing. She'd had enough. She was going to bed and Charlotte was coming with her.

'Where the fuck do you think you're going?' Kathleen roared as Linda and Charlotte disappeared into the bedroom and climbed into the bed their mother had shared with Farah. It still smelt of him. His blood was all over the floor and bed covers.

Kathleen followed and screeched at them to get up and clean up. Linda and Charlotte closed their eyes.

'Let her worry about things for a while,' Linda whispered as Kathleen stormed out.

At first, Kathleen cursed them to high heaven and saved a few choice expletives for her impotent ex-husband. As usual, her family was dragging her down, hell-bent on ruining her life. Her festering anger that had been seething since Farah was killed and butchered now went into overdrive.

She went into the kitchen and turned the kettle on. She filled two cooking pots with water and put them on the cooker, twirling the heat up to high. She removed a bottle of bleach from under the sink, a sponge and some dishcloths. She carried the boiling kettle into the bathroom and sluiced it over the heaviest bloodstains on the walls and floor. She returned to the kitchen, refilled the kettle and put it on again. She heaved the boiling pots into the bathroom one at a time and did the same with them. She lashed bleach indiscriminately and began to scour and scrub. As she worked, her mind concocted her alibi. She wasn't worried about the other residents in the house of flats and what they might or might not have noticed or heard. One flat was occupied by two Russians, Dilmurat and his friend Alex, but they didn't have much English and drank a lot. A single girl called Donna lived in another flat but she was never around and kept to herself. The last flat was vacant.

If anyone reported Farah missing and the gardaí knocked at her door, Kathleen would say she had parted company with Farah on O'Connell Street, that he promised to phone but never did. She would say that they were friends, nothing more. Farah was a ladies' man, she presumed he'd taken off with one of them, thought nothing more of it. He had an ex in Kilkenny with a sick child, she presumed that was where he'd gone. She would say that when she got back to her flat it had been turned over and most of his clothes were gone. She would say she knew nothing more about it. As long as she cleaned the flat of all the blood and body parts, she did not believe she would ever have to worry about him being identified. The girls had done too good a job with the hammer and knives. Farah had been butchered beyond all recognition. By the time she had finished scouring, there was virtually no trace left of the man she had known as Farah Noor.

*

An hour and a half later, she rooted the girls out of the bedroom, telling them she needed to make a start on it. Curiosity got the better of Linda and Charlotte. They got up to see how much their mother had done and got a new lease of life when they discovered the transformation. The place looked better than it had when Farah was alive. The sisters sprang to action, taking over the cleaning, giving the bathroom another going over with six to seven more pots of boiling water. The grout between the tiles was the hardest part to clean because Farah's blood had soaked right into the porous surface.

They also needed to unblock the toilet, which was threatening to overflow with every fresh deposit of flesh.

In the bedroom, Kathleen discovered that trying to turn the clock back was not going to be so straightforward. The blood had soaked into the carpet, the covers and the bedclothes. The carpet squelched with Farah's blood. She tried soaking it up with towels, but realized even industrial equipment wasn't going to work here. It would have to be taken up and dumped. There wasn't time to move all the furniture out and pull it up. She began slicing little strips with the Stanley blade. Her mind kept plotting. She would blame a cockroach infestation if anyone asked. The pest control had been out the previous month to the upstairs flats. She would say she had discovered cock-roach eggs under the carpet and got rid of them.

It was back-breaking work and the girls took turns helping to remove just the bits that were stained. She wasn't made of money, she told them. The landlord, John Tobin, was going to go ballistic as it was.

As the girls worked away on their hands and knees, Kathleen focused on the wardrobe, removing all of Farah's clothes, mostly football jerseys. She went through the pockets of everything, including the trousers Charlotte had pulled off him before dismembering him, and removed his loose change, bank card and mobile phone, setting it all aside with some chains and rings. Farah might be dead, but he still owed her money. She would have her due.

She fetched a fresh roll of bin liners from the kitchen and instructed the girls to strip. Their clothes would have to go out too. Charlotte had plenty of choice; she kept outfits here because she slept regularly in a bunk beside Farah and Kathleen's double bed. And Linda had left a purple polo neck in the flat that Kathleen had previously given her as a present.

In fresh clothes they started to feel more human, and with the clean-up going better than expected, the mood started to lighten – but when the buzzer went just after 6am, they all froze in fear.

'Stay calm,' Kathleen warned.

The buzzer continued to sound impatiently and Kathleen peeped out the dirty net curtain. She saw her ex-husband shuffling nervously on the doorstep and released the lock. John burst into the room, highly agitated.

He had spent the last five hours battling his conscience. Now he was willing to help for Linda and Charlotte's sake, not Kathleen's. His daughters were not going to spend the rest of their lives atoning for their mother's sins if he could help it.

'Thanks, Da,' Linda and Charlotte blurted.

There wasn't time for chat, John responded, not waiting for directions. It was clear from a glance what had to be done. He marched into the murder bedroom, pulled off the duvets and pillowcases from the bunk bed and stripped the double bed down. He dumped them with the towels used in the mop-up and the knife used in the murder, then began whisking the bin bags stuffed with clothing, towels and bed covers out and into the back of his van. The body parts they would have to dispose of themselves.

He barely acknowledged Kathleen but he hugged Linda and Charlotte, got into his City Glass work van and drove away.

When he was gone, the women started discussing where to dump the body. They couldn't drive, but they wouldn't be able to lug the bin bags far without attracting suspicion. The canal, a few minutes' walk away, was their only option. They could walk right up to the water's edge, in the shadow of Croke Park, and tip it in. There were obvious worries: what if they were seen? What if one of the bags floated on the surface? But the most important thing was to get rid of them all before the traffic began to build up.

Just under an hour later, at 7am, the three women emerged into the sleepy, cold, blustery city. Kathleen wore a cream jacket with fur collar, a grey polo and denims. Linda was wearing a black leather jacket and the purple polo. Charlotte was wearing a V-neck denim jacket, dark jeans and white runners. The sisters carried two rectangular sports bags over their shoulders. Linda's contained Farah's two arms bound in a bin liner with a vest and a pair of pants. Charlotte's was heavier: she lugged Farah's torso, dressed in the blood-soaked football jersey. Kathleen carried nothing. What was done was done but Farah had been the man she loved; she was here for moral support, not to dump him.

It took only a few minutes to walk to Clarke's Bridge over the Royal Canal in Ballybough, where the water is about eight foot deep. Croke Park loomed over them on their right.

Linda was nervous and kept glancing back over her shoulder to see if anyone was watching. She walked up to the water's edge first, unzipped her bag and shook out the grisly contents, still wrapped in bin bags. Next, Charlotte swung Farah's chest out into the canal and watched it sink.

The women didn't hang around to see if the bags could be spotted from the bank, it was too risky. It didn't really matter if they were found, as nobody had seen them dump the bags. Nobody would know who it was. They walked purposefully back to Richmond Cottages, amazed they'd managed to get away with it.

Charlotte hurried Linda and her mother on. They weren't finished yet, not by a long shot. Back inside the flat, they packed the sports bags with a second load of body parts, repeating the process until, by the time they were finished, all eight pieces of Farah were in the canal's murky waters, bar his head.

Kathleen was emphatic the head was the most important part in identifying Farah. Back in the flat, they spent the next couple of hours trying to decide where to dump it. There was a new confidence now Farah was gone and the flat cleaned up. It had also taken the panic out of the situation.

'I'm starving,' Linda said.

Kathleen shot her a look of disgust. A dark camera bag they'd stuffed Farah's head into sat on the floor.

'Me too,' Charlotte agreed, to spite her mother. 'And if you think I'm eating anything you've got here you've another think coming.'

Linda laughed.

Kathleen berated them. If they thought they had got away with it, they were very wrong, she warned. They could have some respect for the man she had spent over three years of her life with. Not to mention that if Farah was identified, they'd be knocking on her door and that of her daughters.

After a long discussion they vaguely agreed that Sean Walsh Memorial Park, opposite the Square in Tallaght and on the far side of the bypass, was the best place to dump the head. They often drank there and knew it like the back of their hands. It was criss-crossed with streams and ditches and had a couple of lakes. It was also close to home, so they could keep an eye on any developments.

They decided to get the 77 bus and to dump it straight away. But events were having a weird effect on Linda. She felt like a different person. Someone strong, for a change. Nobody was going to mess with her any more. She slung the camera bag over her shoulder as she headed for the door. 'Does it suit me?' she joked.

Charlotte laughed.

Kathleen's lips disappeared in disapproval. Already she could only remember the good times with Farah.

Her mother's attitude was really starting to piss Linda off. She stopped at Summerhill Parade to spite her and ducked into the Gala supermarket. After queueing at the deli counter, she ordered a breakfast roll.

'Have you any tomato ketchup?' she asked.

At the till, she paid for the roll, six packets of crisps and twenty Superking cigarettes. Kathleen followed her nervously, grabbed a bottle of water, bought and paid for it and waited outside.

Linda put the bag on the ground outside the shop and tucked in hungrily. For the first time in years, she had a hearty appetite. Kathleen and Charlotte smoked but didn't eat.

After four-odd hours traversing Sean Walsh Park, searching for the best place to dump Farah's head, Linda and Kathleen were locked in silent sulks. Charlotte was pissed off too, trying to keep the peace between them. But there wasn't one spot they could agree on after fine-combing every inch of the park's perimeter and grounds. Charlotte was up for anywhere, she just wanted rid of it. But when Linda suggested bushes, Kathleen would remark they were regularly trimmed. If Kathleen wanted a ditch in the stream, Linda would argue a fox might pull it out and into the open. Linda wanted a spot near trees but Kathleen said there were always people around the Shamrock Rovers football pitch. Linda also put her foot down at any point her mother suggested that she considered too close to the school grounds. What if a kid accidentally came across the head? Her own childhood had been screwed up, she didn't want to be responsible for anyone else's nightmares.

Kathleen was raging that she was once again being partly blamed for Linda's past. She could take that one up with her father. Then Charlie started to lose the rag.

'Shut the fuck up, both of youse,' she said. She was cold, starving, acutely aware of the approaching dark and today was her birthday. She still fancied a night out.

Linda's back ached twice as much when she sensed Charlie was turning on her as well. 'Get this fucking thing off me,' she said, tugging at the camera bag containing the head and plonking herself down on a bench in front of one of the park's lakes. She refused to budge. What was wrong with the water?

Kathleen sat, lips pursed, arms and legs crossed, at the far end of the bench and took exception. The problem was they hadn't got a concrete block to weigh it down. It would float. Once the head was found, Farah could be identified and the trail would lead straight back to Richmond Cottages.

'Fuck this,' Charlotte remarked, behind them. She dropped to her knees and started to claw at the earth with her bare hands. She'd had enough. It was going in here and she was going home.

Linda stared at her in horror. There was no way Charlotte would be able to dig a hole big enough with her bleeding hands and she told her so.

Kathleen pulled her sleeve down over her hand, rooted around in her bag and tossed Charlie the Stanley knife.

'What are you doing?' Linda berated her mother. 'We can't leave it there. People sit on this bench. They'll see it.'

The sound of them starting up again made Charlie twice as determined. She used the knife to dislodge stones and pulled more earth aside. After digging a wide enough hole, about the depth of her hand, she unzipped the camera bag, pulled Farah's head out by the hair and jammed it into the hole, scooping and slapping the mud around it. The top of his head stuck up over the surface but she didn't care. She tried stamping it down to flatten it, nudged more earth over it, then slapped her hands together and brushed her knees off. She was knackered and she was off.

Kathleen picked the Stanley knife up with her sleeve, walked over to the pond and tossed it in. At the edge of the lake she also dumped the hammer from her bag, again using her sleeve to obscure fingerprint evidence.

Linda watched them stalk off together towards the Square in disbelief. There was no way Farah's head could stay there, sticking up like that. But there was no way she was digging it up on her own. It would be just her luck to be caught with it. She headed off in the opposite direction, towards home.

7

The Body in the Canal

On Monday, 21 March, 43-year-old Margaret Gannon was walking her seven-year-old son Evan to school on North William Street. With them was her niece.

Evan pointed into the water as they walked over the bridge. 'Look at that.'

Margaret saw a black bag wrapped in brown tape. Dogs were regularly drowned in the canal, but it didn't look like a dog. It was the shape of a body without a head.

'Is that another body?' her niece asked, reading her mind.

It was a reference to the infamous case of the body in the suitcase found at the same spot in the canal less than four years previously, in July 2001.

A cyclist peddling over Clarke's Bridge had thought he saw an arm floating in the canal. It was Good Friday, 25 March, and 24-year-old Paul Kearney, a local, pulled up and studied the object in the water. It was definitely an arm. The fist was clenched and sticking out above the surface and there was a leg there too. He got back on his bike and cycled off. People were always dumping rubbish in the canal but a mannequin took the biscuit. He thought about it all day, then rang his father.

'Da, you're not going to believe me, I was riding along the canal when I saw part of a body.'

'Go 'way out of that,' his father replied.

Marie Mulhall trudged up the stairs to her bedroom in Kilclare Gardens, exhausted after a long day's work. The 21-year-old mechanic needed to change. Her overalls were in the garage, but the oil and smut from engines got everywhere.

The youngest of the Mulhall sisters looked nothing like Charlotte, Linda or Kathleen. Her long, light brown hair was untreated, she didn't wear much make-up and she wasn't under- or overweight. Marie had a trade and a life and was fiercely independent. The only reason she stayed in Kilclare Gardens was to protect her father from the others, who she felt walked all over him, and to keep her youngest brother, Andrew, on the straight and narrow. Marie was more of a mother to Andrew than Kathleen had ever been. She didn't want him to end up like the rest of them. The only other one Marie had any time for was Charlotte. Everyone thought Linda was the soft one, because she looked better, had four kids and wasn't as brusque, but Marie hated the way she tortured their father and blamed him for her problems. Charlotte might have been hard as nails on the outside but she had a heart of gold.

When her frizzy-haired sister arrived in the bedroom, crying, Marie could tell she'd been drinking. Charlotte was always drinking.

'What's wrong?' Marie asked.

But Charlotte couldn't speak, she was so upset.

Marie sat next to her on the bed and put her arm around her. 'What happened?' she asked.

Charlotte looked her in the eye. 'We killed Farah,' she whispered.

Marie threw her eyes up to heaven. When Charlotte was drunk, the stories got wilder and wilder. This one left the others out in the cold though.

'Me and Linda went to Mam's flat,' Charlotte continued. 'Me and Mam wanted chips and we went out. When we came back, Farah was trying to rape Linda. We killed him.'

Marie didn't suffer fools gladly. She believed it was the drink talking. But she didn't want to tell Charlotte to cop herself on when she was this distressed. So she let her talk.

'We cut him up and threw him in the canal,' Charlotte said.

Marie suddenly began to wonder. How could Charlotte make up something like that? Was this why her father hadn't been himself for the last few days? Did he know something about it? Was it true?

She jerked away from Charlotte and ran out of the house to get her head straight. She drove around for hours, praying it wasn't true but unable to quell the fear rising in the back of her mind. The problem was she knew her father too well. She had stuck to him like glue as a child, knowing he was the only stable one in a madhouse. He was the reason she had qualifications herself. She had spent so much time outdoors with him, turning into a tomboy while watching him disassemble engines, that she could have done the job in her sleep.

When her parents' marriage split up and her father moved out, she moved with him to take care of him. When John got an €80,000 compensation payout from an accident he'd had in Carlow, he was able to rent a house in Rathminton Court in Tallaght. Marie had moved with him. They'd stayed there for six months. She'd persuaded Andrew to move in too. For a while it was perfect with just the three of them. There was no arguing or fighting, no drink or drugs.

Then Kathleen and Farah moved out of Kilclare Gardens, leaving the house completely wrecked from all the fighting and with everything of value sold. It was Marie who helped her father try to turn it back into a home.

After everything they'd been through together, Marie understood her father. The more she drove, the more she suspected his strange behaviour was because he had something big on his mind, something really terrible.

When she got home, Charlotte was on the couch talking normally to their father and had calmed down. Marie had had enough of her sisters' problems. She went straight to bed. But she couldn't sleep. Her mind was still racing. Charlotte ranting and raving and telling lies was nothing new. But what was eating John up?

At 6.30pm on Wednesday, 30 March, a group of teenagers fishing in the canal in Ballybough called up to a man standing on the bridge that there was a dummy in the water underneath. Twenty-three-year-old James

O'Connor wandered down for a closer look. It was a bright evening and he saw an arm and a leg about three feet below the surface. James knew from a glance it was no dummy and he immediately dialled 999.

Linda was growing more and more pissed off with her mother. Every time she rang to try to get Kathleen to help her dig up and move Farah's head, Kathleen kept putting it on the long finger. Charlotte had point-blank refused, saying it was grand where it was – but Kathleen knew as well as Linda did that they couldn't leave it sticking up in the open like that. Nine days after dumping the remains in the canal, she decided to go back to Richmond Cottages to force her mother to face the music. Her nerves were shot worrying about it and she also suspected she was pregnant after a casual fling.

She was walking from the 77 bus stop towards Ballybough Bridge when her heart moved up to her mouth. She could see a big crowd gathered on the bridge staring into the water. The air was flashing siren-blue and the closer she got the more her fear grew that Farah had just been found.

She tried to keep it together as she crossed, registering the navy and white plastic crime scene tape spooled around the banks and the forensic men dressed in head-to-toe white jumpsuits and TV camera crews filming for RTÉ and TV3. But it was no use. She broke into a trot, then a race, sprinting down to Richmond Cottages.

Kathleen already knew. The story about the body in the canal had been on the radio. Linda made a frantic phone call to Charlie, but she was out drinking with friends and wouldn't come back.

The women were climbing up the walls in the flat so they walked up to the bridge to see how much people knew about what had happened.

Detective Inspector Christy Mangan watched a colleague in the Garda Sub Aqua Unit scoop another grisly parcel from the canal with a hand-held net. The officer with the peppery grey hair was based in Fitzgibbon Street station. He had been involved in a huge range of criminal investigations over the years and spearheaded the investigation into the notorious 'Dublin riots'. But in all his experience, he had never seen anything like this.

A lower leg was the first body part removed, followed by a thigh, the other leg, and an arm. Each was marble white, the skin washerwoman-wrinkly from being submerged and separating from the muscle. On recovery, the parts were placed in plastic evidence bags. A bulky black-plastic-wrapped parcel was sitting on the bank, bound tightly with duct tape. The impression the contents were making through the shiny black sheath was unmistakable. It was the top half of a man, his midriff, minus his head and arms. It had been ferried out of the water on a stretcher, the only part to have floated away from the rest of the body on the current.

Mangan's eyes moved to the garda attached to the forensic squad who was closest to it. He sat in his white jumpsuit on the bridge wall, his body language speaking a thousand words. He leaned forward, elbows on his knees, his protective mouth and nose cover pushed up over his head, staring straight ahead.

Directly behind them, Croke Park's towering Canal End stand dwarfed the detectives clustered on the water's edge and gave a sense of scale to the enormity of the task lying ahead.

The last time a body had been dismembered in this way was in 1963, when student doctor Shan Mohangi strangled and then dismembered his sixteen-year-old girlfriend, Hazel Mullen, and boiled and burned her body parts in a restaurant on Harcourt Street. Another decapitated body had been found in July 2004, near Piltown, Co. Kilkenny, but the head was the only part missing. (The victim was identified because her fingerprints turned up on an asylum application. She was 25-year-old Paiche Onyemaechi from Malawi, the daughter of the Chief Justice of Malawi, Leonard Unyolo.)

The stretch of canal where Mangan's team was working now had already become infamous. The body of a 23-year-old Romanian man, Adrian Bestea, was found stuffed in a suitcase and dumped in almost exactly the same spot in July 2001. In Bestea's case, a posthumous picture of his face had to be released to establish his identity. Ironically, it would emerge that Bestea had died because he was a woman beater. His Russian girlfriend, Maria Tsouretseva, had hired two Ukrainian men to teach him a lesson, but the plan had gone badly wrong.

As he watched the divers search for a head, the DI suspected this case would be more baffling than any of the others. The only certainty right now was that the brutality of what had gone on was terrifying. His only way into the investigation would be to find out the dead man's name.

Two park rangers, Brian Molloy and Robert McGovern, on foot patrol in Sean Walsh Park emptying bins, went to inspect something sticking a few inches out of the ground.

They had a smoke while they studied the shape, trying to figure out what it could be. Brian Molloy nudged some of the earth around it away with his boot. Black hair was clearly visible on the crown. It looked like someone had buried a dog and not bothered to cover his belly.

'Looks a bit like a human head, doesn't it?' Brian remarked.

It drew a laugh. Neither of them believed anyone would half bury a human head in a public park. They threw some clay over it and continued their patrol.

Detective Inspector Mangan scoured the results of the post mortem carried out by the Deputy State Pathologist, Dr Michael Curtis. The report was the first solid thing the streetwise detective had to go on. He was surprised to learn that the remains were probably those of a black man, possibly African, aged between twenty and forty. The body pulled from the water had looked white. The pathologist reckoned it had been in the water for one to two weeks.

Mangan scanned the cause of death: 'Penetrating wounds to the trunk', and the conclusion: 'This man's body had been dismembered. Dismemberment would have occurred after he had succumbed to multiple penetrating wounds. In the course of the dismemberment, the soft tissues had been cut relatively cleanly with a sharp knife or similar implement while the bones had been severed relatively clumsily by repeated chopping actions from an instrument or instruments such as an axe or a cleaver. The head and neck had not been recovered at the time of post mortem examination. The penis had been amputated and was not recovered.'

Mangan absorbed what the report meant for his inquiry. The ferocity of the attack suggested a grudge killing. He noted that the victim had received twenty-two stab wounds, eighteen of which landed between the nipples and the neck. That number of stab wounds would have been interpreted by a forensic psychologist as personal. Virtually all of the internal organs had been punctured with a blade, possibly a kitchen knife. The stomach had been punctured and a stab wound in the back was eleven inches deep. Did the killer know the victim? The lack of defensive wounds on the victim's hands suggested an element of surprise in the attack.

The incident room was chasing a different, uncharted line of inquiry. But there were undeniable parallels between the body in the canal and an infamous murder hunt which began in London after the mutilated remains of a young boy were pulled from the River Thames in September 2001. All that remained of the tiny boy in that case was his torso. Investigators had christened him 'Adam' to restore some of the child's dignity. His head, arms and legs had been removed with chilling precision and the body drained of blood. The lack of teeth and fingers made identification seem impossible.

In Adam's case, the post mortem results revealed traces of a toxic plant, Calabar bean, in his stomach, leading investigators to conclude he had died in a voodoo '*muti*' killing. Was the body in Dublin's Royal Canal also a victim of human sacrifice? Mangan directed the murder squad to touch base with the Ritual Killing Unit of the South African Police Force in Pretoria. Superintendent Gerard Labuschagne examined the details of the file. Some aspects of the Royal Canal body were typical *muti* – the severing of the genitalia and the cuts on the back. In black magic cases, the killer's purpose is to acquire the victim's intellect or strength and to please the gods. Organs are removed while the victim is still alive. But Labuschagne concluded the gardaí were probably not dealing with a *muti* killing. The internal organs had not been removed but all had been damaged in a frenzied attack, not a laborious, ritualistic murder.

So was the body in the canal the victim of a gangland slaying, Mangan wondered? The bodies of Darren Carey, aged twenty, and Patrick Murray, nineteen, had been unceremoniously dumped in a similar manner in the Grand Canal after a botched drug deal in December 1999 or January 2000. But they'd been shot in the head and their bodies left intact. If this was an underworld hit, it marked a chilling new departure even by Dublin's vicious standards.

A forensic psychologist could try to get into the killer's mind at the time of the killing, to see what clues it yielded about his relationship with the victim. What did the dismemberment of a man's body say about the way the killer saw him? A CIA document, *The Human Exploitation Training Manual*, describes the defilement of the dead as a deliberate psychological ploy. Destroying the sanctity of the dead is intended to terrorize the living. The CIA maintains that desecration of bodies is used by armies all over the world. When an army wants to subjugate a people, it dismembers the dead. By denying the respect usually afforded to the dead, the killer sends out a message to the world that he's now the top dog. Was a drug dealer sending out a message that he was not to be crossed?

All avenues were hypothetical without the victim's name. And the clock was ticking. Mangan needed to make the most of the public's horror, before complacency set in and people started to switch off. His best hope of identifying the dead man was to ride the wave of shock, when there was still a chance someone would pick up the phone and offer some piece of information they might consider small but that could turn out to be the missing piece of the jigsaw.

House-to-house calls were already under way and Crimestoppers had offered an award of €10,000 for information leading to an arrest. African pastors were asked to help relay the appeal through their churches, and articles had been placed in newspapers like *Metro Éireann* targeting the immigrant community readership. But still nothing.

Mangan organized a press conference like that used in

the earlier Adrian Bestea case. But he had no face to show the press so he was relying on replicas of the dead man's clothing: a white Eircom football jersey, his white underpants, his grey towelling sports socks. They were fast becoming his last hope.

A man sitting on a bench in Sean Walsh Park having a drink and a smoke noticed what looked like a dead bird on the ground. Laurence Keegan, an ex-army man, was wearing steel-capped boots. He went over and started kicking it. Some earth dislodged. He could see hair.

He had read all about the headless torso in the canal and it struck him this could be the head the gardaí were looking for. He went and reported it to the rangers but they insisted it was a dog.

He visited it every day for the next three days, growing more and more convinced it was human. The bluebottles had begun devouring it. He asked his daughter to help him.

'I bet you it's the black fella they found in the canal. Will you help me to dig it up?'

His daughter told him to get a grip.

8

The Investigation

Linda chewed her stinging fingernail butts as she sat glued to the TV in Kilclare Gardens. Farah's case was being featured on *Crimecall*, RTÉ's crime-fighting programme. Her heart was going like ninety. Superintendent John Leahy was appealing for help identifying the body. It was freaking her out. There couldn't be too many missing black men last seen wearing an Ireland jersey. If any of Farah's friends were watching, they would easily click it was him. Some had already contacted Kathleen asking where he was, and then there was his family in Kenya and his boss who had also been in touch.

Linda was not prepared to wait any longer. The head was going to have to be moved. But she would have to do it on her own. Charlotte and Kathleen had gone to Holyhead. They'd all bought ferry tickets when she'd had the pregnancy scare so she could go to England for an abortion. When she found out in the Coombe that she wasn't expecting, her mother and sister decided to use the tickets anyway.

Linda went into the kitchen and reached under the sink. Pouring herself a stiff drink, she ripped a new bin bag from the roll and downed the alcohol like water. If Farah's head was found, everything else was going to unravel and since it was still sticking out of the ground in Sean Walsh Park it was more a question of when, not if.

On their first night away, Kathleen and Charlotte walked for an hour and a half until they arrived at a homeless hostel in Holyhead. They were a sorry sight. Blocky Charlotte carried her belongings in one of Linda's sons' schoolbags. Kathleen was off her face all of the time. They slept rough in a park for the next two or three nights, then got a train to Manchester and went drinking.

Their cash quickly dried up but they resorted to old habits. Charlotte slept with an Englishman who bought them drink one of the nights. But there weren't too many more like him. And she had a new boyfriend back home, one of the Russians who lived upstairs in the flat over her mother. They became acquainted after Kathleen complained to the landlord about her 'cockroach' problem and he suggested she move in with the two foreigners. Kathleen was doing a line with the other one herself. After ten days away, they ran out of options.

They contacted the social welfare to buy them tickets back from the emergency fund.

It was after 10pm, cold and dark. Linda sat on the bench in front of the lake, shivering and the worse for wear after the *Crimecall* experience.

Farah's head was sticking up out of the ground looking back at her.

'Hi, Farah,' she said.

'Hi, Linda, thanks for coming to see me,' Farah answered.

'Did you get your hair cut?' Linda asked.

'No,' he said.

'You did,' she answered. 'You got it shaved. It's much shorter than the last time.'

Farah laughed and kept talking to her. Linda started to cry. He was being nice to her and making her feel really guilty.

'I'm sorry, Farah,' she said. 'It should never have been you. It's my ma's fault. It should have been her that died, not you.'

She scrambled down on to her knees and started clawing the earth on either side. The head was really embedded and it took ages. When she finally managed to tug it free, she pulled the bin bag from her pocket and tucked the head inside before returning to Kilclare Gardens. At Killinarden Park, a housing estate on the way home, she hid the bag in some thick bushes.

Linda had the best night's sleep she'd had since the murder. She felt a hundred times better now Farah's head was no longer sticking out in the open. But what if someone saw it in the bushes?

She poured herself a cure for breakfast, then emptied the copybooks, pens and ruler out of her son's schoolbag, slinging it over her shoulder as she headed back to the bush in Killinarden. It couldn't stay there either. Rooting it out, she placed it in the schoolbag and went back home. Once there she got the hammer from the shed and tucked it into the bag with a bottle of vodka. She headed off to a field in Killinarden that she knew from her teens. It had been one of her favourite places as a teenager. It was where everyone went drinking and joyriders burned out stolen cars. After climbing the gate, she headed for a ditch at the far end and sat down. She could hear Farah talking to her again and she started kissing the bag.

'I'm sorry, Farah,' she said, swigging the neat vodka from the bottle. She repeated the words constantly for the next hour.

The head talked back to her and told her not to worry when she explained what she had to do. Having made her peace, she started to smash the bag with the hammer. She needed to crush it so if it ever was found, it wouldn't matter. The noise was a horrible cracking and the smell from the flat kept coming back to her. She bawled her eyes out as she drank.

When she was finished she tipped the contents of the bag into the earth and lit a little fire with her lighter, throwing the schoolbag on top of the blaze. Linda blessed herself. 'Our lady who art in heaven, hallowed be thy name,' she prayed.

She was knackered by the time she'd finished and she lay down on the ground and went for a sleep beside Farah. When she woke it was freezing and getting dark. She brushed herself down and headed back, stopping off in Heatons on the way to buy two schoolbags. Two of her sons were currently carrying their books to school in plastic bags.

Mohammed Ali Abubakaar was growing increasingly worried about his friend, Farah Noor. He finally decided he was going to have to report him missing to the Gardaí. It was almost two months since Mohammed, from Somalia, had last seen or spoken to him, after they bumped into each other on O'Connell Street on 20 March.

The 36-year-old from Kismayo, who worked for Dublin Bus, had hugged Farah after spotting him in his white Ireland jersey on the central median. Farah was with his older girlfriend and her two daughters, who were carrying plastic bags of beer. All four of them seemed drunk but Farah could barely walk. Mohammed knew what Farah could be like in that state.

'Relax,' he told Farah. 'Don't cause any trouble.'

'I'm fine,' Farah slurred. 'I'm going home now to Ballybough.'

Kathleen kept pulling at Farah, trying to get him to move off. She seemed in bad form.

Mohammed worried as he watched the women stoop to help Farah back to his feet. Anything could happen when Farah was that drunk. And he'd heard nothing from him since. He'd tried repeatedly to get in touch, but Farah hadn't returned any of his calls. It was playing on Mohammed's mind because of the trouble between Farah and his girlfriend's former husband.

On 16 May he made a statement to gardaí and referred to a row between John Mulhall and Farah: 'Farah's girlfriend Catherine [sic] is older than him and she is separated from her husband in Tallaght. She has blonde hair. About two years ago, Farah moved to Cork. He told me that Catherine's ex-husband had threatened to kill him. He told me that the ex-husband said to him, "I will kill you and nobody will be able to identify you." Catherine at this time was in dispute with her ex-husband because she wanted the family home to be sold and she wanted half the money. I advised Farah to leave the country or to move down the country. Farah was concerned at the time about the threats. At this time Farah and Catherine went to live in Cork.'

In the absence of any new leads, the investigation team were relying more and more on any clues the scientists could give them.

Samples of water were taken from every Garda station in Dublin and sent to a laboratory in Belfast where they were compared to the minerals deposited in the victim's bones. The results showed that the dead man had been drinking water in the Fitzgibbon Street area for the last six months of his life. The body found in the canal was someone local.

Kathleen Mulhall always felt low when she visited her sons in Wheatfield Prison. All of the people she really loved in life had been taken from her. Thirty-four-year-old James was her firstborn and to Kathleen's mind shouldn't have been inside at all. He'd been drinking with the man he was serving time for killing – 52-year-old Tony O'Brien – and had offered to drive him home, out of the goodness of his heart in Kathleen's opinion, in January 2002. Tony was supposed to have been the one giving James a lift home, but when he couldn't even turn his car alarm off he handed over the keys to his BMW, climbed on to the back seat and went to sleep. James sat behind the wheel and took off without tax or insurance with his girlfriend Tanya Whelan in the passenger seat. The car ploughed into a garden wall on the South Circular Road. Tony O'Brien was killed instantly. James had committed a string of other road traffic offences and had another conviction for assault causing harm. He went on the run in England when the case came to court. When he was caught, the judge jailed him for three years.

Her 28-year-old, John, was always in trouble, but that was because of the drugs. He needed help.

Kathleen snivelled as she looked at handsome James, who was a lot like her.

'How you keeping, Ma?' James asked. He had a pinched nose, a shaved head and a goatee.

'I've been better,' she replied.

Both boys looked at her for an explanation. Kathleen felt her sons were the only ones who ever cared about her and opened up.

'Charlotte and Linda killed Farah,' she said. 'They chopped him up and threw him in the canal.'

In early June, three African men were stopped in a stolen Nissan Micra in Abbeyleix. They were from Somalia and in the station they claimed they hadn't known the car was stolen when they bought it. Their story checked out. In passing, they also mentioned that they were worried the body pulled out of the canal in Dublin might be their friend Farah Noor. They hadn't been able to contact him.

*

The murder team had been unable to track Farah Noor down. His mobile phone records revealed he hadn't made any calls from a date in March up to early June 2005. The individual using the phone wasn't Farah Noor. It was a man called Florian Williams, who'd bought the phone in good faith off a work colleague, John Mulhall.

They needed to establish if Farah was the body in the canal before they could move. Their records revealed that a barring order had been taken out by a previous girl-friend of Farah's who had borne him a son.

Two gardaí called to Sue's home. Her child's DNA could prove if Farah was the body in the canal. 'They had a picture of an Ireland jersey and asked if Farah ever wore clothes like it,' she recalled. 'I said he did.

'At that point, and I still remember it to this day, one of them said, "We think it may be him." I froze because I just knew it was him. I just knew. I was shocked. I suppose it was the manner in which he was killed.

'I first met Farah when I was sixteen years old. I was in third year in school. I was only a schoolgirl. I actually met him when I was walking through town with my friends one day. He came over and started talking to me.

'He told me he was twenty. He was very charming at first. We started going out and it became very serious fast. I suppose now I realize it was puppy love but at the time it was very real.

'He didn't get me pregnant just to claim asylum. He was very careful not to be seen to have a relationship with me just for that. Instead, he became part of my family. He would spend a lot of time in my parents' home. You could say he was a full member of my family.

'We got a flat in Dublin and everything was great. I suppose you could say it was good for a period of time. Then he began to change.

'I remember what happened the first time that things started to go seriously wrong. I was out with my friend and he started saying that one of my friends was a lesbian, who wanted to sleep with me. I just stood there, thinking that I was hearing things. He kept shouting abuse at my friend saying that she wanted me. It was stupid. That night I was too afraid to go home so I stayed with a friend.

'The next day I went back home and he beat me. This happened every day from that day onwards. Then the sexual violence started.

'He would just force himself on me no matter how much I'd resist. He would force me to be with him and would never take no for an answer. This happened every day. It was a nightmare. I thought this was normal because I was very young. I also had a baby to care for and I just was too young to handle the situation. I also didn't want to admit that I'd made a mistake.

'I left twice but when I came back he'd beat me up. He'd then say he was sorry. When he'd hit me, I would fight back. It got so bad that I began to tell my friends and they demanded that I do something. One of them said she'd call my parents if I didn't leave him and in the end that's what happened. She did.

'When my parents found out, my dad came down and collected me. I had been with [Farah] from 1998 to 2001.

My father and mother could not believe what had been happening because they had treated Farah like one of their own. They were upset. They had no idea of the way he was treating me.

'Farah was a good father. He was a very loving father to his son and he doted on him. He had his own problems with alcohol but I don't think he was evil or anything like that. He just changed when he drank alcohol. It made him into a different man. There was a time when he was the nicest bloke in the world but he turned into something else when he drank.

'He started to follow me around. Everywhere I went he would just turn up. He'd come to the house but then he'd hang around the area. If I went out for a drink he'd turn up at the bar. I was afraid of him. I knew what he was capable of.

'There were three of us outside a pub. He knew one of my friends had known Raonaid Murray and he started shouting: "You're the reason why she's dead." My friend went straight to the Gardaí because he was trying to suggest he was the killer.

'When I met my husband, he [Noor] virtually vanished. He knew there was no point, that I had met someone else. He didn't even come to see our son. It was over.'

The caller on the other end of the phone was agitated and was whispering. 'I've got information about the body in the canal,' he said. He sounded in his twenties and his voice was nasal.

It was 7.47pm on 11 July and the 999 call had been rerouted to Harcourt Street station.

'I want to talk to the Gardaí,' the voice continued. 'My name is John Mulhall. I'm serving a prison sentence in Wheatfield with my brother James. I can tell you who the dead man is and I can tell you who done it, where it happened and when.'

Detectives travelled to the prison and interviewed both brothers, who told them everything they knew.

They said they were 'disgusted' by what their family had done. Charlotte had killed Farah. Linda had chopped off his penis to punish him for raping Kathleen. John had taken bedspreads, carpet and towels from the flat.

They wanted to be moved out of Wheatfield to Shelton Abbey open prison in Wicklow.

John Mulhall Sr had deposited the bin bags he'd removed from Richmond Cottages in his wheelie bin out the back and in his shed. He was waiting for the first opportunity to get rid of them but two days after his son John tipped gardaí off about what had happened, it became incumbent upon him to dump them.

John knew his boss, Harry Byrne, was on holiday and that his home in Castle Park in Leixlip backed on to the Liffey. John knew because he did odd jobs and gardening about the place.

At 7.30pm on 13 July, he went to the bottom of Byrne's back garden and began to fire the bags into the water. He also dug into an embankment at the bottom of the garden and buried some other items taken from the murder scene, including a large knife with a black handle, a photo of Adolf Hitler in a Scooby Doo frame, a blue plastic bag which contained a pair of gloves, a lighter from Gala in Ballybough and a brown paper bag containing clumps of hair and maggots.

Two houses up, Harry Byrne's neighbour, Vincent Mahon, noticed a white duvet floating by and saw a stocky, tanned man firing rubbish into the river. A week later, Vincent saw a wheelie bin with '31' painted on the side in the water, stuffed with strips of carpet. He decided to put a stop to the dumping and rang his neighbour's daughter, Niamh Byrne.

Linda sat on the far side of the table in the interview room of Store Street Garda station with a stunned expression on her gaunt face.

Gardaí had swooped on 31 Kilclare Gardens on 3 August and arrested her, Charlotte and her father, John. Kathleen had also been picked up from the city centre. After being fingerprinted, photographed and having a cheek swab and blood sample taken, Linda was interrogated. She was playing dumb, maintaining she couldn't remember if she was in her mother's flat on 20 March, when Farah was last seen on O'Connell Street.

The detectives were taking a softly, softly approach with the mother of four, convinced it wouldn't take much to crack her. The last thing they wanted was to get her back up too early on.

'I honestly can't remember being there,' Linda said. 'Unless I must have been drinking. I'm not supposed to drink when I take these tablets [for blood pressure].'

The interviewer held up a photograph of Farah's Ireland jersey and pointed out the holes they believed had been made with a knife. What could she tell them about how they got there?

'I didn't even know he'd been murdered until today,' Linda exclaimed, keeping up the pretence.

Did she admit she'd been in her mother's flat?

'A couple of times.'

A photograph of bloodstains on the bunk bed in the bedroom was held up. Could Linda explain how they got there?

'God, I don't know anything about that,' she maintained.

The photo was placed to one side and a shot of Clarke's Bridge was produced. Did she recognize any of the onlookers? Linda and her mother could be seen studying the officers working on the bank underneath. Murderers often returned to the crime scene just like that.

The photo took her by surprise. It was almost 8.30pm.

'No, no, no, no, no.'

The interrogator needed to keep her emotions running high and took a different tack.

Did she know Farah had been cut up into eight pieces?

'I knew there was a body found but I didn't know the way it was cut up. Was it really Farah? I would like a solicitor because I just can't believe any of this.'

After she called Kevin Tunny, in Tallaght, the detectives feared the moment might have passed. They played the tape recording of the call to emergency services made from a mobile phone in Wheatfield Prison.

'That doesn't sound like my brothers,' Linda said, visibly shaken.

The detective played it again.

'That's not my brothers, that's not my brothers,' Linda insisted. 'That sounded like a junkie to me, my brothers don't sound like that.'

Didn't she believe that her brothers would shop her?

'They don't know anything to tell about murders. I don't know anything. I don't believe what you're saying to me, I don't believe any of that.'

She was shown Farah's Sagem V55 mobile which her father, in another interview room in Store Street, had said one of his daughters had given him before he sold it on.

'I've never seen that phone before in my life,' Linda said scornfully. She knew nothing, either, about withdrawals from Farah's bank account after he'd died, she claimed.

After twelve hours, when they reached the end of their right to hold her, gardaí reminded her of the case against her: 'So your two brothers call the Gardaí and tell us that you and your mother and Charlotte killed Farah at Flat 1, 17 Richmond Cottages. We go to that address and search the same. This is where your mother lived and we find splatters of blood everywhere and the indication we have is that there was a violent struggle or assault there. Farah's body is found in the canal very close to the flat. You are the last people seen with Farah. He is found wearing the jersey he had on when last seen with you. You were in the Ballybough area after he was last seen and your father states that you or Charlotte gave him Farah's phone and Charlotte takes money out of this account after he goes missing. We can prove all of these allegations very well indeed. What do you say to that?'

'I don't know.'

In Mountjoy station, Charlotte was being subjected to a very different style of questioning. After their interview with John and James Mulhall in prison, gardaí believed the busty woman sitting opposite them was the key player on the night of the murder. They didn't know she was also the most vulnerable. Charlotte was almost two months pregnant.

Why would her brother have shopped her, Linda and Kathleen unless it was the truth, a detective asked baldly.

Burly Charlotte wasn't fazed. 'He must be fucked in the head,' she said.

The questioning got less tolerant.

Was Farah's penis cut off for a 'sexual' reason or out of 'pure spite'?

Charlotte shrugged. She didn't know what they were talking about.

'Did she [Kathleen] get enjoyment when Farah's penis was cut off? Was that the ultimate revenge? Were you hungover after your birthday, was it a treat for you to clean up the mess?'

Charlotte eyeballed the questioner.

'Did ye enjoy cutting him up? When you cut off his head, did you talk to it?' he pressed.

She sneered.

'Do you find that funny?'

She stuck to the same story throughout. She last saw

Farah in February. Her mother said he'd gotten back with the Chinese girl he had a child with.

What did she think when she heard about the body in the canal, the interviewer asked.

'Not a lot.'

Did she think it was gruesome?

'God, yeah.'

When it came to specifics, she blamed drink for her memory loss.

'I can't remember any of my birthday this year because all I done was drank.'

'Surely you must have woken up at some stage sober?'

'Not if ya drank as much as I do . . . I don't really do much but drinking so there's not much to remember.'

She said the only thing she could remember about the month of March was meeting her boyfriend on 31 March.

'Did you feel guilty on your birthday?'

'I'd nothing to feel guilty about.'

She didn't recognize Farah's jersey or a pair of socks or any of the exhibits but she had an answer for the reason the wallpaper and carpets were removed from the bedroom of her mother's flat in Richmond Cottages: 'Problems with cockroaches.'

She never saw blood in the flat and her mother never asked her to murder Farah. 'Well, I think you'd remember something like that, wouldn't ya.'

She didn't give her father Farah's phone and she didn't change the voice message on it.

Didn't it get to her, the way Farah was treating her mother?

'Obviously it concerns me, everyone has arguments though . . . I wasn't there twenty-four hours.'

Kathleen was also being held in Mountjoy.

'That my kids may die, I did not hurt a hair on his head,' she swore, claiming Farah was 'a friend, a companion'. They both came and went as they pleased and had no ties to each other, in her version of events.

'Do you think if I did anything I would still be in the country?' she persisted. 'Why would I stay here? I have a passport. I could have left. I was waiting for him to come back to me. Three years of my life I gave him . . . I can't understand that you'd think I'd hurt him. Farah was harmed enough times and what did anyone do? Irish lads beat him and they [the Gardaí] did nothing. He has enemies, his so-called friends who give him drugs.'

She never saw him in the white soccer strip and couldn't explain the bloodstains in her flat. 'I'm not going to tell you bullshit . . . it must have happened when I wasn't there.' She admitted Farah hit her but she insisted: 'I didn't do nothing, I don't know how he ended up there. I never murdered Farah. No one touched Farah, no one in my family. You're looking in the wrong place.'

She said on the day he died they'd been drinking together, but after he went into an off-licence on O'Connell Street she went home. 'He went to see the Chink. I was drinking, drinking vodka. I can't remember. I was on the street that night with a man. I was with a man, someone I went off with.'

She agreed she'd bought bleach and bin bags and

aerosols in the Gala in Ballybough after the murder but said she'd spilled cranberry juice on a pair of white cords and 'Everybody buys bin bags.'

Taking the photograph of Farah in her hand, she said: 'I did nothing to that man. That man knows I didn't kill him. I never hurt a hair on that man's head.'

She claimed the number in her mobile phone contacts list recorded as 'J', which was the same number as that which dialled 999 and linked her to the crime, was a 'close friend', later admitting it was her son John's number.

'I never told my sons anything. My sons know nothing about me. When I do see my sons I will tell them that my boyfriend Farah is dead, something I only found out today.'

When told her sons informed on her because they were 'genuinely horrified', she replied, 'Not as horrified as I am. My sons told you nothing. They would tell you nothing because they don't know anything.'

John Mulhall was working on a job in Terenure College when gardaí arrested him in connection with the murder of Farah Noor. Some of the detectives involved believed he must have carried out the dismemberment of the body. An analysis of the times of the calls made and received on his mobile and CCTV footage of his van arriving outside Richmond Cottages placed him at the murder scene in the immediate aftermath.

They had no idea during his interview that he was experiencing more remorse than any of the people actually culpable. But his initial instinct was to deny everything.

*

Linda stuck a CD on, closed her eyes and danced around the kitchen in Kilclare Gardens when she got home from the interview. She felt absolutely brilliant and was on a complete high.

'What are you doing?' Marie chided, arriving in the room and turning the music off.

Linda laughed. 'They've nothing on us, we're in the clear.' She didn't need the music anyway. She could bop away without it.

Marie thought she was going to be sick. She slammed the door shut on the way out. She couldn't bear to look at her any more.

9

Confessions

Marie stalked up to Linda and eyeballed her. 'You are ruining our lives,' she yelled. Their rows were now occurring on a daily basis.

Linda shrugged.

'If you don't hand yourself in, I will,' Marie warned.

'Don't even fucking think about it,' Linda hissed back.

Marie stormed upstairs. The only person Linda cared about was herself. Her selfishness was destroying their father.

'Loads of people are being dragged into Farah's death,' Marie had bawled at her. But there was no getting through to her sister.

A week after the arrests, the Gardaí had started hassling John about his driving licence. John was convinced it was just to see if he'd crack and tell them what they wanted to hear. They'd pulled him in on Sundrive Road to check his tax and insurance. When he produced his documents in Tallaght Garda station they'd accused him of having a forged licence.

John argued the Carriage Office had already checked the authenticity when he needed a pass for a job in Dublin airport.

'We have to be very thorough when we're investigating a murder,' the garda told him, asking if he could help.

'It had nothing to do with me,' John insisted.

Marie could see him ageing with worry in front of her eyes.

There was only one way to get through to him. She decided to put it up to him, instead of Linda.

'It's her or me, Dad. Either she owns up to what she's done or I'm off.'

John Mulhall Sr phoned DI Christy Mangan on 17 August and told him Linda had agreed to tell him what happened.

He had gone to his daughter and told her he couldn't take any more. But when the Gardaí showed up, Linda had disappeared. She was in Tallaght hospital after another self-harming episode had almost led to her death.

Two days later Mangan came back. She sat on her bed in the shed out the back and talked and talked.

She told him how drunk Farah was.

'We walked up O'Connell Street where the cinema is. Some time after that we met a little Chinese boy playing with his friends. Farah started saying to the boy, "Kathy, this is my son; this is my son." My ma said, "Go away, you bleeding eejit, that is not your son." Farah said back to my ma, "It is my son, I know my own son." My ma said, "This is not your f**king son." The little boy was roaring and crying, he was really screaming. I think he was about five years old. Charlotte was still linking me at this time. I said to Charlotte, "Come on, let's walk." '

She explained how the situation suddenly spiralled out of control back in her mother's flat.

'Farah was holding on to me with one hand and the other hand then went on to me. It was just a grip I could not get out of. Charlotte said, "Get your hands off Linda." I told him to get his hands off me as well. He was never like this before. Charlotte said, "Get your hands off." It was like they were not there; it was like he could not see them. He frightened me, he did. Me ma said get his hands off me as well. It was a hold I could not get out of and then Charlie said again, "Get your fucking hands off," and he whispered. I remember it different some days, I remember in all different ways. Because of the E we took that night, I remember it in all different ways. When we were sitting in the chair, me and him, before he stood up, he whispered something in my ear that me and him were two creatures of the night and he whispered something else in my ear, I know it was something dirty he said to me. I could not really understand the language. Farah was saying, "You are so like your mammy." Charlotte was sort of putting it up to him, you know like, she has big shoulders and me ma put her hand on to his arm and he still would not let me go and Charlie was roaring, "Get your hands off Linda." Charlie must have seen the blade on the sink. She picked it up. Charlie opened up the blade and she cut him on the throat. The bedroom door was sort of open and me ma was like, "Get him in, get him in," and he sort of tripped. He did not fall on the floor, he sort of fell on to the bunk beds. Before he fell on the floor me ma was still trying to push him into the room saying, "Get him away, get him away from me." I had seen the hammer and hit him on the head. Charlotte got a knife from the kitchen. That Sean Paul CD was still playing. She stabbed him. I hit him loads of times with the hammer on the head. I don't want to keep talking about this. It is driving me mental. I don't want to be alive any more. I don't.'

She detailed the rationale behind the dismemberment.

'We got Farah into the bathroom. Myself and Charlie dragged him by the legs and me and Charlie cut him up. It was Charlie's idea. Me ma kept screaming, "Get him out, get him out." When I hit Farah with the hammer, Charlie stabbed him in the chest with the skinny knife. She cut him up with another knife, with a rugged blade. She cut into his legs with the knife. She got tired. The smell was . . . it won't go away, I think about it every night. I can't even look at a black person any more. I done that to my arm [pointing to slashes]. I did not want to wake up. I then used the hammer and hit his legs a number of times. It took us a few hours to do it. Me ma did not cut him up. We had to put a towel over there when we were removing his legs to stop the blood rushing out. We cut him on the knees and on the elbows. Me ma had told me already that he had raped her and I said, "He won't rape my ma again." I cut his private parts off. The long piece, not the balls. We threw it in the canal with the rest. I was sitting in the shower part and Charlie was sitting on the toilet. Me ma done nothing. I had the towel over his head, over his face and kept using the hammer. It would not come off. Both of us had to take turns with the hammer. I did not think about chopping it up but Charlotte said to do it. Me ma said, "Get it out of here." Me ma had sports bags. Charlotte started putting the heavy pieces into the sports bags but into black plastic bags first. I took the light bits and Charlotte took the heavy bits. We walked down to the canal. Me ma walked with us. You asked us to tell the truth. I am telling you the truth. We walked down to the canal a few times; it took a few times to go up and down. I see him every night in me mind before I go to sleep. I don't see him as a bad thing, just when he and Ma were happy. The smell won't go away. It just won't.'

She spoke about the fear when she realized Farah's body had been discovered.

'I rang me ma and said I have to go back down [to dig the head up]. I asked me ma to come with me. I went to my ma in Summerhill and asked her to come back down with me. The day I asked me ma to go with me was the day the guards were pulling Farah out of the canal. We were in the house crying. We went down close to the bridge, close to where the guards had the tape. We walked on the side, away from the Gala. We asked some people what was after happening. We went home and watched the news. We watched the news all the time.'

She outlined her own efforts to dispose of the head: 'I walked into a far field and kissed the bag and I told Farah I was sorry. I stayed there for ages, a long time. I had a bottle of vodka with me. I drank all of it. I took the hammer out of the bag. I left the head in the bag and hit the head loads of times to try and break it up. I fell asleep and woke up cold. It was starting to get dark. There was a mucky patch there and I turned away and pulled the head out of the bag. I put the muck over it and said a prayer and told him I was sorry and said, "It should not be you, it should be me ma." I burned the plastic bag there and the schoolbag and I ran home to bed. I am sorry for what happened. It is not my fault it happened, I'm sorry. If I could turn back time, I would. I am sorry.'

It was 17 October before John Mulhall managed to track down Charlotte and persuade her to follow Linda's lead. Linda had been charged with murder for over a month, since 13 September. She was out on bail, living in her father's house, awaiting trial.

By this time, Charlotte knew she was going to have to talk to the Gardaí. Her relationship with her mother had completely disintegrated. Charlotte had not seen her mother or heard from her since she had broken her big news – that she was pregnant. Since then, she had not been able to get hold of Kathleen, and didn't even know where she'd moved to. It was the ultimate betrayal for Charlotte. She no longer felt any loyalty to her mother and she planned to blame Kathleen for everything, including murder. She told the detectives how she and Linda accidentally stumbled upon the murder scene.

'Me and Linda thought Farah was after hitting her and they were fighting as usual. She [Kathleen] was like, she was screaming and crying like a mental case in the flat when we went back and we said, "Mam, what was after happening?" She said she was after killing him.

'. . . We didn't believe her and finally when we got her to sit down she said she was after killing him with a hammer and cutting his throat. We kept asking her where he was and she wouldn't tell us. She kept saying if she got locked up she was going to kill herself. Then she told us she was after putting the body in the river.

'. . . She said if she didn't kill him he would have killed her. Then she asked us would we help. Would me and Linda help her clean up the flat and we were cleaning up the flat. And me and Linda said that she wouldn't go to prison, we'd say we did it. We told her that we'd say that we killed him so she wouldn't go to prison. I didn't think Linda would really say it, really say that she done it because when it came to it, I didn't.

'. . . She told us that she hit him with a hammer and cut his throat . . . She said when he was dead she cut him up, she panicked . . . With a knife she said . . . Just a knife and a hammer . . . There was blood everywhere . . . Pools of blood . . . In the bedroom, in the middle of the floor and everywhere in the bathroom, the bathroom walls, all the walls were just red . . . She had blood on her clothes and on her hands . . . There was blood in her hair . . . Just everywhere – her clothes were soaked, all her hair was soaking . . . [There was] only a little bit [of blood] on her face.'

Charlotte denied knowing where the head was. 'She [Kathleen] won't tell us where the head is.'

She admitted helping to dump the body. 'We did bring the body down to the canal with her . . . When we came back to the house she had it all in bags. She had all the pieces in bags and the three of us had a bag and we just walked down and put it in the canal. Yeah, but I really don't know where she put the head . . . She said they were fighting and she hit him with a hammer and she cut his throat . . . There was a disgusting smell.'

Charlotte continued to maintain the only reason Linda had owned up to a crime she didn't commit was to shield their mother.

'I think she's fucking mental to be honest with you because she's saying she done things that she didn't do, just to protect Mam.'

She admitted she no longer had a relationship with Kathleen. 'Things are after changing now, sure the woman hasn't rang me, hasn't done nothing . . . I've tried to get through to the woman so many times, no one ever knows where she is, well I don't.'

Amazingly, the tough nut who had kept her cool when the Gardaí played hardball finally cracked when they showed her some kindness.

'You love your sister . . . you're trying to help her . . . Are you all right? . . . Do you want a glass of water? Will you tell us the truth . . . what happened?'

'Everything that Linda said,' Charlotte admitted, breaking down. '. . . He [Farah] was drinking for ages and everything was grand and the two of them started arguing as usual and Farah started saying shit to Linda and he wouldn't let her arm go.

'Something like "We're two creatures," something similar. Everyone was just arguing, me mam kept saying to me and Linda, "Just please kill him for me, kill him for me."

'Then she got the hammer and the knife. She gave them to me and Linda but he wouldn't let Linda go and I cut him . . . on the neck . . . I don't remember how he died in the bedroom. Then we didn't know what to do with him . . . Me mammy just said, "Just cut him up." '

She continued: 'I just remember cutting. I cut him up with the knife . . . We just cut him up and brought him down to the river . . . We cleaned up. We went back and we just started cleaning up, just cleaning up for hours . . . We had everything in the flat cleaned up. Then we went up to Sean Walsh Park and buried the head. After we done that we went back and started cleaning the flat again.'

She didn't know where the head was.

'Linda put it somewhere. At first the three of us went to the park and put it there but Linda moved it.'

She emphasized the dismemberment was Kathleen's idea: 'Me ma said the only way to get rid of this is you're going to have to cut it up now.'

She didn't blame her: 'I can't be annoyed with her. We're the stupid ones that done it.'

What was the switch that drove her to kill him?

'The way she [Kathleen] kept going on, just telling us, "He's going to kill me, he's going to kill me, youse have to kill him." '

After owning up, Charlotte admitted she felt 'a lot better'.

Linda was having one of her meltdowns in Kilclare Gardens and her father was bearing the brunt of it. It was

8 December. She was convinced Charlotte had stolen her Christmas present money for the kids.

John had just arrived in from Ryan's pub on James's Street, where he'd had a couple of pints with Marie and his brother, Eric. John had bought takeaways for the kids and Linda on the way home. But Linda was pissed and screaming.

'It's all your fucking fault. You've never done anything for us.'

John Mulhall walked out, claiming he was going to find Charlotte. Instead, he walked around to the back garden and took the clothes line down.

He drove to the Phoenix Park, leaving the car on Wellington Road. He walked into the forest and strung the rope from a tree. He pulled a €50 note from his pocket and used it as paper for a suicide note he wrote to Marie, tucking it back into his pocket.

10

Trial

Linda and Charlotte clasped hands in Dublin's wood-panelled Central Criminal Court as Judge Paul Carney prepared to hand down his sentence. Both had pleaded not guilty to the murder of Farah Noor, also known as Sheilila Salim. Their trial got under way on 12 October 2006 and had lasted thirteen days, with the jury deliberating for eighteen hours and one minute.

Linda had checked her nails as she waited for the verdict, and read celebrity magazines *Heat* and *Bella*. Expressionless, Charlotte was regularly hugged by Marie. A memoir about alcohol and drug addiction, *A Million Little Pieces*, sat on the bench between them. For a while it looked as if the case could swing either way. At one stage the exhausted jury forewoman reported that they were 'talked out' and the 'air was blue', indicating an impasse in the jury room. Judge Carney reminded her that 'Five children have a vital interest in this.'

The defence had argued that if the jury believed the Mulhalls had been provoked into the killing, they could acquit them or find both guilty of the lesser charge of manslaughter. They had called two of Farah's previous partners, 'Mae' and 'Sue', to corroborate his portrayal as a violent rapist, requesting that their real names should not be revealed to respect their privacy.

'He tried to do something on me,' Mae had told detectives. 'He tried to do something, make sex with me . . . he forced me to do it.'

Sue also testified. She had revealed to gardaí that Farah Noor raped her on an almost daily basis and she feared he might kill her. She said he had also been interviewed as a suspect in an unsolved murder case in Dun Laoghaire, Co. Dublin. The now-married mother of three said he changed when he had drink on him and agreed that the deceased carried knives.

She said she had taken out a protection order against him and had secured full custody of their child. She agreed she had been raped on numerous occasions and had had 'very brutal sex' with the deceased at his whim and that she feared her son was being abused by him.

She said the mother of the two accused, Kathleen Mulhall, had contacted her on a number of occasions, making complaints about Mr Noor and seeking advice. The medical treatment Kathleen had received after her beatings at Farah's hands was also entered as evidence.

The sisters' lawyers argued that it was possible, since Farah's head had not been found, that he had died before being stabbed from banging his head and that this could make them accessories after the fact.

None of Farah Noor's relatives was in court. They could not afford the flight from Kenya. Kathleen Mulhall was also noticeably absent. She had fled to the UK, where she was living in the London area.

But when the jury returned its verdict, it found Linda guilty of manslaughter and Charlotte guilty of murder. Linda whispered, 'Thank God it's over.'

Charlotte reminded her lawyer to make an application for her five-month-old baby boy to join her in the Dóchas Centre at Mountjoy Women's Prison for up to eighteen months.

As he prepared to hand down their sentences on 4 December 2006, Judge Carney took into account what the head of the murder inquiry, Detective Inspector Christopher Mangan, told the court of his knowledge of the two accused.

Mangan said Linda Mulhall was unemployed and a mother of four. She had a conviction for larceny dating back to 1993. She had not shown up for the start of the trial and a bench warrant had been issued for her arrest. A doctor gave evidence that she smoked heroin and drank up to three litre bottles of vodka a day.

DI Mangan said she came from a 'very tough family background'. He suggested that the mother of four had met little but trouble, tragedy and brutality for much of her young life, citing the 'drugs-related' death of her husband and her subsequent relationship with a man who ultimately got seven or eight years for burning and brutalizing her four small children.

He said Charlotte Mulhall had a conviction under the Criminal Damage Act and for a public order offence. She had received probation for both. She also had a problem with drugs and alcohol and came from a 'troubled' background.

Referring to the death of their father, John, he said: 'John Mulhall was probably in my view the mainstay of the family.' He believed the current case had contributed to his death.

'It was a very long trial and we're happy it's been brought to a conclusion,' DI Mangan continued. 'We're still actively seeking the whereabouts of Kathleen Mulhall. Anyone who has information about her whereabouts, we'd be delighted to receive information from them.'

All that was left now was to translate the verdicts into sentences and when the round-faced, balding Judge Carney looked over the rim of his glasses and declared it was the 'most grotesque case' ever to have come before him, the Mulhall sisters must have envisaged long years stretching ahead. The sisters' lawyers tried to adjourn sentencing until psychiatric reports were ready but the judge refused. The judge gave Charlotte, who was dressed in a pinstriped suit, the mandatory life sentence. He refused to go easy on Linda because of her dysfunctional family background or life of disadvantage. The judge pointed out that Linda had tried to stop or postpone the trial from the beginning by not showing up and threatening to go 'cold turkey' during it.

In fifty previous cases before the courts, the longest sentence imposed for manslaughter verdicts in murder trials was fourteen years. He gave her fifteen. He said it was open to him to impose a life sentence on her too but he had to respect the fact that the jury had allowed the defence of provocation. He added that the only reason he wasn't giving her eighteen years was because she was 'very frank in her admissions' once she began co-operating with gardaí.

'Any time the police called she took them to point out locations and on the final occasion when the police came to arrest her, she said she had had her bags packed on the first day.'

But he took issue with the claim by Linda's barrister, Brendan Grehan SC, that she was a good mother: 'I don't regard this as particularly persuasive. If she was a good mother she would not have got herself into a situation of this kind.'

Dressed in a white shirt and black leather jacket, Linda wept inconsolably behind her long, blonde hair.

11

Bad Girls

The best picture of what makes the Mulhall sisters tick emerged in Mountjoy Women's Prison. Far removed from the spectacle of a trial and with no prospect of parole before 2013, Linda and Charlotte, now dubbed the 'Scissor Sisters' by newspapers, instantly became top dogs even among society's most damaged and dangerous women.

They faced down some tough competition from Catherine Nevin, the Black Widow and self-styled Queen of the Joy. The scheming landlady of the Jack White pub is an arch manipulator who plotted for ten years to kill her publican husband, Tom, and managed to create her own human pyramid-style power structure behind bars.

The Mulhalls quickly knocked young killer Kelly Noble's ambitions for the top spot on the head. They regularly confronted devil-may-care Kelly over dropsies (drugs thrown over the prison wall) and stories appearing about them in the papers. The baby-faced 21-year-old, who has two children, was jailed for ten years for knifing nineteen-year-old Emma McLoughlin from Laytown in June 2006. She boasted (in the *Sunday World*, in her only interview), 'Emma thought she was Big Miss Large. I was selling drugs and she thought she was bigger than me. She was always pushing it.'

Kelly's problems went back to her tragic childhood; she was abused by her father, Derek Benson, who was subsequently murdered by her mother, Jacqui. Benson also subjected Jacqui to horrific acts of cruelty and violence at their home in Ballymun before Jacqui hired a man to hack him to death for IR£800 when Kelly was just fourteen. Although the pair were reunited behind bars, the mother–daughter relationship is less than harmonious. Kelly is regularly transferred to Limerick because of her behaviour; she has even challenged Jacqui to fight her in a grudge match.

Another inmate jockeying for poll position in the race to the bottom when the Scissor Sisters were first jailed was Martina O'Connor, a stunning teenage tearaway with a death wish. She'd racked up seventy-two previous convictions, including one for setting a girl's hair on fire and another for making life hell for her elderly neighbours.

Unlike the male prisoners on the far side of the yard, who still slop out in overcrowded, Victorian-style cells, the Dóchas Centre accommodates the women in their own rooms in seven separate houses. Linda and Charlotte had a clear choice to make the best of a bad situation. They could have availed themselves of a huge range of educational courses if they wanted. Instead they carved out a new role as a female version of the Kray twins.

They instilled fear into the other prisoners by befriending the other 'man killers'. Their first close affiliation was with 'She-Devil' Christine Williams, a paranoid schizophrenic. The 29-year-old Welsh woman is serving life for murdering a complete stranger, 54-year-old Andrew Foley from Leitrim, after offering him sex if he bought her a pint. When Foley took her back to his flat on Dublin's Nelson Street, Williams stabbed him thirteen times, once in the eye, then doused the father of four in boiling water from a kettle. She mutilated his eye, face, shoulder and genitals in a frenzied attack, laughing openly during her trial, even telling the judge to 'fuck off'.

'Linda, Charlotte and Christine go everywhere together,' a prison source said after they were first jailed. 'It's weird because Linda and Charlotte are supposed to have been driven to their crime because they were pushed over the edge that night. But Christine is definitely not the full shilling.'

Linda would find love in the arms of other women, perhaps because of her experience on the outside of men like her brutal ex, Wayne Kinsella.

'Linda has been having an on/off relationship with Tanya Lamb inside,' a source revealed.

Lamb, aged twenty-nine, from Mountainview Park in Rathfarnham, is serving life for murdering her ex-partner, Anthony Jordan, in May 2003. He died at his flat in Balbutcher Lane in Ballymun after Tanya bashed his head in with a hockey stick and a mop.

When Lamb was viciously attacked in a row inside prison and had a cement block smashed over her head, she required ten stitches and her mother Sandra went public. She claimed her daughter had been victimized for not taking part in lesbian sex romps and appealed to the authorities for more protection. Lamb would also suffer regular beatings at the Mulhalls' hands.

'They gave her a serious hiding, worse than anything she'd ever had before,' a source said. It was the Mulhalls' way of sending out a message – nobody messes with us.

The sisters have been causing mayhem in other ways too. During a school trip to the prison, designed to warn youngsters about where a life of crime could lead, Charlotte flashed her breasts at an eleven-year-old boy.

'This young fella was horsing about during the trip,' a source revealed. 'He was a bit hyper. He pulled his T-shirt up when he saw Charlotte, just messing, and she did the same thing back. There was uproar. The kid shouldn't have been exposed to that.' Worse was to come when a grinning Charlotte posed for a photograph holding a carving knife to another prisoner's throat.

In their new home, where notoriety is a form of currency, the Mulhall sisters shamelessly played up their own infamy to force themselves up the prison's ladder.

'Whenever there's a fight, Charlotte and Linda start chanting, "Cut the throat, cut the throat," which freaks everyone out because that's how their victim died,' the source said.

They have also talked openly and casually about their own crime.

'They're always going on about the smell after they killed him,' a prison insider said. 'Linda went on and on about hitting him with the hammer. She wasn't sorry. She just said he was a bastard and that's why they did it.'

Seemingly at home in this inverse hierarchy, the sisters

perversely revelled in their infamy. They got a huge kick out of a show put on by comedian Tommy Tiernan.

'He cracked them up by making a big laugh out of what they did and made them feel like superstars,' a prison insider revealed. 'They were the main source of his material. The whole show was about the prisoners' crimes. He joked with the Mulhalls that washing in the canal gave you blackheads.'

Paradoxically, prison life is the most protected, structured environment the sisters have ever known, presenting them with many opportunities. They showed an interest in the martial arts and beauty courses. Linda got a job in the salon doing the women's colour but abused her position by stealing a GHD hair straightener. Beauty courses are extremely popular in the prison, which in 2006 forked out €9,520 on beauty products such as fake tan and hair dye. Prison insiders say that inmates use the courses to give one another facials, makeovers and other treatments like waxings and body rubs.

'They are designed to give them a skill for when they get out of jail and could allow them to start apprenticeships or get work in hair or beauty salons. But the reality is that they are a great way of getting free treatments,' a source said.

In June 2007, Charlotte christened her one-year-old son in the prison chapel.

She celebrated the occasion by getting stoned, and was not allowed to keep her son with her overnight, having already lost one of her two weekly meetings with him after trying to smuggle drugs into the prison during one of his visits.

Linda and her on/off lesbian lover, killer Tanya Lamb, both attended the ceremony, which was performed by the prison chaplain. The baby's grandmother, Kathleen, was still on the run.

Kathleen Mulhall was finally tracked down in February 2008. She was living in London and found by gardaí and the Metropolitan Police through social welfare records. After being interviewed, she agreed to return to Ireland voluntarily and was remanded in Mountjoy Prison with her daughters.

She pleaded guilty to helping to clean up the crime scene in order to conceal evidence to protect her daughters, and in May 2009 she received five years' imprisonment. Sentencing the Scissor Sisters' mum, who gave her address as St Mary's Park, Carlow, where she'd moved after breaking contact with her family, Judge Paul Carney once again described it as 'the most grotesque case' he'd ever seen.

As snapshots of Irish crime go, the picture in the Central Criminal Court on the day she learned her fate was as grisly as it gets. Fifty-three-year-old Kathleen shared the court with a Galway father of four, Edward Griffin, aged forty-five, who left the man he'd killed in a walk-in freezer behind a city centre fish shop for five years. Also ongoing was the murder trial of Gary Campion, a 26-year-old member of one of Limerick's feuding gangs. Campion shot the man he was on trial for murdering twice in the head from the back seat of a car the victim was driving. Campion had only been released from prison the previous Friday after a two-year sentence for threatening to kill a prison officer. He is also now serving another life sentence for the murder of Limerick nightclub bouncer Brian Fitzgerald, killed in 2002 because he refused to allow drugs to be sold in the club.

Gary Campion's brother Noel was shot dead in 2007. His brother Willie is serving life for the murder and torture of prisoner Paul Skehan in 1998. Skehan was blindfolded, beaten and suspended over a banister with TV cable in an inverted crucifixion position, having also been doused with petrol. He was discovered later by a neighbour but never regained consciousness, dying just under two months later.

Kathleen appeared in court heavily made up, her hair dyed dark brown and pulled back, wearing a pale pink blouse and light brown pinstriped jacket, and bedecked in costume jewellery. Having previously adopted some of the outer signs of the Islamic religion, presumably in deference to the fact that Farah had been a Muslim, Kathleen had switched from Islam back to Christianity while being remanded for sentencing and her hair was once again visible – this time in a ponytail of long extensions.

Judge Carney compared the case to other landmarks in criminal savagery – Shan Mohangi, who boiled his girl-friend Hazel Mullen's body parts in a Harcourt Street restaurant in 1963, and the cross-dressing killer Michael Bambrick, recently released, who also dismembered his victims.

The judge reminded the court that he had the advantage of having been the trial judge for Kathleen's daughters, Linda and Charlotte. The fifteen-year sentence he'd given to Linda was one of the longest ever imposed for manslaughter and had been upheld in the Court of Criminal Appeal, the judge went on. Kathleen had pleaded guilty to carrying out an act with the intention to impede the prosecution of another for murder. 'She helped clean up the flat . . . the scene of evidence . . . and the maximum penalty is ten years,' the judge said. The DPP had submitted that she be treated at the higher end of the scale.

'She laid a false trail suggesting that Farah Noor was still alive . . . supporting the DPP's case for a longer sentence,' Judge Carney said, adding that he was also bound to look at the factors in favour of the accused. These factors were as follows: she'd pleaded guilty in a case that would have been difficult for the DPP to prosecute; there was a lack of previous convictions; she'd returned from England to face the charges; she'd acted out of the desire to protect her daughter and her family; she had suffered violence at the hands of her family or men with whom she was in relationships; she'd made good use of her time behind bars.

He gave Kathleen five years, backdated from 13 February 2008 when she was remanded to Mountjoy Prison. With her automatic entitlement to 25 per cent remission for good behaviour, she'll be free by 2011.

12

Last Pieces of the Jigsaw

I wanted to know what made Linda, Charlie and their mother, Kathleen, tick. In court their defence was that Farah Noor had provoked them, but how did they explain the elaborate cover-up afterwards? How could they have chopped up someone whom they had known for years, socialized with and, in Kathleen's case, professed to love? What was going through their minds when they packed Farah's body parts into sports bags and dumped them into the canal like household rubbish, stopping afterwards to buy a breakfast roll? Why stuff his head in a schoolbag and transport it on a bus like a trophy?

My starting point was the woman who knew Farah as well, if not better, than anyone else, his ex-girlfriend 'Sue'. How bad was he? How much more could she, the woman who claimed to have escaped an attempted rape by Farah in Dun Laoghaire on the same night Raonaid Murray was murdered, remember about the night in question?

I find her living a short distance from the Kilclare cul-de-sac in Tallaght where the Mulhalls themselves grew up. Sue answers the door of her home, in a white polo neck and jeans, looking younger than her twenty-six years, with shoulder-length brown hair and piercing light blue eyes. It is immediately obvious why Farah Noor had targeted her. She is polite, softly spoken and nervous as I explain why I am here. A handsome little boy of about ten years with gorgeous coffee-coloured skin sits listening on the stairs, his resemblance to Farah Noor striking. Two other younger children are playing in the background.

But Sue does not want me to come in. She wants to put the past behind her, she explains. She's frightened that members of the Mulhall family might take a grudge. She is desperate to save her family from any further embarrassment. Most of all she wants to protect her three children and her husband from her past, she says. I tell her I need to talk to her about Farah's involvement in the Raonaid Murray case, because as a potential suspect he seems to tick all the right boxes. As I discuss the parallels, she becomes alarmed.

'Was she stabbed?' she asks about Raonaid, genuinely surprised.

It seems hard to believe that given how important Sue might be to unlocking the Raonaid mystery, she doesn't know something so fundamental. I need to talk to her more than ever.

She agrees to think about it overnight, and when we next come face to face she lets me in – explaining she is going to go over things for Raonaid's family's sake. She wants to help.

Sitting across the table in her immaculate kitchen, she begins sifting through the memorabilia of her life with Farah – tickets, photographs, letters. She hands me a snap showing the two of them together. Farah is dressed in a tuxedo, and Sue in a glamorous olive green, crushed velvet dress. He grins at the photographer like the cat who's got the cream. He looks playboy handsome, confident and cool, and he has his arm gripped tightly around her waist.

'That was taken the night of my debs,' Sue explains. She was only seventeen years old at the time, and already the mother of Farah's one-year-old son, the boy on the stairs. 'He's the image of him,' she agrees.

I ask when her debs took place. She can't remember the exact date, but given that most debs are held in September, the picture I'm looking at has to have been taken within weeks of Raonaid Murray's death.

Sue thought Farah was twenty years old at the time, when in reality he was thirty-three, she says. That night, like the relationship, was destined to end in disaster.

'All I remember about the debs is Farah getting into a fight with another fella,' she says. Her tone is not bitter, it's weary.

'But he didn't deserve that death,' she states categorically. Even after everything he put her through – rapes, beatings, the torture of her son, she adds: 'If it was anybody that had to kill him, it should have been me. I honestly thought sometimes we would die at his hands. I fought back, I can tell you, but nobody deserves what he got, not even him.'

They met on O'Connell Street, on her sixteenth birthday in April 1998, she recalls. 'I waved at him. I was just a kid. I thought he was good-looking and I was just messing, the way kids do. He was over straight away, asking me did I want to "go for a drink?" I was delighted with myself. We all went up to his friend's flat and had a drink. That was where it started.'

By June 1998, she was pregnant. 'He was delighted and when I had a son, he was over the moon. He was brilliant at first, buying him clothes and a pram. All he spoke about was "my son, my son". But then his drinking got very bad.'

Thanks to her parents, she explains, she managed to sit her Leaving Cert, even though she was now a young mum living with a violent man. She dreamed of becoming an architect, but Farah had his own ideas about her future.

'He wanted me to have more babies,' she says. 'I used to have to hide my pill from him because he wanted me to get pregnant again.'

Did she want more babies?

'Then? No!'

And she was beginning to suspect there was more to his past than met the eye.

'When I first met him he told me his wife had been killed after she was knocked down. But every time I asked him about it I got a different version of the way she died, so I started to suspect he was lying. I wrote letters to his sisters and his mother asking them about it but they never told me his wife was still alive.'

She believed everything else about the story he'd told her. 'He said he'd come to Ireland because of the war in Somalia, that he was being beaten up and thrown in and out of camps where there was no food or water and that the soldiers had been giving him grief.'

She refers to a set of knives he kept in the wardrobe of his room in the Rosepark Hotel in Dun Laoghaire. 'He used to carry a Swiss Army knife everywhere. He said it was for his own protection if he got in a fight. He used to say he could cut a person up like a chicken because he used to work as a butcher in England. He kept them in a sort of plastic sleeve he could roll up, like a GHD thing with pockets. One was a carved blade knife about twelve inches long. It was bigger than an A4 sheet. It had a dark handle with cuts into the sharp end like shark's teeth. There was a butcher's knife with a long black handle and a straight blade carved at the end with a serrated edge and small teeth. He would show them off and say, "These are my butcher knives." '

Sue now realizes this behaviour was bizarre but says at the time she was 'very naïve'.

By now their relationship had spiralled into a 'living nightmare'. He was raping her on a daily basis, beating her, but was 'always careful not to hit me on the face where the bruises would be seen', she says. 'I never told anyone. I didn't want people knowing my business.' He also wanted sex whenever she was bathing the baby, she recalls. 'It was disgusting.'

She was very reluctant to discuss the following memories, and agreed to share them only because it would help to show what Farah was capable of: 'Whenever he wanted sex he would have it,' she says. It didn't matter if she didn't want it. He could see that he was hurting her and she was crying and he would continue. 'We would be watching TV or whatever and he would just turn on me and demand sex, there and then, he wouldn't wait.' She would tell him no and he wouldn't listen, she says. 'I didn't know any different, he was my first boyfriend. I can honestly say he raped me, he forced himself on me, he would hurt me. I would kick him, screaming at him to get off me, and he would hit me with his hand, slap me on the face and head.' This happened at least once a day and sometimes twice a day. 'There was no normal sex, no love, there was no kissing or touching, just brutal sex.' She says he did not care if she had her period, or was sick. 'This was my life.'

She reveals the non-stop cruelty: 'I remember one time, I never told anyone about this, but I was in bed and trying to sleep and he threw alcohol all over me and all over the bed, vodka, and he kept trying to light it with a lighter.'

She admits becoming really worried by the two-way conversations he conducted with himself in the mirror. 'It used to freak me out,' she says. 'I was terrified. He'd be speaking in a different language but he used to be really into it. He was admiring himself and telling himself how gorgeous he was, I'm convinced.'

She only left Farah for good when her friend 'Melissa' moved in and witnessed the abuse and informed Sue's parents. Although she got a barring order, Farah continued to stalk her and make her life a misery, even targeting their son. 'He still had visitation rights and my son was two when he came back and I noticed about five cigarette burns on his leg. I was sick. My son had eczema anyway so I couldn't be sure and I asked him, "What happened?" and he said, "Daddy smoke." He was only two.

'Farah used to burn himself with cigarettes whenever a friend died. The inside of his arms were all dark scars.'

Sue remembers clearly the incident in the Penny Black pub, when Farah again referred to Raonaid Murray during a row with Melissa. 'We were going for a drink and he said to her, "No wonder your friend was murdered. You're like a lesbian whore." '

Sue also remembers the phone calls she got from Farah's new girlfriend, Kathleen Mulhall. 'She rang me and said he'd locked her in a bedroom, that she was pregnant with twins and that he'd beaten her and she was bleeding, she was losing the babies. I told her she had to get away from him, that he would never change. She wanted to know how I got away from him.

'She sounded really nice. She would ring other times just for a chat, asking me how I was and saying we should meet up. We just never got the chance.'

Amazingly, even after everything she endured, Sue says: 'I never hated Farah. There were two Farahs. Sober Farah and drunk Farah. He was like Dr Jekyll and Mr Hyde. Sober, he was loving, caring and fun-loving. Drunk, he was violent, possessive, angry and jealous. At the end he was always drunk.'

She went to his funeral. She says there is no excuse for the way he met his end. She found it 'scary' to come face to face with the Mulhall sisters in court 'because of the way they kept looking at me'.

'What happened to him was disgusting and grotesque,'

she says. She hopes that his head will be found so it can be buried with him. But most of all she wants the parents of Raonaid Murray to get justice.

'For me there could be nothing worse than the thought that Farah might have done it [killed Raonaid]. It's bad enough I am going to have to tell his son that his father was murdered, but to have to tell him his murdered father was a murderer would be just too much,' she says, as our conversation comes to an end.

I need to speak to Linda, Charlotte or Kathleen Mulhall more than ever. There are huge outstanding issues of public importance involved, including the Raonaid Murray link, and the problem of locating Farah's missing body parts. But the prison authorities operate an un-written rule enforcing a blanket ban on journalists' attempts to interview prisoners. I believe it's draconian, and it's anti-democratic – it also means that people suffer-ing miscarriages of justice never get the chance to talk. My interview will have to be carried out covertly. I begin to try to establish contact with the Mulhalls behind bars, when suddenly an unexpected avenue for further investigation presents itself.

Linda Mulhall's fiancé, 'Constantine', contacts me at the *Sunday World*. He is a 29-year-old Moldovan and he wants to discuss the stories I've run in the paper. He's been Linda's partner since before Farah's death, and now I want to find out did their paths cross? And does he know anything about Raonaid Murray?

We meet in a Kildare hotel. It's the first time

Constantine has come out of the shadows. He's here because the *Sunday World* has been running stories about Linda's on/off relationship with the shaven-headed Tanya Lamb and Constantine is not happy. He does not believe Linda would be unfaithful to him. He wants to know my sources.

Constantine is not what I expect. He's short, sallow-skinned with dark eyes and a goatee and clearly in a state of emotional distress. He doesn't want a coffee or any lunch because he's not paying for it, and won't accept my offer to buy it for him. He works in a garden centre, and doesn't want to enter the lounge because he's embarrassed about the state of his clothes.

He has been in Ireland for seven years, he explains in broken English. He met Linda before she killed Farah Noor through her late father, whom he worked for. He stayed with her after the crime, which she never properly explained to him, and he visits her every Saturday or Sunday and brings her children.

'I love Linda,' he says. 'She is very soft and very easily led. Charlotte you would find on the street fighting and drinking vodka but Linda is very different.'

Constantine wants me to tell him that Linda is not a lesbian. This I cannot do. And when I refuse point-blank to name my sources, he becomes increasingly agitated. Linda is the love of his life and he's prepared to wait for her as long as she's not having an affair, he says.

'We filled in the papers to get married but we were too late. The court case came before we got the chance. I don't believe she is a lesbian. I give her everything she wants.

I've spent thousands of euro on her cosmetics on the internet.'

He has an immediate answer for why Linda is in prison for the most gruesome killing in recent memory. 'It was the drugs. When I met her she didn't take drugs but when she started she changed. I don't touch drugs. I brought her to the GP to try and get her off them. The morning after she'd taken them she wouldn't be able to remember anything. She'd be so embarrassed about things, crying. She never spoke to me about the murder.'

Constantine tells me he lived with Linda for a year. He explains the real source of her problems. 'Her first husband just wanted her to have children. The more the better. Wayne [Kinsella] hurt her and the kids and got her on drugs.'

And her father? What does he make of Kathleen Mulhall's claim to detectives that Linda didn't have a good life thanks to her father? Does he believe Linda was abused by her father, John, who committed suicide before the case came to trial?

'Yes,' Constantine says.

With tears in his eyes he describes how she had no life and how he intervened on numerous occasions to stop her self-harming, cutting her arms and attempting to take her own life. 'She didn't want to go drinking with Charlotte that day,' he says, adding that Charlotte bullied her into it.

He says her drug addiction has gone from bad to worse since she was locked up. 'But she has the best of everything. Any clothes she wants I bring her.' He says the other female prisoners actually cut all her clothes up out of badness but he can't resist a grin when he describes how they put chocolates in her washing 'just to be bad'.

I ask him what he knows about Farah Noor. Constantine says he refused to have anything to do with him. 'The first time I spoke to him he asked me to sell drugs,' he says in disgust. This is all he knows about him.

My request to interview one of the Mulhalls has reached Mountjoy. By now even James, Kathleen's son and the Scissor Sisters' brother, is back in prison, jailed for attacking prostitutes. The father of six from Ardmore Walk who with his brother had turned his family in after Kathleen confessed to him in prison is now serving five years for robbing the women in 2006. He dragged one by the hair when she tried to escape. A psychologist might point out the connections between these incidents and the fact that his mother and two sisters all sold themselves to men.

I speak to a professional who's come across the Mulhall women behind bars, about who he considers would be the most reliable source. He doesn't hesitate: 'Charlotte's the best of them,' he says. It seems incredible that the woman who played the worst part in Farah's murder and who got the stiffest sentence should be considered the most balanced.

But as it turns out, Charlotte has her own reasons for wanting to speak to a journalist – her son. The woman who swaggered into court sucking a fag with a devil-may-care attitude, dressed in skin-tight clothes, black eyeliner curling into Cleopatra slits at the sides of her eyes under a sloping scar across her forehead, is pining for her little boy . . . She's in big trouble with the prison authorities. That photograph of her holding a knife up to another inmate's throat and grinning over a birthday cake has appeared in the papers and she's been transferred to Limerick as a punishment. But the destination is considered too far for the two-year-old to travel. After nine weeks without a visit, she's prepared to talk to me in the hope she can highlight the flouting of a court order protecting her access rights to her son.

It's her first ever interview, and so as to ensure it's not the last time I infiltrate the prison system I can't describe exactly how it was done.

'What was Farah like?' she asks, repeating the first question I put to her in a high-pitched, light Dublin accent. 'He was an evil bastard . . . He broke my ma's ribs with a hurley, her hand with a hammer . . . The things he done!'

No remorse then, it was still his fault in her mind?

'We were very high . . . What I done, I think I was that out of my head really, I didn't really realize what I was after doing until the next day. I still can't believe that it's true . . .'

Why?

'He was trying to strangle me ma . . . dragging out of Linda and pulling out of her and saying mad shit to her, he was a weirdo.'

And afterwards?

'My memory . . . the most I remember about it is that Linda and my ma, they were that panicked and afraid, they were just screaming basically, what are we going to do with this [the body]?'

So she felt she was being the strong one, by chopping him up?

'Yeah, kind of,' she explains, 'the two of them were just really losing it altogether, I dunno, it was just a spur of the moment thing like and me ma said we're going to have to cut him, cut him up like . . .' Here Charlotte breaks down crying. 'I dunno, I think it was just panic trying to get rid of it and cut him up basically.'

How does she live with what she did?

'I don't sleep, you always see it in front of you, just like flashbacks all the time. It is really hard to deal with. I try to tell myself that it's not real kind of but it's very hard though really . . . I'm on anti-depressants, I was never on that stuff in my life.'

If she still hates Farah, does she feel she got a raw deal in the courts?

Yes, she says. 'We were convicted before the trial even started. The jury didn't hear his two ex-partners give evidence. They were sent out for that part.'

This is not in fact the case. Although Sue and Mae – both of whom bore a child for Farah – had their identities protected, their evidence was heard in court. Both agreed to testify about the violence they suffered at his hands.

'I mean that girl told of how he was molesting his own child and everything,' Charlotte says. 'He broke her arm, raping her when she was only sixteen.'

Did she ever hear Farah Noor boast about killing Raonaid Murray?

She did, she says.

I press her for a date.

'The whole time they were living in Cork. Soon as he was drinking he'd always be talking about the girl that he killed in Dun Laoghaire. You'd never know whether to take him serious or not. He'd been fine when he wasn't drinking, but then when he was drinking, he just used to go ballistic.'

Did she believe him?

'He was very convincing like, talking about it to his friends, they used to say don't believe him, but you'd never know with him, he'd be talking to himself in mirrors, a total lunatic when he was drinking.'

I ask her again to try to pin one of Farah's Raonaid confessions to something else that happened that night, so that I can try to work out the date and corroborate the claim.

'One night, with friends, we were all drinking up there. The Gardaí even have a report on it and there was travellers living across the road in Grattan Hill and he fought the travellers, stabbed two of them 'cos he always carried knives, and he smashed up the van and tried to stab two of the boys. He [Farah] was on about it [killing Raonaid] that night, and he was always on about it, like the minute he'd start arguing he'd say I'm going to kill you like I killed her.'

Her story tallies with the records – on 3 November 2003, Farah contacted the Gardaí claiming he had been assaulted by two men in Cork. But when he sobered up, he refused to make a statement.

Did he ever brag about killing anyone else?

'Oh, in his own country he said he killed a man and took his identification and that's how he got here like, but then again he'd change his story ten minutes later and say his wife was shot and killed over there. And he'd say that's why he was here, and then he'd say again, "Oh no, I killed another man, a fisherman." And that's how he got here and took his papers and he was very mad like that, you'd never know what to believe and what not to believe.'

But she continued to socialize with him. Does she believe her blind loyalty to her family and especially her mother is at the heart of all of her problems?

'There was always trouble growing up with my brothers and the police and my eldest [brother], he's been locked up the best part of my life . . . I've always worked and that, I've always had jobs and that but there was always something happening in my house, do you know that kind of way . . . there was always trouble in the house,' she agrees.

What did she want to do with her life?

'I always wanted to be a chef. I was on a three-year chef course in the Joy. I worked in the kitchen, I made all the cakes.'

Was that how she had access to knives, as in the one she held up to another prisoner's throat in the photograph? Yes, she says, explaining that she held the knife because the person taking the photograph told her to.

'It was taken about a year before it came out, by another prisoner.' She says that it was done as a 'joke', and that she did it without thinking. The truth may be more complicated as a number of rumours have since emerged as to why and how the photo was taken.

Charlotte keeps portraying herself as a victim. I ask her if she blames her mother for what's happened. But she jumps to Kathleen's defence.

'Me ma was a great ma, so was me da, that's one thing I will say to them.'

But Kathleen has been telling detectives she still loves Farah. How does that make Charlotte feel – serving life for killing a man to protect her mother, when her mother says she still loves him?

'She does not [still claim to love him], she doesn't even talk about it. It's too hard for her. Even if I try and mention something to her about it she'll just break down in tears. She is taking it very bad now, I don't think she can really cope with it. She's been drinking and all. She's lost an awful lot of weight. She slimmed down an awful lot. She's changed an awful lot since I last seen her. I think she's very withdrawn and all. She used to be very happy-go-lucky and all but I think she's very different ... I hadn't seen her in nearly two and a half years anyway ... The last time I actually seen her was when I found out I was pregnant. I told her I was pregnant in town. After that, I never seen her again until she went to prison and she was just a totally different person.'

How could she forgive her mother for absconding and leaving her in that state to face the music?

'We wasn't even charged at that time [when Kathleen fled],' Charlotte says, again jumping to her mother's defence. 'We'd only been questioned on it. I wouldn't have even I don't think really admitted to it, only for Linda. Because Linda actually walked into a Garda station and told them the story. She just couldn't cope with it like.'

But I know that Kathleen still sees Farah through rose-coloured glasses. Why else would she have converted to Islam, wear her hair up in a cap, and insist on a Halal diet in the prison? I ask Charlotte if Kathleen put her on the game as a teenager, and not the other way around.

'That's a lie,' she blasts. 'I was out working, me mother never did . . . I only actually started going out working on the streets after all that hassle [her parents breaking up] – that's when I started on heroin and heavy drugs, and it was just to pay for my habit really.'

Again the answer doesn't add up, since Kathleen herself admitted to detectives she was selling sex. Didn't Kathleen kick Charlotte's father out of his home, so Farah Noor could move in?

'Me da was having an affair with her sister so there was always trouble in the family . . . But to me that was a long time ago. We were kids when that happened. Me ma was ten years with him, he was very good to her out working and bringing her out but he just kind of went off the rails out drinking and meeting fellas, and she was very cruel to me da before she left because she threw him out of the house and left him homeless, and me little brother and younger sister.'

I remind Charlotte that she also killed Farah and chopped him up at her mother's instigation, according to Charlotte's own version of events. Of all the things that have happened to Charlotte in her short life, I ask her what was the worst.

'You'd get upset at me child basically being taken away from me but I think me da [his suicide] was the hardest thing. That nearly killed me, I have to say. That's making me worse, I'm not over that . . . He was never the same after my mam left. He was a very happy man, he'd go to work and that, but when my mam left, he got real cranky and that, he'd be hanging around the house.

'He was very caring and hardworking and if we ever needed anything he'd get it for us and bring us off to bike rallies, he looked after us well, he was a very hard-working man all his life.

'He actually wrote on a fifty-euro note and he just says everything was too hard and he loved us all and that he wanted to go.'

Was her father involved in disposing of the body, as detectives suspected? Was there more on his mind than his daughters' pending trial when he took his own life?

'He had nothing to do with it whatsoever,' she states.

But Kathleen rang him and he came . . .

'Literally just a phone call, no involvement whatsoever,' Charlotte insists.

Charlotte makes it clear that apart from Farah she doesn't blame anyone else for what happened; she attributes most of the madness of the night to drink and drugs.

'It [heroin] ruined my life altogether, it really did, I thought it would work and everything else but it just really depresses everything and then when you come off it everything just hits you again, it's like best of reality with a bang. I was on a methadone programme for a year and a half in the Joy and I ended up coming off that as well when I got that job in the kitchen . . . I'm not on anything, I would not touch drugs at all because really I did not want the baby coming up seeing me stoned out of my head in the prison either. That's what made me snap out of it.'

The only joy she has in life is her son, she says. Her voice lifts when she talks about him.

'Ah, he's a great young fella, he's very good. Just a great young fella, real happy and that. He loves Iggle Piggle [a character from the *In The Night Garden* series] and that sort of thing . . . He loves dogs. Up in the Joy they used to bring them in on the visits.'

She has no contact with her son's Russian father, who has left the country.

'Curly hair like me, that's about it. He's the head off his da.'

She talks about the torture of having a screened visit with her son in Limerick.

'You know, behind a glass frame where you can't even touch the child . . . Perspex and then two locked doors. I swear to God. I think it's terrible, I swear . . . couldn't even touch the child or nothing . . . I thought he would have been real distant with me but he wasn't, calling me Mammy and telling me about Santy. I was delighted, he's getting real big . . . yeah I swear I can't believe the difference.'

I remind her that whatever Farah Noor was like, his

mother in Mombasa feels as strongly for him as Charlotte does about her own young son. If she revealed where Farah's missing head was, she would be giving that family closure.

'I don't think it would actually make a difference though at this stage . . . not after being sentenced, they won't even let me appeal against it, so I really don't think it would make a difference . . . I think it's just gone too far. It'd only just start another whole load of publicity again. I think it's just best to leave it be really.'

Pressed on the subject, she admits she can't tell because 'I swore I wouldn't.'

To whom?

'To me ma and Linda really . . . I'm the kind of person if I give someone my word I just can't go back on it.'

But all her life her family have been letting her down. It was her brothers who told detectives who'd done it, Linda who walked into a station and confessed their part, and her mother who told her to kill Farah Noor.

'I know so I basically try not to let them down, 'cos Linda and me ma has had a bad old run of it as well, Linda especially, like every fella Linda has been with has been abusive to her, know what I mean, she's had a bad old life and like I just wouldn't like to cause her any more heartache.'

What about her son, what about her sense of loyalty to him?

'I know, but it wouldn't change my sentence in the slightest . . .'

*

Shortly after the interview with Charlotte is published in the *Sunday World*, it is rumoured Linda has told fellow prisoners she put the head in a bin bag in the Phoenix Park – the place where her father took his own life. Other sources have since rubbished this notion.

Meanwhile, the Raonaid Murray case is being reviewed. The Cold Case Unit has trawled through the mountains of paperwork – statements, door-to-door inquiries, questionnaires at checkpoints, the claims of suspects.

Farah Noor's role is being investigated again, and Sue's school records sought in an attempt to corroborate her claims that she was out drinking with him on Sandycove Strand on the day Raonaid died.

The Rosepark Hotel no longer exists, so it proves impossible to establish if he was there on 3 September.

The findings suggest that too much emphasis was put on trying to track down one suspect – a man who was described as looking like Noel Gallagher from Oasis, and who was believed to have argued with Raonaid as she walked home. The feeling is that the whole investigation may have been skewed.

Members of the Cold Case Unit travel to the States and consult with a psychological profiler, among others. Could the desecration of Raonaid's grave just months after her burial have had anything to do with the killer?

The Murray family are also reinterviewed, and have a list of queries about the original investigation. I call to their Glenageary home on two separate occasions, but Raonaid's father, Jim, a school principal, does not want to speak either time. He suffers from a heart attack shortly afterwards.

Then an unexpected breakthrough occurs which throws things in a completely different direction.

Epilogue

More than eight thousand people were interviewed during the Raonaid Murray murder investigation. Over three thousand witness statements were taken. There were twelve arrests. But the case remains unsolved. The seventeen-year-old's grave in Shanganagh cemetery was desecrated several times after her brutal murder. A carved oak cross which had been inscribed by a neighbour with one of Raonaid's favourite quotes was ripped from the ground and vandalized. It read: 'I believe that when death closes our eyes we will awaken to a light of which our sunlight is but a shadow.'

Farah Noor was interviewed twice about the killing. He fitted the profile. He was arrested for threatening a woman with a knife at Patrician Park in Dun Laoghaire in the early hours of 18 August 2002. On a separate occasion, he was again arrested in Dun Laoghaire for carrying a knife. He also had a history of violence towards previous girlfriends. His ex-girlfriend Sue's statements about his attacks on her were on file. During one interview, Farah Noor said: 'I have never killed anybody, either in Ireland or Somalia.'

He was questioned a second time, after Sue's friend Melissa told gardaí what he had screamed at her during the row in the Penny Black pub. Detectives travelled to Cork on 29 May 2003, picking him up at Wellington Terrace, one of the addresses he shared with Kathleen Mulhall. They took him to Anglesea Garda station and interviewed him under caution.

He remembered where he was on the night in question because 'that was when the girl Raonaid Murray was murdered. It was all over the papers, on the news. I didn't kill Raonaid Murray. I didn't even know her, I have never met her and I have never even seen her. I can't really remember that well but I think that on the day that Raonaid was killed I was out at my girlfriend's house. I think I got the bus to the Rosepark Hotel. It was the last bus leaving at 10.30pm and it is about forty-five minutes on the bus. I went straight into my room in the hotel. I was on my own. I went direct to my room and didn't speak to anybody. It was a long time ago so I am not fully sure but I think that's what I did. I didn't go back out until morning time.'

When he was reminded that his ex-girlfriend, Sue, and a friend of hers had spent the afternoon drinking with him on Sandycove Strand and had been in the Rosepark Hotel with him that evening he said: 'I don't think it was the day that Raonaid was killed but it might be, I don't remember. Anyway I never had an argument with Sue that time. I was not drinking in Dun Laoghaire that night either. I don't have the money anyway. I was not drunk in Dun Laoghaire that night and I didn't ring her at her home that night from Dun Laoghaire to say "I'm sorry." I have met a friend of Sue's called Melissa. She is a fat girl. I don't like Melissa. Melissa made Sue leave me for a South African man. I know that Melissa knew Raonaid Murray because she told Sue that they were friends and Sue told me.'

Asked why he had bragged about the murder he said: 'Before me and Sue split up I met Sue in the Penny Black pub in Tallaght. It was our son's birthday. He was two years old. Sue's family was there and so was Melissa and two South Africans. I was upset because I didn't want the South Africans there but they had all the money. I had an argument with Sue because I didn't want them there. I told Sue to be careful because Melissa was a bad girl and her friend was killed. I mean Raonaid Murray and I don't know how. Did Melissa know something because she was her friend, I don't know. Melissa then left with the South Africans and me and Sue went home. A couple of months later we split up. She has married one of the South Africans. She broke my heart and I never see my son now. All I know is that I didn't kill Raonaid Murray. I was arrested last year in Dun Laoghaire with a knife. The garda has the knife now. I got the knife as a present from my girlfriend. Before I used to go climbing and fishing with Sue's father.'

Detectives studied his form. He first came to the Gardaí's attention on 2 December 2000. He refused to pay a bus driver on the Harold's Cross Road and he pushed and assaulted a female garda who attended the scene, attacking another garda who arrived to help her. He was charged with assault, convicted and sentenced to three months but the jail term was suspended. Instead, he was bound to the peace for a year and fined €190.46.

Less than two years later he was arrested for threatening a woman with a knife in Dun Laoghaire in August 2002. He could have gone to prison for breaching his earlier agreement, but Noor denied the knife was his, the woman was too frightened to make a statement and he was not prosecuted.

On 30 November 2002 he was cautioned at North Gate Bridge in Cork for being drunk and in another incident on 4 March 2003 he appeared before a judge at Cork City Court charged with being drunk in public on 20 February on Leitrim Street when he was making a nuisance of himself and not wearing a top. He was fined €75.

Farah contacted the Gardaí himself on 3 November 2003, claiming he had been assaulted by two men on Cork's Lower Glanmire Road. When he sobered up he refused to make an official complaint.

Gardaí hunting Raonaid's killer concluded that Farah Noor was not their prime suspect, focusing their inquiries instead on the Noel Gallagher lookalike reported to have been arguing with Raonaid on Corrig Avenue. He was blond-haired, in his late twenties and has never come forward to explain what the row was about.

The reasons why Farah Noor bragged about the killing or claimed to have been interviewed immediately after Raonaid's murder have never been explained.

During her interviews with gardaí about Farah's murder, Kathleen Mulhall remembered: 'He told me he killed someone, some girl in Dun Laoghaire. I one hundred per cent believed it. He told me he stabbed her, she was a friend of an ex-girlfriend. He told me I would end up the same way. He said he was too good to be caught. He told me it was somewhere down a laneway and he killed her with a knife. When he told me he killed a girl in Dun Laoghaire he told me that if I told the police he would get my family, my children and kill them and I would be the first killed,' she said.

Kathleen said Farah was drunk during this first confession but he brought it up again during an argument a week before his own death.

Kathleen Mulhall and Raonaid Murray came from different planets. Raonaid came from a loving family and grew up in a leafy south Dublin suburb. Her whole life was full of potential and she was planning to pursue a third-level education. Kathleen was a hardened alcoholic and a prostitute who set the worst kind of example for her daughters. But Kathleen believed Farah had killed the teenager and she also believed Farah would kill her.

The Mulhalls were reinterviewed about the case by gardaí. Farah Noor's DNA is on record – it led to his positive identification. Farah was finally ruled out as a suspect.

On the other side of the world, in Mombasa, when Farah's wife Husna heard of her estranged husband's murder in Dublin, she stayed inside for four months and twelve days in mourning, as is the custom. Her eldest daughter, Somoe, died of a fever, which her mother attributed to her grief on learning of the death of her father.

Back in Ireland, the Cold Case Unit could not confirm

that the girl seen arguing on Corrig Road was Raonaid, and determined that the emphasis on finding the Oasis lookalike had skewed the entire investigation. Focus shifted to another suspect, a then teenager believed to have harboured a grudge against Raonaid's father, Jim.

Fresh hope was also placed on new DNA techniques that may finally yield a breakthrough. Mitrochondrial DNA traces under Raonaid's fingernails indicated she was in contact with someone female. Some forty women would need to be swabbed and their DNA compared to the sample.

In August 2009, almost ten years after Raonaid's murder, the investigation continues.

Wife Killer

I was chilled to the bone watching The Late Late Show *interview of the mother and husband of a young house-wife, Rachel O'Reilly, who'd been brutally murdered in her own home.*

As if the murder wasn't terrible enough, the body language between Rose Callaly and her son-in-law, Joe, made it clear that Rose believed that the man who'd killed her daughter was sitting right next to her.

But if the successful advertising executive was brazen-ing out a public plea to find Rachel's killer on national TV, having murdered her himself, what did it say about his ego? As Joe O'Reilly appealed for help to find his wife's murderer, what stood out most was the dead look in his eyes . . .

Niamh O'Connor
August 2009

Prologue

Bloodstained fingers froze on the shower switch. The killer's eyes were out on stalks. He'd just been startled by an unexplained noise. *Was someone coming?* Craning his neck towards the door, he strained to hear over the thud of his heart. Seconds later he heard it again and breathed a long sigh of relief. The gurgling sound was coming from the bedroom. It was only Rachel. She was still alive.

Pacing back down the hall towards her, he stalled outside the little boys' empty bedroom and glanced around. A giant Winnie the Pooh plonked on the lower bunk bed was even bigger than its usual occupant, two-year-old Adam. Luke, the four-year-old who slept in the bed above him, had already outgrown teddy bears.

Rachel moaned again. He closed his eyes momentarily, drew a sharp intake of breath, and continued on in to her. Hot blood pooled from her head, congealing in the carpet and dying her long blonde hair scarlet. He reached again for the weapon and crouched back down on his hunkers to finish her off.

Stepping over her body, he felt moved beyond words. With her death, his own life was finally beginning. He was free. But she was in his debt too. Like Peter Pan, she would never grow old. Now she really was Tinkerbell, the cartoon character she loved so much.

He returned to the shower with a spring in his step, humming as he tilted his face into the jet of steaming water to wash away the blood. After a quick towel dry and change, he wrapped the murder weapon in two towels to take with him. The entire process, from entering to leaving the house, transforming himself utterly and taking a life in the process, had taken just eighteen minutes.

1

Murder

Rose Callaly's heart raced as she inched past a quarry truck lumbering down the narrow road that led to her daughter Rachel's new home. In her bones she knew something was wrong. Her grandson, Adam, hadn't been picked up from crèche at 12.30am, an hour and fifteen minutes earlier. Rachel would never simply not show for her children. It was a twenty-minute journey, traffic permitting, from Rose's Dublin home in Collins Avenue, Whitehall, to Rachel's at Baldarragh, near The Naul. The slowest part was navigating the last two hundred yards past the steady stream of heavy trucks.

The caring grandmother with an open face and tight-cropped, light blonde hair felt a wave of relief as she pulled up outside the cream bungalow. Rachel's Renault Scenic was parked in the usual spot. Hurrying around the side of the house, she barely registered that the curtains at the front were drawn. Rachel's two dogs, a springer spaniel and a Labrador, panted behind her as she bustled around to the back.

She didn't worry when she saw the patio door was pulled open. Rachel had moved to the country almost a year and a half earlier so that she wouldn't have to worry about locking doors. Steadying herself against the spindles of the new deck, she climbed up the steps and entered the house, surprised when Rachel's dogs, who would normally race ahead, did not follow.

Inside, the sound of the tap gushing full throttle in the kitchen made the hairs on the back of her neck stand on end. She glanced around at the clothes folded on the kitchen table and things strewn across the floor that did not belong. Something was definitely wrong. Breathlessly, she called out, 'Rachel?'

No answer.

Rose entered the utility room tentatively, 'Rachel?'

She continued out into the hall. 'Rachel? Are you here?'

In the sitting room she noticed more items scattered across the floor. She called out louder, 'Rachel?' heading back into the hall. She hurried down towards her grandsons' bedroom, filled with trepidation. Still no sign. Turning to enter the last room in the house – Rachel and Joe's bedroom – she tried to make sense of the shape in the doorway. It was unrecognizable and unmistakable at once. Her heart stilled. 'Rachel!'

Rose fell to her knees in horror. Her daughter's lifeless body lay face down on the floor covered in blood – her head in the doorway, her bare feet pointing back into the bedroom. She was twisted sideways, on top of her car keys, one arm protruding grotesquely behind her back, the other bent underneath her. There was so much blood that Rose could not even make out where her beautiful face was.

Choking grief broke into a wail as her terrified eyes ran

over the ransacked bedroom. The pine bedside locker and dresser drawers had been pulled out; chairs were overturned; the bed was dishevelled. The peach-coloured carpet, the turquoise walls, even the ceiling were stained in blood. Rachel's grey tracksuit leggings and long grey T-shirt were sodden.

Desperately, Rose tried to rub warmth into Rachel's freezing arms, horrified that her normally sallow skin looked white as marble. All the while she kept talking, jabbering, begging Rachel to cling on; to stay with her; to come to. Her hands hovered over her daughter's precious head, but did not touch, terrified she would hurt her more. Instead she clutched and patted her daughter's stiff hands and arms, scaly and dry from the psoriasis that she'd contracted in the previous months, and now cold as stone.

Suddenly Rose was back on her feet – she had to get help. She looked around frantically for a phone, then scurried up the hall in a state of blind panic, hysterical as she grabbed the landline and dialled 999. Her hand was trembling so much it almost proved impossible. Nothing happened; she didn't know how to use it and was too distressed to concentrate long enough to figure it out. In her mind she must have prayed as she called out, panic-stricken, for help.

Dear Jesus, not Rachel. She was only thirty years old. She had two children who needed her. Someone. Please. Help her.

Rose darted in and out of the rooms again until she spotted Rachel's new mobile on a press. Grabbing it, she jabbed at the buttons as she struggled with a flood of emotions. Had Rachel slipped after a shower or bath? She'd seen more blood in the bathroom.

Eventually, someone, a man, spoke back at the other end.

'I think my daughter is dead,' Rose sobbed, and he promised to ring for an ambulance.

Then Rose dialled her own home number. Her husband, Jim, answered.

'I think Rachel is dead,' she bawled, dropping the phone and running back to the bedroom to try to will Rachel back to life. Deep down the realization was dawning that this was no accident, that Rachel had been murdered. It was 4 October 2004. The nightmare had begun.

Joe O'Reilly had risen at 5.20am. His office was twenty-five miles from his home in The Naul and an early start was the only way to beat the traffic to Citywest. The day was going to be a long one and he wanted to get a head start with a sauna and a jacuzzi in the gym.

His wife of seven years, Rachel, was still sleeping in the master bedroom as he pulled on his sweats in the spare room and organized a navy jacket, pair of dark trousers and lilac shirt for work. The couple slept separately because one or both of their sons inevitably woke during the night requiring attention. As the breadwinner, Joe needed an uninterrupted night's sleep if he was to perform in work. There were other reasons for the separate rooms too, and this day they played heavy on his mind.

He was thirty-two years old and an advertising

executive with the leading outdoor billboards firm, Viacom. He'd come a long way from his days as a dogs-body in Arnotts stores. As Viacom operations manager, he now headed a team of twenty-six people. With no third-level qualifications, he put his success down to hard work, the gift of the gab, and to always, always being on call.

He threw his mobile phone on to the dash of his Fiat Marea as he pulled open the door, and ducked to climb in. At six foot five, with the span of a heavyweight boxer, he dwarfed the driver's seat. His physique had also stood to him in his choice of career in that he could command respect the minute he walked into a room. It was a crucial advantage when making a pitch in the advertising game. A taste for the good life had contributed to a recent paunch, but had never affected his ability to pull any piece of skirt he wanted.

Joe was the first to admit that marriage had never dampened his enthusiasm for the ladies. There was just too much temptation in the advertising game with all the after-hours 'networking'. Currently, the other woman in his life was one Nikki Pelley, a busty, blonde stunner he used to work with and had started seeing romantically at the beginning of the year. The year before, he'd had a fling with a golf pro, Barbara Hackett, but she lived in Limerick and the distance was not conducive to romance. The affair had fizzled out after five months.

The way men like Joe saw it, any man who denied having a little bit on the side was either a liar or dead. And in no way did he ever let his affairs affect his priorities. Family was everything to him, having come from a broken home himself. The boys – Luke and Adam – came first in his life. He was going to do whatever was required to keep it that way.

He was completely preoccupied as he drove, stopping off only once for petrol at the Tesco Clearwater garage in Finglas village. He and Rachel had rowed the night before, over the usual – him not spending more time at home. They seemed to be fighting non-stop these days.

He and Rachel had two fantastic sons, and the same circle of friends. They'd traded up their three-bed semi in Santry for a cracking new place in the country. You didn't just walk away from all that.

As he pulled into the Jackie Skelly gym at 6.20am, the colleague he'd arranged to meet, Derek Quearney, was already in the car park and Joe was glad of the diversion. Derek was a 43-year-old ex-soldier and now Viacom's delivery manager. They got on great and Derek often covered for Joe when he was 'unavailable' during work hours. Derek looked over his glasses as Joe approached and waved. They had a chat about their planned in-spection of the ads on the buses at the depot in Broadstone, Phibsboro, later that morning.

It was almost twenty to eight when Joe arrived at Viacom in the Bluebell Industrial Estate. He read his emails, had a coffee and cereal, and just after five past eight left, telling colleagues he was headed for Broadstone. Derek told Joe he'd see him there, he had to sort out work rosters and schedules first.

Joe's thoughts must have drifted to his wife. Rachel would have been up to her eyes right now, getting the boys dressed, fed, and ready for school. It was a typical, hectic Monday morning. Rachel had to drop Luke to Hedgetown National School in Lusk for around ten past nine, and Adam to the Tots United crèche in Swords for half nine. Her friend Celine Keogh was due to visit at elevenish and Rachel had also mentioned that she wanted to drop a present over to her best friend, Jacqui, along with a suitcase and a hedge trimmer. Jacqui was a neuro-surgical nurse in Beaumont and had been on night shift last night, so she didn't intend calling too early. Rachel was also due to go to the gym but had hurt her bum play-ing hockey and Joe told her not to. He texted Rachel just after five past ten. 'Hope you and the boys slept OK. Wish Jacqui happy birthday for me.'

Joe and Derek hooked up later that morning and finished up just before ten past eleven. They drove in convoy down Church Street, arriving back in Viacom by midday.

'Jesus! You look like shit,' the receptionist, Michelle Slattery, told Joe.

'Oh shit,' Joe answered, deciding he'd better touch base with home again.

'Hiya, Rach, it's just twelve o'clock. Ringing to see where you are. Obviously you're just in Jacqui's chewing the fat and not listening to messages from me. Give us a shout. Let me know how your morning's been, all the usual sort of stuff. Don't forget to wish Jacqui a happy birthday. OK, goodbye.'

He was up to his eyes in work when the principal in Adam's crèche called. Rachel hadn't collected him. It was

1.15pm. Helen Moore needed to leave. Joe expressed his surprise and rang Rachel's mobile, which diverted to the answering service.

'Hiya, Rach, it's only I just got a call from Helen in Montessori. She says you haven't picked up Adam. Was Sarah meant to pick him up or something? Give us a shout. I'm going to try the home number. You've no doubt left your phone at home or in the back of the car or something . . . Helen has to go and pick up her kids so she can't stay there. So if you get back and she's not there, don't panic. I will try the home number, thanks.'

Next, Joe rang Jacqui to ask if Rachel was there. The call woke Jacqui up, but she got up to check if Rachel – who had keys to her place – had dropped by and left the stuff over.

'No, she never called,' Jacqui explained, sounding concerned. Her friend would never have been late for her children.

Joe next phoned Rachel's brother, Anthony, who was with his parents, Rose and Jim, helping to paint the house. Joe spoke to Rose who said she hadn't seen or heard from Rachel.

'I rang her myself this morning but she still hasn't got back to me,' Rose said, really worried. She got a fright when she heard Adam hadn't been collected and told Joe she'd drop straight over to The Naul.

Joe rang Helen back in the crèche and told her he was on the way and would pick up Adam. He rang Rachel again. He left another message at 1.24pm.

'Rach, this is Joe. I tried your number now I don't know

how many times. You're not in Jacqui's and not in your mother's. I'm now really, really worried about you. Please call me, please call. This is not funny. This is not like you.'

Twenty minutes later, he phoned again, this time from his car. 'Rach, it's me again. I'm just on the M50. I've spoken to your mother. She's going to pop out. Please ring. I've been crying. You have me worried. I don't know, talk to me please.'

When Joe arrived at the crèche he looked flushed. The teacher handed over Adam, and Joe hung around for twenty-odd minutes until she reminded him that he was going to be late for his other son, Luke, whose class finished at two – five minutes ago.

Just after ten past two, Joe came to the door of Luke's classroom in Lusk but was told by teacher Aine Doyle that another mother, Michelle Mulligan, whose daughter also attended the school, had taken Luke with her. Rachel and Michelle had an arrangement to pick up each other's children on alternate days to give each other a dig out. Joe finally headed home.

Michelle Mulligan pulled into his drive just ahead of him and Joe grinned at Luke in the back seat. His eldest son ran towards his car and Joe tousled his head, before lifting Adam from the car seat. He gripped the toddler's hand tightly as he headed towards the house and smiled at his mother-in-law Rose as she appeared at the door and walked out to meet him.

Rose looked wretched. She said something to Michelle, then opened her arms to Joe, blocking the children's path.

'I think Rachel is dead,' Rose blurted to her son-in-law, sobbing.

Joe pushed past her into the house. His neighbour, Sarah Harmon, was in the kitchen on the phone to the emergency services, distressed and begging them to hurry.

'Where's Rachel?' he demanded.

'In the bedroom,' Sarah replied, helplessly.

Rose ran after Joe as he paced down to the bedroom. When he reached Rachel's body, he put his hands to his head. 'Jesus, Rachel, what did you do?'

Rose looked at him, appalled. 'I think she must have fallen in the bathroom,' she explained, bewildered. 'There's more blood in there.'

Joe reached over to a box of books beside Rachel's head and chucked them into the boys' room. He trampled around the body, pulling stuff out of the way, then knelt down and put two fingers on Rachel's neck. Suddenly, he was back on his feet, trying to heave her up, but he couldn't move her. Jacqui appeared on spec, having let herself in the back door with a key Rachel kept hidden. Rachel's friend was shocked by the unfolding pandemonium and shook her head in dread when she heard what was going on.

'See if you can do something,' Joe instructed.

Dazed, Jacqui made her way to the bedroom. She'd been knocking around with Rachel since they were fourteen. She was her bridesmaid and Luke's godmother. She struggled with her emotions when she saw the body. There was congealed blood around Rachel's head and a big gash behind her right ear. Jacqui managed to go into automatic gear with Joe towering behind her. Trying to find a pulse, she reached for Rachel's hand. It was cold. She pressed her fingers on Rachel's neck, to try again to locate a pulse. She knew Rachel was dead but she could not believe it. She looked desperately under Rachel's T-shirt to see if her ribcage was moving, if she was breathing.

Finally, she checked her pupils, which were fixed and dilated. She tried to turn Rachel over, Joe trying to help, but Rachel's body was stiff and unyielding.

'She's gone, she's dead, what happened?'

The paramedics burst into the hallway and Jacqui briefed them while struggling with her own shock. They needed space and sent everyone down to the kitchen.

Outside, Luke and Adam would have watched, fascinated by the flashing blue light of the ambulance, while inside the crew applied ECG patches to their mother's body and bounced electric shock pads off her chest. The machine flat-lined.

A paramedic steeled himself to break the news, then headed into the kitchen to inform the desperate group there was nothing more that could be done. 'I'm sorry, she's dead,' he said.

Rose became inconsolable. The other women did their best to comfort her, breaking down themselves. Joe felt himself levitate out of his body and watched as if the unfolding tragedy was happening to someone else. The gardaí arrived and the first officer on the scene, Thomas Cleary, gently explained that they would all have to vacate the house to begin the process of preserving the crime scene.

Joe declared he had touched the body and thrown things around, destroying any potential forensic reconstruction of Rachel's last moments. 'I'm really sorry. I'm probably after ruining it for ye,' he announced.

2

Rachel and Joe

Rachel used to take a drag from one of her sneaky Silk Cuts as if her life depended on it. Joe hated her smoking so, officially, she didn't smoke. Technically, she fully intended giving up completely when life was a little kinder. This day she would have been excused for having a little weep, and a glass of red wine too sitting on her own out in the garden. She could not believe someone had reported her to social services for being a bad mother. Her sons were her life.

She glanced back through the patio door to make sure Luke and Adam – her Velcro boy and her baby – were still asleep. Not a stir. She was going out with her friends tonight, if her husband ever arrived home from work. He was always like a dog when he had to babysit, so she'd have to humour him anyway from the minute he walked through the door. Normally she backed down to avoid an argument, but tonight she was standing her ground. After the showdown with social services in Coolock yesterday, she needed to talk to her friends more than ever. They were her lifeline.

Heading back into the kitchen, she rooted out her emergency stash of chocolates from the fridge, cursing herself for forgetting to leave her cigarette outside. She jabbed at the smoke frantically as she ran back out into the garden. If Joe smelt it, there'd be hell to pay.

She tucked into the chocolates as her self-esteem took another nosedive. It wasn't that the social worker had been judgemental. Far from it. When Rachel admitted she did have problems managing the kids, and that she did shout at them on a daily basis, the social worker's response was 'Sure, we all do it.' She had reassured Rachel that she was satisfied the boys weren't suffering any abuse and that the anonymous allegation against her was now rubbished so there'd be no unexpected inspections or house calls. *Just as well.* The house always looked like a bomb had hit it. Still though, it was so upsetting to think that somebody she knew considered her an unfit mother and had reported her to the authorities. *Who? Why?* It was such a nasty thing to do. Even the social worker admitted they only got involved in cases of suspected sexual abuse or unexplained hospitalizations.

She started to weep again, playing things over in her mind, as a pang of guilt shot through her. Was she too rough with her sons? Did she shout too much? Was she a bad mother? If she didn't do things as well as she wanted, it was just because she found it so hard to manage everything on her own. Joe worked so much and slept in the office several times a week, most weeks. She felt like a single mum half the time. She'd hoped, dreamed, that the move to this house would mean a new start. Instead, it had just widened the cracks in the marriage . . .

She closed her eyes and breathed the fresh scent of lemon geranium, the only plant she could ever grow. When she opened them again the sight of the stunning view from her garden took her breath away. She was looking out on dazzling Lambay Island and the rolling Meath plains. She decided to take her half-brother Thomas up on his offer to build a deck, in this very spot. Maybe then Joe would start to love the place as much as she did.

Rachel knew the new house, Lambay View, wasn't perfect. The quarry was too close for comfort and she hated the mobile phone mast that had gone up 850 metres away. And she shuddered every time she thought how the previous owner, a pilot, had died playing in the garden with his children. But she always looked on the bright side. These were the things that brought the bungalow with its giant garden, in a beautiful countryside setting, into their price range.

The only real problem with it was the remoteness. Rachel had grown up surrounded by people – as one of five children and with loads of friends. Nobody had prepared her for the isolation that came with giving up work to become a stay-at-home mum. She'd loved her old job as a legal secretary in Donnybrook, but she loved being a mother more, so she had cut work down to one day a week. Being an Avon lady and holding Tupperware parties supplemented her income, but they didn't get her out of the house much. She had brilliant neighbours and friends, and her family were always calling, but she still craved adult company. If Joe came home at night, she knew they could make it work. But every time she pressed him, it just led to another row.

She tucked into another chocolate and felt instantly guilty. Joe was always commenting on her weight. No wonder he didn't want her in bed any more, she thought self-critically. She wouldn't mind but she'd been trying to lose a few pounds before their romantic meal out in Wongs in Clontarf on Friday. Rachel was going to surprise him with a big night out and had already organized his mother Ann to babysit. This was one occasion she was not going to take any of Joe's usual excuses for an answer. He'd been promising her a special night together to mark her thirtieth birthday, for the last eight months. He'd been in Florida on a softball trip on the actual day. Better late than never, she thought. A bit of quality time was exactly what they needed, especially after yesterday's blazing row.

Her eyes welled up again at the thought of the shouting match in the car park after the meeting with the social worker. She couldn't believe he was still knocking her maternal instincts, when she'd just been told by a complete stranger there was no substance to what had been said about her.

'Did you hear them? Everybody does it and I am a good mother,' she'd argued defensively. She regretted shouting at him, but he knew how sensitive she was about wanting to be a good mother, having been adopted herself as a newborn. She had made her peace with her birth mother, making contact with Teresa Lowe when she'd turned eighteen. Rachel understood completely why Teresa had given her up. Ireland was a different place in 1973. When they had met, Rachel was already older than Teresa had been when she'd given birth. Teresa was just a scared teenager. Rachel had written all her feelings to Teresa, in a series of letters. If Teresa hadn't given her up, she'd never have had the Callalys, Rose and Jim, a plumber, as parents, or for siblings the other children they had adopted – Anthony, Declan and Paul as her brothers, and beloved Ann as a sister. She had grown to love her half-brothers from the Lowe family, Thomas and Patrick, and sister Sandra too. Thomas was a carpenter and had been a brilliant help to her with the move. And Sandra was so stylish, great at helping her shop for girlie clothes, where Rachel hadn't a clue. But the Callaly family was everything to her. Her own childhood had been like one long, happy Disney movie. Jim was her hero and Rose had turned into as much a friend as a mother. They were brilliant role models. She remembered her mam sitting in a cold hall for an hour and a half so Rachel could do gym in the winter, or waiting in the car outside the swimming pool so she could practise.

She went back inside to check on the boys. The sight of their downy heads tucked under their duvet covers brought on an overwhelming surge of love. Darling, blond-haired Luke, her firstborn, with his gigantic blue eyes, so brave about starting school in a couple of months; a mammy's boy, the spitting image of her; giggling uncontrollably as he tried to copy her cartwheels and now going through a scary spider phase. She'd taught him to respect bugs and not to tread on them, so he'd taken to collecting them and took delight in scaring the living daylights out of anyone squeamish. And sweet little Adam with his chunky hands and gorgeous smile. He had started talking and was coming out with the most hysterical things.

She sniffed as she kissed their heads and resolved to try harder for their sakes. She couldn't have it all, she realized. If she wanted to bring up her boys in a dream home, she would have to get used to having a hotshot husband who worked a lot. Rachel decided she was going to give Luke and Adam a childhood like her own if it killed her. If that meant cutting Joe some slack, then that was what the 'new' Rachel was going to do. After all, his childhood had been a nightmare. His father had moved to Wales, after splitting from Joe's mother, Ann. No wonder Joe was such a perfectionist when it came to the boys. He just wanted everything perfect for them. His background explained why he was such a workaholic too. His own mother, Ann, had to drive a bus to support her four kids – Martina, born blind with Down's syndrome, Joe, Ann and Derek. As if things weren't bad enough for him growing up, when Joe was six, his mum's brother, Christy Lynch, was twice convicted of murder then acquitted by the Supreme Court. Joe's only escape was movies like *Star Wars*. He'd worked his way up the ladder from Arnotts to Oracle, then Microsoft and now Viacom – the hard way. She remembered him working nights in a video shop after his day job.

Rachel closed her eyes and tried to recall the good times. They'd met thirteen years previously, through softball, a sport like baseball in which she excelled. She was only seventeen and Joe nineteen when they'd started dating. They seemed to have so much in common then. They were both born in St James's Hospital, only a year or so apart. They were both giants. He was six foot five, she was five foot eleven. He was from Kilbarrack, she lived close by, in Whitehall. She thought he was gorgeous, hilarious, larger than life.

It was hard to imagine life without him. They'd spent their entire adult lives together. When they finished school they worked together in Arnotts. Joe proposed to her in Paris, up the Eiffel Tower. She insisted he get down on one knee, then told him she'd think about it. They'd married in 1997, in the Church of Blessed Margaret Ball. Her wedding day was one of the best days of her life. She giggled at the thought of Joe posing for the photographer with her garter between his teeth and went in search of her photo album, poring happily over the memories when she found it.

She smiled wistfully at the pictures of herself in her bridal gown. She was so slim in her off-the-shoulder silk dress. She'd worn her hair up with a full billowing veil and carried a bouquet of lilies. Her four bridesmaids were dressed in bottle green. Rose wore a lemon dress and white jacket and hat. Her father beamed proudly. She was giggling in all of the pictures. It had been one big party, surrounded by family and friends, her life with Joe full of potential and hope. Her only regret was that she hadn't invited her birth mum, Teresa. She'd just wanted it to be Rose's day as much as her own.

Her eyes brimmed at the sight of the 'old' Rachel, the sportswoman – on the hockey pitch; swimming; competing for Leinster in shot and discus. She looked so strong in the pictures of herself on the softball pitch with her red cap on, eye fixed only on the ball, bat swung back at the ready.

There were more pictures of Joe – striking a karate pose; he was a black belt in Kempo. There was one of him dressed in his Darth Vader outfit; he was a *Star Wars* fanatic and kept all his paraphernalia in a spare room in the house with his collection of sci-fi movies. There were millions of snaps of them together on the softball pitch, smiling and carefree. They'd had so much craic with their team, the Renegades, over the years. But now, every tournament ended up being a battle about who would travel and who would stay home to mind the children. If they fetched up on the pitch together with the children on the sidelines, it always ended in a screaming match. 'Are you stupid or wha?' he'd shouted at her in front of everyone. It was mortifying, they'd actually been taken aside and asked to tone it down. She hated the way he referred to her jokingly as 'the dragon' and made out that he wasn't 'getting any at home'. She couldn't bear him being crude at the best of times, but what made it even worse was that he had no interest in her.

She grinned at the picture of Adam's first Christmas. He was only weeks old, in Santa's arms while she tried to get Luke to look at the camera. Life before her children was great fun, but emotionally empty compared to the joy they had brought. She wondered would she ever fulfil her dream and have a third baby. She'd love a girl.

She studied a picture of her and Joe on the couch a couple of months after she'd brought Luke home. She looked tired; she hadn't lost the baby weight. But she was smiling. She and Joe had their arms around each other. They were still happy then.

She sighed heavily. The new Rachel missed the old, smiling Rachel. What had happened, she wondered. They were living the dream, weren't they? Teenage sweethearts who'd married, had two children and were bringing them up in a house in the country. She wondered if he was having an affair. Women were always coming on to him, at least according to himself. He always told her whenever he got invited out and he was convinced half of her friends fancied him. At least if he was telling her, he had nothing to hide, the new Rachel chipped in. She reminded herself of him joking about an affair her family thought he was having with his friend Nikki, because one of the children had referred to her as 'dad's girlfriend'. It was purely platonic, he'd reassured her. She believed him. But he made so many trips away to Limerick and Cork, sometimes it was hard. And he didn't even wear his wedding ring any more, claiming his physiotherapist said it was bad for his shoulder.

There were pictures of her thirtieth birthday, celebrating with her friends. Her smile looked forced. She remembered becoming maudlin that Joe wasn't there and trying to recall when they'd last kissed. Their beds were like musical chairs. One got in and the other got out. She'd asked her friends at her party for their opinion – if they thought he was having an affair. But they were so fond of Joe it was hard for them to be impartial. He'd helped Celine Keogh move house; she considered him a friend too. He was the life and soul of her murder mystery nights. And Brid Horan thought he was really kind, always the one to run out to help someone injured on the softball pitch.

The new Rachel decided if she was ever going to move on, she was going to have to stop fretting about other women. Deep down, she didn't believe he'd do that to her. Anyway, why would Joe, who had no interest in sex, have an affair? She believed him when he said he was working because as long as she'd known him he'd been a workaholic.

Rachel headed into her bedroom to get ready, eyeing herself critically in the mirror. She looked worn out. She touched the dry patches of flaky skin under her eyes. When she had told Joe the doctor said her psoriasis was stress-related, he had laughed out loud. She was a lady of leisure, he reminded her. The house was like a kip, hardly a sign of someone stressed out.

As she put on some make-up and brushed her hair, she resolved to stop worrying about everything and to start thanking her lucky stars she didn't have any real problems. She would enjoy tonight with her friends, forget about the social worker and have a good carefree bop to Madonna. Tomorrow, the new Rachel would start her diet, pack in the fags and go easier on Joe. She would forgive him for the things he'd said in the car park. She would take on the DIY jobs herself. She would turn this place into a home he couldn't resist coming back to. And she would arrange something they could both look forward to . . . say, a party for the Renegades. Here in the house. They might not have beds, but they had loads of space outside. They could bring their tents. It would be great craic; they could have a sing-song, a barbie. She'd organized loads of events for the Irish Softball Association; this would be a piece of cake and just what the doctor ordered. She might even get the Tinkerbell tattoo, the one the old Rachel had always wanted. She felt her spirits lift. She went to the wardrobe to try to put something together that would hide her horrible bits. She picked out her favourite dark trousers, mauve top, and her amethyst stone and matching earrings, then decided to put it aside for Friday night's meal with him and to wear something else instead.

In her mind she went through her start-afresh speech. She would remind him that it was no wonder they were fighting all the time, that moving house was one of the most stressful things you could do. But they'd get through it, for the boys. If things went well, she might even mention just how much she longed for another baby, to make their lives complete.

3

Stone Heart

State Pathologist Marie Cassidy plays light music like Tom Jones in the background to keep her emotionally detached from the job in hand. On the slab awaiting post mortem on 5 October 2004 lay a fit and healthy, tall, heavy-set, young mother of two, with medium-length blonde hair pulled back in a ponytail and perfectly manicured nails. From the first glance Dr Cassidy could tell the victim had been beaten about the head so savagely that it was not going to be easy to determine how many blows had been inflicted.

The petite Scot, dressed in morgue overalls and a face mask that looked like a welder's helmet with an inbuilt microphone, weighed and measured the victim's body first, then removed plastic bags from the victim's head and hands, collecting the debris that fell from them into specimen jars. If skin or blood cells cross-matched with the DNA of a suspect, it would be central to any prosecution.

Next, she moved slowly from the top of Rachel's body towards the feet, recording into the microphone what she was witnessing – noting the locations of the bloodstains and injuries. All her observations would be related at an inquest or, hopefully, a trial. Dr Cassidy studied Rachel's face closely. She noticed an injury on the victim's mouth. It indicated she had been hit in the face to stun her, probably punched. The victim's face was also extensively bruised, she observed. 'Injuries to the forehead indicate the victim may have been standing upright when the first blow was struck,' she speculated.

After swabbing the stains and taking scrapings from underneath the fingernails, she cut the clothing free, depositing it in clear plastic labelled bags, and began her external examination of the body.

Her hands, covered with rubber gloves, probed and prodded Rachel's injuries gently as she counted out loud the number of lacerations to the head. 'Eight.' She lifted Rachel's arms, noting the bruising and scratches on them – consistent with the victim having tried to defend herself. She could tell from the extent of the patching on the skin that the woman had fought hard for her life.

Dr Cassidy tried to see if she could find a pattern to the injuries, but there was none. The victim probably made several attempts to escape, she realized, noting the marks on one side of Rachel's neck – she'd been gripped in an arm lock. Bruising on her wrist suggested she was held tightly there.

She took swabs to establish if there was sexual assault, and samples from around the nostrils and mouth. She examined the inner eyelids for signs of bloodspots indicating asphyxia. The colour of the body also indicated the presence of carbon monoxide at death.

Next she washed the body clean of the blood and the

sticky residue from around the ECG patches on the chest where attempts had been made to resuscitate her.

After carrying out X-rays, Dr Cassidy prepared for the more gruesome internal examination. She began with a Y-shaped incision in the torso to access the organs. She deduced from only a little fluid in the victim's stomach that this was a busy mum who hadn't even had time for breakfast.

After collecting a range of body fluids, she concentrated on the victim's head where the real answers lay. The skull was slightly thicker than average, but it hadn't stood a chance against the savagery. It was fractured in two places. There were heavy blows to the top of the head and more over the right ear. She found a fracture to the right and back of the skull, which had damaged the victim's brain. She estimated a minimum of four separate blows but maybe more than twice that. The first blow to the top of the victim's head was not fatal but could have caused concussion.

Dr Cassidy spoke carefully into the microphone: 'These blows, while she lay on the ground, were forceful and heavy and inflicted with a weapon. She would have fallen and once down on the ground, more blows rained down on her head as she lay prone on the floor, rendering her unconscious.

'The victim's injuries did not kill her instantly. She may have lain unconscious for several hours before dying,' she continued. 'Death would have been caused by choking . . . as the victim inhaled her own blood.'

She wound up with the information she suspected the

gardaí wanted. 'The murder weapon . . . something blunt, something heavy . . . possibly a wooden post from the deck, or something similar.'

Rachel's memory was honoured by the vast crowds who turned out for her funeral at the Holy Child Church in Whitehall on 11 October to pay their last respects. The sight of bewildered Luke and Adam looking so grown-up in their formal clothes filled everyone with sadness. Rachel hadn't only been robbed of her life, the boys were robbed of all hope of a happy childhood.

A Tweetie Pie stuffed toy sat on Rachel's coffin along with a piece of paper on which Luke had written the word 'Mammy'. Everyone whose life Rachel had touched felt moved to write too. They had all placed personal messages and cards inside the coffin. Rachel's neighbour and friend Sarah, who had helped Rose so much on the day she found her body, had summed it all up. 'Remember, Luke and Adam, that mothers hold their children's hands a little while, but hold you in their hearts for ever, and know that Rachel, your lovely mummy, loved, adored every hair on your heads, from the tip right down to your toes, and will always be with you.'

Rachel's dad, Jim, broke down during the service and Rose squeezed his hand. His heart was broken like everyone else's in his family. Rose resolved to stay strong for them all, for the boys, but most of all for Rachel. She had to find out who did this if they were ever going to have closure. She could be forgiven if she raised an eyebrow as her dry-eyed son-in-law walked over to Rachel's coffin to give an oration. Joe had taken no part in the funeral arrangements and had argued with the undertaker, even refusing to pay for the coffin. Rose and Jim had paid for the funeral, the afters and the plot. Joe announced that he didn't want Rachel to be buried in Balgriffin cemetery on the Malahide Road, so wouldn't be paying the bill. Perhaps he was still in denial, Rose could have thought charitably, acutely aware that grief affects people differently.

'Rachel had achieved everything she wanted in her short life,' Joe told the congregation. 'She had travelled widely, achieved a number of sporting goals, got married, had children, got a house in the country with a sea view. "Mission accomplished, Rachel. Well done,"' he said.

To the Callalys the words sounded strange and inappropriate but they had to give Joe the benefit of the doubt. He was always a bit of a showman. That was why Rachel had fallen in love with him.

Then the hushed church listened as Joe O'Reilly spoke directly to his wife's killer. 'Unlike you, she is at peace. Unlike you, she is sleeping. She forgives you and I hope she gives me the strength to forgive you one day.' He pleaded to the congregation, 'Please help find my wife's killer.'

At the reception afterwards, his asides to Rachel's friends were also setting off alarm bells.

'It's ironic,' Joe told army corporal Tara Kennedy, who went to school with Rachel at St Mary's Convent in Glasnevin, 'we were at the funeral at 10am and she was killed at 10.05am and here we are at two o'clock and the body was found at ten past two.'

Fiona Slevin, a friend of Rachel's, was shocked that Joe knew so much about the murder weapon. 'I don't know why they are looking in the fields,' he remarked about the Garda search. 'It is in the water.' Registering her horror, Joe then quickly added, 'Well, if I did it, that's where it would be. There's water all around us. That would get rid of all DNA.'

Gardaí kept a low profile at the funeral. But the incident room in Balbriggan was a hive of activity. The head of the Louth/Meath division, Chief Superintendent Michael Finnegan, led the team which included some of the force's finest – Superintendent Tom Gallagher, Detective Garda Sean Fitzpatrick, Inspectors Sean Galway and Oliver Keegan, Detective Sergeants Patrick Marry, Austin Foran and Peter McCoy, and Chief Superintendent Martin Donnellan of the National Bureau of Criminal Investigation (NBCI).

Closing this case was fast becoming a priority for every garda involved. It wasn't as if any of the assembled could remain detached. Anyone who had met the salt-of-the-earth Callaly family took this crime personally.

Pictures of Rachel O'Reilly's body were on display alongside a vibrant family snap. It was important that everyone involved in the investigation kept to the forefront of their minds exactly what this killer was capable of. The Garda Code specified that they must keep a distance at all times during an investigation. But they must come to know the victim if they were to feel any sense of loss. Outrage would spur them through the darker days ahead. The scene-of-crime pictures would be their starting point – the ransacked items strewn on the floors: Rachel's jewellery; a black glove; a china press opened, the contents carefully scattered.

'Keep an open mind,' the team was advised, as they were briefed as to why, despite appearances, murder, not robbery, appeared to be the motive. There was an order about the way the items were scattered, suggesting their killer had staged the attack. And the phantom burglar or burglars had stolen a digi-camera, six or seven years old, found dumped in a culvert up the road with the O'Reillys' name and address tagged on it. It looked like the killer not only wanted it found, but wanted it returned. There was €450 in cash in Rachel's purse. Any perpetrator hell-bent on ransacking the house would have found it. The money wasn't hidden.

The preliminary forensics results were in. Thirty areas of blood spattering were identified, mostly in the main bedroom where the body was found, and on the floor of the children's bedroom too. Another smear of Rachel's blood was discovered on the washing machine; the clothes inside were slightly damp and smelled of washing powder. There was more blood on the bathroom floor, a towel, baseball bats and a hockey stick. On the living-room floor there were two bloody footprints – one left by a sports fashion shoe.

Nobody wanted to believe Rachel's husband was capable of giving the mother of his two children such a horrific death, but for someone catapulted into such a tragedy he seemed to have a heart of stone. When questioned in his mother's house on the night of the killing by Sergeant Pat Marry, he had initially denied an extra-marital affair. But he quickly changed his story, admitting he had had a relationship with Nikki Pelley which he said was over. His phone records on the day of the murder were suggesting otherwise. There were eighteen calls and texts between the pair, starting at 5.45am. Other significant times included a call for almost half an hour at 8.12 am and a text afterwards from him at 8.48am, minutes before Rachel's murder. But was Joe O'Reilly so cold and calculating that he was capable of casually texting the mother of his two children at 10.07am, having murdered her minutes earlier?

For the moment, it seemed not. Joe O'Reilly had an alibi. His claim that he was at the bus depot on the morning Rachel was killed had been corroborated by his colleague Derek Quearney.

Rose struggled to keep it together as she neared Lambay View with her son Paul and his wife, Denise. It was Wednesday, 13 October, only two days since they'd buried Rachel; three days after they should have celebrated her thirty-first birthday; and less than two weeks before Adam turned three. Her emotions were as raw as they had been the last time she was here, nine days earlier, when she discovered her daughter murdered in cold blood.

Stumbling up the stony drive, she found herself in the jaws of a flashback. The running tap; the silence when she called Rachel's name; Rachel's mutilated body; the two boys left without a mother. The mindlessness of the savagery, the ferocity. Had Rachel suffered much before she died? She should never have come back here.

She braced herself as Jim approached. He had travelled up with Joe, his own shock still insurmountable. This was the last place on earth they wanted to be but they suppressed their suffering for Joe's sake. He had received the keys back from the gardaí only yesterday. It was at his behest that they had come. He'd invited them to put their minds at ease. He reassured them he had found 'peace in the house'. They would too. 'Rachel was there,' he said. They had brought Paul and Denise with them for moral support.

Joe seemed almost gregarious as he greeted them. Maybe it hasn't hit him yet, Rose may have thought as she swallowed down another wave of loss. Joe's mask hadn't slipped once since Rachel's death, even at the most poignant moments that would have taken tears from a stone. He doesn't seem like a man in mourning because he is in denial, she may have thought sadly. She derided herself for ever thinking ill of him. How could he behave normally after what he'd been through? She resolved to do everything to help him through it. Today she would make herself useful by getting rid of Rachel's clothes, as hard as it would be, so that he and the boys wouldn't be reminded of her horrific killing every time they saw her things.

Joe welcomed his guests, then got straight down to business. The gardaí had taken him around the crime scene yesterday trying to establish what was missing. They were still looking for the murder weapon. Joe had informed them two towels were gone from the hot-press and one of Rachel's dumbbells had also disappeared.

'Would you like to hear the messages left the day she died?' he asked the Callalys solemnly.

Nobody answered. Nobody was interested. They were there for Rachel's clothes. They wanted to get it over with.

'Would you?' he pressed.

When there was still no answer he changed tack, heading down the hall, inviting them to follow him to the master bedroom. They followed, dazed, trying to focus on the reason they'd come – to get Rachel's clothes.

Joe swept his arm around to encompass the appalling vista waiting through the doorway. Rose gasped. Jim turned his head away. Paul and Denise looked at him in horror. Rachel's blood was still splashed all over the walls, clotted on the floor, splattered across the ceiling. Oblivious to the horror he was inflicting on them, Joe then informed Rachel's family that it was possible to tell exactly how she had died from the formations of blood in the room.

'What do you think of the scenario of how she died?' he asked, in a matter-of-fact tone. Pointing to a stain on the wall ringed in biro by gardaí, he commented on how low it was, adding, 'This is the way she must have been murdered.' He raised a clenched fist above the spot where Rachel had died. He looked at the appalled faces around him and then explained, 'She got a blow to the head when she went into the room.' Joe threw an imaginary punch to demonstrate.

Rose's heart must have gone crossways as his fist flew through the air. Jim's stomach flipped. Paul and Denise watched open-mouthed.

Joe crouched down on one knee in the doorway, raising his fist again as he jabbed at the floor.

'He got her down, he made sure she didn't get up again,' he said grimly, looking back at them to make sure they were paying attention, before adding, 'This is what whoever was here must have done.' He drew his hand up and whacked again, up and down, landing blow after blow.

A chill ran up Rose's spine. This was the spot where she had clung to her beloved daughter's body and begged the Almighty to spare her. She knew Joe had not begun to grieve yet, but this was profane. She glanced at her family and knew from their expressions they felt the same. Denise was weeping, her gaze fixated on Joe's clenched fist.

Joe stepped over an imaginary body, anxious to show more bloodstains in the other rooms.

'See here,' Joe told them, pointing out more bloodstains inside the bathroom. 'Whoever was here must have come back, probably to clean the blood off himself, then heard Rachel making a noise, gurgling or whatever, and gone back down to finish her off.'

In the boys' bedroom, he pointed out a bloodstain on the floor.

'He must have knelt here,' he said, 'while he was cleaning the blood or whatever.'

Sisters Charlotte (23) and Linda (31) Mulhall at their trial for the murder of Farah Noor. Charlotte was convicted of murder and sentenced to life imprisonment, and her only son was christened while she was behind bars. Mum-of-four Linda got 15 years for manslaughter.

Left: Farah Noor and 'Sue' at her debs ball. Sue was just 16 years old when she first met Farah, and she became pregnant three months later.

COURTESY OF THE SUNDAY WORLD

Below: Forensic officers remove Farah Noor's body parts from the dump point in the Royal Canal, near Croke Park. Farah's head was disposed of elsewhere and has never been recovered.

MAXWELLS

Right: Farah Noor's lover, Kathleen Mulhall, who was sentenced to five years for trying to cover up his murder. After Farah's death in 2005 Kathleen fled to England, returning three years later only after gardai tracked her down, by which time both her daughters had been imprisoned for the crime.

COLLINS PHOTO AGENCY

Below: The house at Richmond Cottages where Farah Noor was murdered and decapitated. After the murder Kathleen cited a cockroach infestation as the reason why she had removed chunks of the carpet from the floor. In fact the cuttings were soaked with Farah's blood.

COLLINS PHOTO AGENCY

Above: Proud mum Rachel with sons Luke and Adam. Rachel called Luke her 'Velcro boy' because he was so attached to her.

COURTESY OF THE SUNDAY WORLD

Above: Lambay View was Rachel O'Reilly's dream home in 'The Naul'. The rural location seemed the perfect place to bring up a young family, but the remoteness also served Joe O'Reilly's evil intentions.

COLLINS PHOTO AGENCY

Above: Rachel and Joe O'Reilly on their wedding day in 1997. Rachel considered it one of the best days of her life.

COURTESY OF THE SUNDAY WORLD

Right: Joe O'Reilly's mistress, Nikki Pelley, an advertising executive whom he met through work. Joe dreamed of replacing Rachel with Nikki to such an extent that he would bring his young sons on outings with Nikki when Rachel was still alive. Nikki continues to visit Joe in prison.

COLLINS PHOTO AGENCY

Rachel's mother Rose Callaly holding hands with daughter Ann and husband Jim at Joe O'Reilly's appeal, which was thrown out of court, marking the end of the family's quest for justice for Rachel.

Joe O'Reilly outside the Four Courts. Joe displayed the same detachment during his legal appearances as he had when making public appeals through the media for help in catching his wife's killer.

Above: Sharon Collins, who tried to arrange three contract killings after Googling the word 'hitman' on the internet.
COLLINS PHOTO AGENCY

Left: PJ Howard, Sharon Collins's partner and one of her three intended victims, who stood by Sharon and refused to believe that she wanted him dead. He later said he spent €200,000 trying to prove her innocence.
COLLINS PHOTO AGENCY

Above: PJ's sons, Robert and Niall Howard, whom Sharon Collins tried to have killed so she could inherit PJ's fortune. His wealth has been variously estimated at between €65 million and €200 million.

COLLINS PHOTO AGENCY

Left: Essam Eid aka 'Tony Luciano', who offered to carry out the three hits for Sharon Collins after she contacted him on his website *hitmanforhire*.

COLLINS PHOTO AGENCY

2FM shock jock Gerry Ryan, on his way to court to give evidence in the Sharon Collins trial. Collins emailed the DJ four months before she tried to solicit a hitman, describing her partner's predilection for 'strange sex', and his desire for her to 'work as a prostitute'. Ryan told the court he did not remember the email, and that it was not read out on air. Ryan was called 'purely to feed the ego of Sharon Collins', the state barrister said.

It proved too much for Jim, who scrambled away up the hall. The rest of his family hurried after him and tried to steady him.

'Would you like to hear the messages now?' Joe called after them, following closely behind.

Nobody answered. Arriving in the kitchen, he asked Rose directly. 'Would you like to hear them?'

She finally agreed so that he would stop haranguing them.

'Are you ready for this?' he warned, his finger hovering over the playback button. He jabbed before he got an answer.

Rose winced as she heard Joe's voice on the tape, then a bleep, then the tape playing back her own voice, 'This is your mother calling,' Rose heard herself saying. 'If you hear this message could you return the call . . .'

She'd left the message around ten minutes before the horror. When Rachel was still alive. Rose studied the man her daughter had loved so much in utter confusion. She could not fathom why he was doing this. It was pure torture.

In the background, the tape began playing a message from Helen in the crèche asking if she was on the way, then another from Joe, asking Rachel why she hadn't collected Adam from the crèche. There was another message from a friend of Rachel's living in Australia. As the spool wound up, Joe again wanted their attention. He had just remembered something. They were all to follow him to the bathroom.

Rose clung to her husband, Jim, who was still

distraught. Paul and Denise were struggling. She hurried them all towards the door. There was no peace in this house. Rachel was not here. If anything, she was spinning in her grave.

4

Murder Tours

The crime correspondent standing on Rose's doorstep was respectful and deeply sympathetic. It was Monday, 18 October. Two weeks had passed since Rachel's murder and the Gardaí feared the trail was running cold. They wanted the family to launch a public appeal. Reporter Mick McCaffrey knew how sensitive the subject was when he followed Rose into her home and to a room off the kitchen.

Inside, Joe was waiting, dressed in jeans and a baggy fleece jumper. He stood up and gave a weak handshake when McCaffrey offered his condolences. The reporter was struck by his sheer bulk and noted that his eyes seemed dead. No wonder, he thought, he's lost his wife of nearly eight years. As the interview began, Rose found the memories too upsetting and excused herself, leaving the room tearfully.

Joe, in contrast, was a model of composure. He stared into space and remained very calm as he opened up. 'When I saw her body I just went into automatic pilot, I guess, trying to revive her. You just don't think. She was cold and stuff, but you just wouldn't think that a thirty-year-old is dead – your wife's not meant to be dead. It

185

didn't make sense. I just couldn't come to terms with it . . . someone killed her in cold blood for no reason that I can see. What's to stop them doing it again? This is worse than anything I have ever imagined. Absolutely nothing can prepare you for this.'

Nothing moved Joe to tears, McCaffrey observed, not even the revelation that Rachel had already bought the children's Christmas presents. His robotic responses when he spoke about Rachel were at best abnormal and sometimes bordering on the bizarre. 'I have nothing to hide and I think the Gardaí know that,' Joe proclaimed. 'I didn't kill her. Everyone, including myself, is a suspect until this is resolved. I was questioned the same way everyone else was and statistically you know it's usually the husband, boyfriend, whatever.'

That said, Joe ticked all the right boxes when he talked about the boys. He seemed passionate about them, confiding the heart-wrenching questions that Luke had asked, 'Where is mammy?' . . . 'Is her head sore?' . . . 'Is she under the ground?' . . . 'Is she a ghost?'

Although his almost clinical coldness could be put down to shock, the reporter wasn't totally convinced he was innocent, even if he did have an alibi. He told colleagues when he got back to the *Evening Herald* newsroom, 'If it turns out that he did it, I won't be a bit surprised.'

The next day, when the paper hit the streets, McCaffrey rang Joe to touch base. Joe was delighted with the story and very grateful, saying he hoped it would lead to the killer being caught. To McCaffrey's complete amazement, he offered to show the newspaper around the bungalow, which he said was still covered in Rachel's bloodstains, for a follow-up story.

'I couldn't believe it and thought this was psychotic behaviour, but as a journalist it was a fantastic story,' McCaffrey admitted.

Joe gave the paper the grisly tour, matter-of-factly pointing out bloodstains on walls. He let them into the bedroom where the murder took place and calmly stated, 'This is where it happened.' He posed for pictures without displaying any emotion.

'Looking back, it was the textbook behaviour of a psychopath, going back to the scene of the crime and collecting trophies,' McCaffrey recalled. 'Only his trophies were photos that were seen by three hundred and twenty thousand newspaper readers when they appeared on the front page.'

As other reporters came into contact with Joe, they were also unnerved by his strange behaviour. *Sunday World* reporter Jim Gallagher approached Joe at his home on 22 October. Joe was heading out with the boys, to drop them off to school and the crèche. That night he was due to appear on *The Late Late Show*. He subsequently told Pat Kenny that he was only bringing the boys back home for short spells because he wanted to 'make the place habitable' first and 'clean away and paint away the bloodstains' to slowly get them used to the idea of coming back home. As the reporter had witnessed that very morning, the boys were already staying the night.

Crimecall presenter Brenda Power interviewed Joe with Rose and Jim in their home around the same time.

'Rachel's parents were pale and dressed in their Sunday best for the cameras, overawed by all the strangers in their neat sitting room. They politely offered us tea and apple tart and were anxious to do their best for the television, trying not to cry while they talked about their girl,' she wrote. In contrast, Joe looked 'controlled' and was 'neat and groomed . . . he had clearly put some time into looking good for his television appearance.'

Power was struck by the moments in between filming, when Rose and Jim asked Joe all about Luke and Adam, because the conversation seemed stilted. And one gesture in particular jarred with her as she finished the interview. Joe winked at her.

RTÉ crime correspondent Paul Reynolds also got a sense something wasn't quite right when interviewing Joe. He found it highly unusual that Joe was comfortable speaking so clinically about the gruesome details of Rachel's death, which most victims' relatives would have found too upsetting. Reynolds didn't know any man who knew the contents of his hot-press, so how was Joe able to claim two towels were missing? And considering Rachel's head had been covered in so much blood that her own mother, Rose, couldn't see her face, how was Joe able to describe the precise location of her injuries?

Joe's desire to relive what had happened to Rachel was becoming insatiable. At Adam's birthday party on 25 October, Joe told Jacqui Connor he had 'laid down in the spot where Rachel had died and she had come to him in a dream'.

His sister Ann entered the room and the conversation stopped. But two days later he continued his story when Jacqui visited his home. 'I was standing in the bedroom and Joe was standing in the hall close to me,' she recalled. In the dream Joe said he was doing it. He re-enacted two or three whacks. He waved his hand and showed he was enacting whacking to the head. He then went to the bathroom and said they [the attackers] heard her gurgle. He came out and re-enacted whacking again.' Jacqui added: 'He said they held her down. That's why blood splashed all around. He told me that he had told the gardaí there were two towels missing from the bathroom, one brown and one white.

'He said a weight, a bell bar [barbell], which was his, was missing from the spare bedroom, where he slept. He said he believed it was somebody Rachel trusted. And when she went down to the bedroom she may have bent down to get some of her Avon products. He referred to the killer or killers as "they".

'They went down to the bathroom to have a shower. They heard her moan and they came back and finished her off. He said the area behind the ear was the correct place to hit someone if you want to kill them. He said someone with military training would know this,' Jacqui recalled.

When one of Rachel's best friends, Fidelma Geraghty, called to pick up something of Rachel's by which to remember her, she was also given the tour. Rachel had given her scented candles the week before but she had forgotten to take them.

'Joe answered the door to me and invited me in. I didn't want to come in because of what happened but Joe insisted. He said people felt at peace when they came in.' Joe said he would give her the 'tour'.

Fidelma said, 'No, I don't want to.' He responded that a lot of people found it peaceful. He talked about the forensics and what he had to do for the guards. He pointed at bloodstaining on the walls. He showed her where a section of carpet had been cut out because it was saturated with blood. Then he re-enacted Rachel's murder again. 'He went to the bedroom. I was standing at the door. He said Rachel was possibly bending down to get something from the table in the bedroom and that she was hit from the back and to the side,' Fidelma recalled.

Fidelma said Joe got down on the floor and told her: 'They went into the bathroom to take a shower and they heard her moan and they went back to finish her off.' She was flabbergasted. 'I could not understand how he was talking about that,' she said.

Rachel's friend and neighbour, Sarah Harmon, went to visit him with her three-year-old daughter, Sophie, in the weeks after the murder. He left her alone in the bedroom where Rachel died. She left Sophie with him in the kitchen.

'I sat on the bed. I was quite upset,' she recalled. Joe then appeared at the door without Sophie. 'He got down on his knees in the bedroom where the underlining was cut from the carpet. Using his left hand, he showed me the blood spatter on the wall and said this must have been Rachel's blood. With his right hand he did the same and said this must be the killer's blood. He said they must have been short and they must have beaten her repeatedly. He moved his hand down quite violently. I was quite shocked. I was shocked by the physicality of the situation. I found it quite hard to deal with. Sophie arrived at the door. I didn't want her to come into the room. Joe picked her up and put her into Adam's room . . . I switched off at that stage. I did not want to take any more in.'

Another friend subjected to a re-enactment was Alan Boyle, who visited Joe two weeks after the murder. Joe stayed calm throughout the entire episode. Boyle asked if Rachel could have been killed by a lover, to which Joe replied that he 'couldn't give a fuck' what Rachel got up to.

Later Boyle found out from Joe's mother that he had had a fling. 'I said to Joe, "All the gardaí had was circumstantial, but if they got something else I would have difficulty believing you." '

Joe replied, 'When you stop believing me, let me know.'

The investigation was being held up by the time needed to analyse Joe's mobile phone movements and by the painstaking trawl of the hours of CCTV footage from around the city. Suddenly, a breakthrough came from somewhere unexpected – Joe's work computer. A series of vicious emails exchanged with his sister Ann uncovered a motive, spelt out by the man who was now the prime suspect. In a nutshell, they revealed that Joe O'Reilly hated his wife, but refused to separate because he wanted full custody of his children.

The correspondence had taken place on 9 June, the day after Rachel and Joe had met with a social worker to answer an anonymous complaint made against Rachel by Joe's mother, alleging the children were being abused.

Ann had emailed Joe at 10.16am:

I'm just asking how you got on yesterday. How are you?
   Concerned Banana.
   Wanted to leave you alone yesterday to
get your head together, but trust me, I
held back on calling or mailing you. Let
me know how things are and if you need
anything.

Joe responded at 10.41am:

In a nutshell, it was a big steaming
pile of shite. They told us both, that
shouting at the kids was OK, 'Sure, we
all do it.'
   Hitting kids is OK in the eyes of the
law, as again 'We all do it.' They never
come out and visit the homes of kids
reported as being abused unless the
allegation is of a sexual nature or
after several cases of non-accidental
hospitalizations.
   Could it have gone any worse?
   Yes!!!

Rachel is a 'good mother' because she
admits to having problems dealing with
the kids and confessed to shouting at
them on a daily basis. There is some
Mickey Mouse course run once a year, to
help parents cope with 'difficult kids'
and 'parenting difficulties', and Rachel
has volunteered to go on one. She was
also playing the 'home help' card but
didn't get anywhere.

The best I got was commitment to
getting the district nurse to pay a
visit, as Adam is due his developmental
check-up. Should have got it last year,
but in the words of his mother: 'You
know yourself, what with the house move
and so on, it's easy to forget these
things.' Anyway, I gave them the go-ahead
to drop out whenever they want to see
the kids. Hopefully the DN [district
nurse] will see her at her 'best' or
else the state of the house that the
lazy cunt leaves it in etc. Positives?
Very few. At least it's on record that I
don't need to attend the courses, I've
no issues in dealing with the kids, and
the complaint had nothing to do with me.

To answer your question as to how I am.
Well, to be honest, I wasn't expecting
much, as you were no doubt aware, so I

wasn't too shocked with the apathy displayed by our wonderful child protection people.

That said, I think matters may get worse, as she told me in the car park that 'I knew you were overreacting going on to me about shouting at the kids. Did you hear them? Everybody does it, and I am a good mother.' Instead of giving her a slap on the wrist, it appears that they've forgiven her and patted her on the back for a job well done.

Did you get to talk to Derek by the way? Had to physically restrain him on Saturday night, not good. He's too much of a hothead, but you really couldn't blame him.

As usual, I had a right go at her, but as usual, by that stage the damage is already done. Shouldn't really complain though, she is a 'Wonderful Mother' in the eyes of the state.

PS Interesting choice of terminology used by the Social Worker, everything was 'Rachel is the main care giver and I was the secondary care giver.' I'm already Mr Weekend Custody in the eyes of the state. Doesn't bode too well does it? Oh, nearly forgot, the case is now closed to their satisfaction.

Ann replied at 11.01am:

Well at least you get the DN coming out
on unexpected visits, that can't be too
bad really.

Dan was talking to her yesterday and
she told him she now counts to ten and
examines the situation with the kids, so
let's hope something good, even if it's
little, will come out of this.

So you're going out for a meal on
Friday night with her. Should be good
fun, all nice romantic (not). Try again
to talk to her about her lack of
motherly instincts. Have you told her she
has none? Does she admit to it?

Try a bit harder to talk to her about
it. Tell her everything, be open and
honest. I know I'd keep on trying
constantly. I wouldn't give her ears a
break from the subject. Otherwise she's
just going to keep on living in cloud
cuckoo land.

Did Derek say anything to Rachel about
her manhandling Adam and Luke?

Ma was very worried about it yesterday.
If you get a minute could you ring her,
put her mind at rest?

I went straight into Ma's yesterday to
see what the story was and she was

saying that Rachel came in and was all over Adam and just blanked Luke (fooking bitch).

That hurt Ma, she wanted so much to say something, but didn't.

Anyway, Rachel stayed for chips, eggs and bread and was very calm and happy so Ma was left thinking.

Call her. She's our mammy and does really worry about us.

Don't let on that I have told you, you know what she's like!

So do I still have to be on my best around Rachel keeping my mouth shut? If I see her hit or manhandle the kids can I speak up?

That afternoon at 3.42, Joe wrote back:

Hiya. So she now counts to ten, eh?

Believe that and you're not my sister!!!

Where the hell did you hear I was going for a night out with that cunt???? A meal? I'd rather choke.

Absolutely no way, never, not happening.

To quote your good self, Ann, never look back, only look forward, eh?

Just to drill the point home, Me +

Rachel + Marriage = over!!!!

I keep telling her, straight as you like, exactly what I think of her mothering instincts. Yes. In fact, to be even a little fair, I'm very aware that I'm overcritical at times, although I don't feel guilty about it to be honest, as she repulses me.

Derek didn't say anything, I wouldn't let him. Bad enough I have to bite my tongue and restrain myself, don't need him losing it. Not for her sake, but the kids wouldn't like seeing their mother abused by their uncle Derek, and I don't want his halo around them diminished in any way.

(You're getting competition, Ann!!) That's where you need to be careful. When Ma reported the incident that brought about yesterday's farce, it nearly came out as to who did the reporting!!!

You are prime suspect number one, you know it. By all means, drag her fat ass outside and kick it into the middle of next week, but not in front of the boys, and don't leave any marks that can and will be used against you in a court of law.

As I've said repeatedly, there is no

talking to her. She doesn't listen.

Mind you there's a lot of that about.
I told you and I told Ma that this would
amount to nothing, and you both knew
better than me and went through the
usual series of questions.

I'm not having a go, Ann, but it
really wound me up last time. Yesterday
proved yet again, the injustices that
exist in this country.

As a mother, you can shout and scream
and smack most as much as you want to,
once you admit to having a bit of a
problem and then volunteer to a lip
service parent's course.

Maybe now, you'll both listen to what
I have to say and not go about with your
heads in the sand.

Being a father in this country, no
matter how good, will land you with
weekend visits and not much else. You
know of one case where full custody was
given, that's great, and good for him. I
know of dozens where it went the other
way.

Yesterday was my first personal
indication of how much I will lose if I
don't try different angles. After all,
I'm only the secondary care giver.

I do appreciate your support; and I

know the boys mean the world to you,
they are my life and I am nothing
without them.

Adam was the one singled out as the
child whom the concerns were about. More
bad news for Luke as proved yesterday,
in your own words and observations.

Ann, there is only so much crap the
kid can deal with and [patience is]
running on empty. You saw first hand the
number she did on him before. I'd rather
die than see him go through that again.
He won't go through that again, end of
story.

Be as good as you can around Rachel
for now, but tell me everything you see,
do not hold back.

If you see her being excessive, then
step in. I want to know as much as
possible, and I can't be there all the
time. Ann, you're my sister, my blood,
she's not. What you tell me will not be
questioned. You have carte blanche
visitation rights to my house, and to my
kids. In fact the more you're around,
the better.

Same with Dan, but I don't want him
knowing too much.

I plan on calling Ma later tonight. I
know she's worried. The 'World's Greatest

Mum' is out tonight, getting laid with a
bit of luck, so I'll have time to talk
to Ma properly when the boys are asleep.

I'll be home in Ma's on Friday with
the boys, so I'll see you then?

Thanks for the concern, sorry for the
long email!!

Ann replied at 4pm:

Your meal is probably a surprise.

Well of course it is.

She got Dan to book it last night for
ye then you are staying in Ma's but she
asked me last week if she ever wanted to
venture up to Dunleer and eat out could
she stay with me???

So she knows the marriage is over then
and it's a divorce. What does she say to
that? Maybe that's why she's taking you
out on Friday. Say nothing.

I do get it now. You're fooked as a
father in this dump. Ask her to move
abroad. I really dunno how you're going
to get out of this one.

So when are you filing for legal
separation then?

If you want I can kidnap you and the
kids on Friday night before she has a
chance to get hold of you. We could

```
go on a trip in my car??
  Or you could just go with her and
ignore the whole night or stare at sexy
ladies.
```

Another email was only a couple of lines long, but just as stunning as the others. Three minutes before Joe left the Viacom building on the morning of Rachel's death, as captured on the CCTV camera in reception, Joe emailed his friend Kieron Gallagher:

```
I will be out and about most of the
morning, and in poor phone coverage
areas, so unless I hear otherwise from
you, lunch at 2pm, usual place?
Got the 40 quid off my brother at the
weekend!
Later
Joe
```

Was Joe O'Reilly so ruthless that he could pre-plan his lunch before setting off to murder his wife? It was more incumbent on the team of detectives than ever that they verify Joe's alibi.

5

The Late Late Show

Pat Kenny lurched on the edge of his seat. The Rachel O'Reilly murder had gripped the nation and now the long-standing presenter was flanked on *The Late Late Show* by Rachel's mother, Rose, and husband, Joe. It was 22 October, less than three weeks since the crime had been committed. For the first time, the bereaved family was speaking publicly on air. It was a huge scoop and against the backdrop of a ratings war, it promised to be box office TV.

Rose sat rigidly to the right of the presenter, dressed in a black and white striped V-neck top, her back straight as a beanpole, her chin held at an elevated height. She pressed her lips tightly together as she stared straight into the audience where her husband Jim was sitting with their daughter, Ann, and Sarah Harmon.

Her clean-shaven son-in-law sat on her left, dressed in a grey shirt open at the neck. He rubbed his large palms together in anticipation. Rose glowered at him and bit her tongue. His behaviour in the green room before the show had been disgraceful. He had devoured sandwiches and laughed and joked with the media. In the background, a television monitor displayed a family snap of Rachel and

Joe holding the boys. In actuality, Joe wasn't even wearing his wedding ring.

After reminding the audience of the tragedy that had befallen his guests, Pat Kenny added that Rachel's 'killer or killers are still at large. The Gardaí are absolutely baffled,' he explained, offering Rose his hand in condolence, then reaching over to Joe. As her son-in-law stretched across her, Rose physically recoiled. Joe shot her a sidelong glance. The audience burst into oblivious, heartfelt applause. A quick smile of relief spread across Joe's face. He pursed his lips quickly and resumed an expression of measured anxiety, frowning slightly. As the clapping faded out, Pat turned to Joe, 'What kind of a woman was Rachel?'

Joe shook his head. 'Just a normal woman,' he replied, exhaling. 'She did extraordinary things in her short life. Great sporting achievements. Mother of two small children. Just nothing out of the ordinary. No lifestyle of the rich and famous. Just an ordinary person.'

Rose had appeared pale from the outset, but now the colour seemed to drain from her face. It sounded like he was doing Rachel down. The camera shifted to a close-up of Joe.

'How did you meet?' Pat probed.

'We met years ago,' Joe answered, with a half-smile. 'About thirteen years ago, at a softball game which is a game like baseball. Rachel took it up. She was a lot better than I was . . .' He grinned.

The audience began to laugh nervously, then thought better of it and stopped short.

'So, eh, I just kept at it until I could catch up but I didn't,' he continued, grinning again. 'But she put up with me and we went out and just took it from there.'

'You proposed to her where?' Pat asked.

'In Paris,' Joe answered, 'up the Eiffel Tower. So it was either propose or she'd throw me off.'

The audience laughed. The camera panned back. Rose looked ill.

'She said yes,' Pat prompted his interviewee, 'and you have two small boys. Everything was going great. You were making plans for the future?'

The TV screen filled with the background photo. Joe was holding doe-eyed Luke on his lap; Rachel clutched Adam. Close up, Rachel's smile looked forced.

Pat asked about their plans.

Joe's eyes bulged. 'I mean, just carrying on life as normal. The last thing we expected was, em, what happened.'

'Any plans for her birthday?' Pat grilled.

'We had, she would have been thirty-one on 10 October which was six days after she was murdered,' Joe replied. 'We missed her thirtieth birthday last year, I was away. Em, we had plans then for this Monday for Adam's birthday as well.' Joe shrugged. 'So, eh, he's going to be three.'

As the camera switched to a wide angle, Rose seemed to be struggling. Her eyes were downcast; her breath laboured.

Pat picked up the cue and turned to her. 'Rose, it's a terrible thing to lose a daughter like this and you have great memories of her growing up. What sort of a kid was she?'

'I was just looking through the photo album this morning,' Rose sighed. 'And she had a very, very happy childhood. She was just a bolt of lightning from the time she could move. She figured everything out. I recall the time we were in Spain. And we'd have to tie the doors of the apartment because she had figured out how to open them. She would only have been a little over a year at the time. So we put her into the cot. And ten minutes after she had figured that one out, how to hop out of the cot, I strapped a harness to her and tied it to tights under the cot and she could only sit up. She figured out how to get the cot from one side of the room to the other and how to turn the light on.'

The audience laughed spontaneously, releasing tension.

'So that was Rachel all her life,' Rose continued sadly, her hands clasped on her lap.

'A bit of a tomboy?' Pat probed.

'A bit of a tomboy,' Rose agreed. 'She had everything worked out and whatever she set her mind to, she got there.'

The camera flicked to a picture of Rachel in her wedding veil. This time her smile was infectious. Her eyes had a spark that was missing from the family shot.

'She was an absolutely brilliant daughter,' Rose went on. 'A brilliant person. Everybody that ever knew her, she touched their lives. It's just inconceivable that her life has ended and the way it did. She didn't deserve that and it should never have been.'

Pat turned back to Joe. 'Bring us back to the morning

205

of the killing,' he quizzed. 'You had already gone to work, you work quite a way away from home.'

A photo of Rachel playing softball appeared on screen. She was wearing a red cap, a black V-neck jersey emblazoned with the red and white Renegades logo and shin guards.

'Yeah, I work about twenty-five miles away,' Joe reeled off, as the camera zoomed in for a close-up. 'So what I usually do, was my normal routine as well, is, I'd leave the house at five thirty, six o'clock. Em, travel across city, go to gym, do quick workout there, shower and a shave, and then into the office. So business as usual really.'

His eyes darted from side to side. 'Rachel would have got up, have the kids washed and dressed and fed, then off to school.'

'She's two calls to make,' Pat coached, 'one to the crèche and one to the school?'

'Yeah, to Luke's school first for around ten past, quarter past nine. Then Adam's school for nine thirty. And that's the last time that we know of that she was seen alive. There's nothing during the day that was in any way peculiar or out of the way to my knowledge. It was her best friend Jacqui's . . . it was her birthday. So when I got the call from Adam's crèche to say he hadn't been collected—'

Pat cut in, 'Which would have been very unusual?'

'Highly unusual,' Joe agreed. 'I mean if she was going to go somewhere for a lunch appointment, she'd get one of the other mothers to pick Adam up. They'd sometimes swap around collecting the kids.'

The monitor filled with a fresh picture of Rachel – holding Adam.

'So I wasn't overly panicked when I got the call from the crèche,' Joe went on. 'I called Rachel's mobile then and went through to message. I called Jacqui, her friend, then to see was she having lunch and Jacqui, who's a nurse, was still in bed. She'd just done the night shift. She said no, she hadn't been around.

'Something didn't feel right so I called Rose and she hadn't been with Rose either. So I was actually on my way out then to pick up Adam.

'Jim, Rachel's dad, he then called me to ask was there a number for the neighbours to see had she fallen down the stairs or had an accident or something.

'And I didn't but I sent a text through for the number for the crèche. Jim then called the crèche to get a number for Sarah who was our nearest neighbour. Sarah was going to pop down to see was Rachel OK but Rose had already left at that point.'

The camera flicked to an audience shot, homing in on Jim's red-faced expression. His mouth was downturned, his eyes blinking rapidly. He gulped back the rising emotion.

'So I went to pick up Adam,' Joe babbled, 'and when I was picking up Adam, Rose had got to home.'

Joe gestured to Rose, who was looking at the ground. Her eyes swept up to Pat tragically.

'What did you find when you got there?' Pat asked. 'Were the doors open?'

The camera closed in on Rose. 'Well, initially, when I

got to the house I saw Rachel's car in the drive,' Rose replied. 'And it was such a relief because on the way out I knew something had to be wrong for her to be late for the children and for her to be that late. When I saw the car initially it was just a sense of relief. I thought she's just here before us. I got around to . . . I never used the front door. I would walk around the back. If Rachel was there it was not unusual for the door to be open. If it wasn't open, you pushed it back. But, as it happened, that day it was open and as I walked into the kitchen, it just looked different.'

Rose tapped her finger off her temple. 'It didn't register with me why. But it was afterwards . . . it was the curtains were drawn. And I'd never known Rachel to draw the curtains. And then, the rest is history, Pat, it just . . .' Rose stalls.

The angle widens to include Joe, who's watching Pat intently.

'You were the one who found her?' Pat pushes Rose.

'I was the one who found her,' Rose nodded, 'on my own in short. You know I went up to the bedroom and to my dying day I'll never forget the scene that met me.' Rose's eyes filled. Her mouth curled.

'Did you quickly ascertain she was beyond help?' Pat prodded.

'I knew as soon as I saw her because Rachel had very sallow skin and when I looked at her she just looked as if she was carved out of marble. And I knelt down beside her and although I knew she was dead I sort of felt her arms. I was afraid to touch her head in case I'd hurt her.'

The camera panned back. Joe was cleaning his upper teeth with his tongue.

'Although I knew ... it didn't make sense,' Rose struggled. 'I knew like she was dead but I knew to look at her before I knelt down she was dead. And Pat, she had a horrific death.'

The camera shifts to Joe, who is now pursing his lips. Back to Rose, 'So I sort of . . . I feel the way she died that somebody out there would have known something. Like it couldn't have gone unnoticed. There must have been . . . Whoever done it must have had some evidence. There was an awful lot of blood involved.'

'So they would have had to . . . ?' Pat pressed.

'They would have had to, I couldn't see, and Joe feels the same,' Rose rushed.

'Joe, when did you arrive on the scene?' Pat quizzed.

Joe looked at him earnestly. 'I arrived on the scene about ten past, quarter past two. 'Cos I went to Luke's school after I had Adam. I got to Luke's school to collect Luke, I had Adam and Luke had already been collected. There was a glimmer. As Rose said, she saw Rachel's car, and thought thank God, the car was there. When I went to collect Luke, I thought thank God Luke has been collected.'

The camera angle pulled back to show Rose, twiddling her thumbs around each other, eyes downcast. It switched quickly back to Joe.

'So I arrived to the house. Rose obviously was there. Sarah was there, a neighbour and Rachel's friend.

Thankfully Luke hadn't got into the house. He just saw my car and ran towards me.

'I saw Rose coming out of the house then and I just knew looking at her face something was wrong.

'So I said, "What's wrong?" and she said, "I think Rachel's dead." So everything else you know, you hear about out-of-body experiences and stuff, I just literally felt,' he patted the air, 'I was at the outside looking in at myself walking into the room.

'Sarah was calling the emergency services as I got to the kitchen and I asked Sarah where Rachel was and she said, "Down in the bedroom," and Sarah looked really, really upset so I knew what I was going to see was going to be bad but not as bad as I actually saw. I went down to the bedroom and it was very bloody. Very violent and instinct just kicked in to try and revive her, give her some kind of CPR, something. And when I checked for some sign of a pulse or something, as Rose said, she looked like marble, she felt very cold, very hard. I tried to move her as well and I couldn't. I don't know if that was because she was so stiff or just the life just drained out of me pretty much.'

Pat cut in, 'You were lifting a dead weight at that point?'

'Quite literally, yeah,' Joe said, sounding chirpy. 'The next thing I remember is Rose coming down and saying, "I think she must have fallen because there was blood in the bathroom."

'There was a box near where Rachel was lying, there was blood on that. So I moved that to, again, to try and move Rachel and then I remember Jacqui arriving, who is a nurse.'

The screen filled with Rose's reaction. She looked like she was going to be sick.

'Jacqui and I tried moving Rachel but Jacqui checked, knew how to look properly, I guess, for pulses and that, and said, "She's gone, she's dead, what happened?"' Joe continued. His expression became overly perplexed as he relived the moment. 'I said, "I dunno. I think she fell." It could have been seconds, minutes, I don't know, but the next thing I remember is the paramedics arriving.'

Rose looked at him intently.

'They asked us to move out of the way,' Joe continued. 'They had to do some work on her. So we went up to the kitchen where we were waiting at the kitchen door and we see the other paramedics coming in with their box of tricks, you know, the electric shock things.'

'But you knew in your hearts?' Pat asked.

'I knew in the back of my head that it was too late,' Joe admitted. 'But there was still hope. You know you see it so much on TV. They come in and give a shock and the person is brought back. I knew if they were going to bring Rachel back, you know that she'd suffered massive brain damage and she'd never be the same again. Em, but within a minute they said, "I'm sorry, you know, she's dead." We wanted to go down then, just to see her.'

Pat asked, 'You were both still thinking this is a fall, this is a terrible domestic accident?'

Rose threw her eyes upwards and shook her head.

'Was the rest of the house trashed in some way?' Pat went on.

'It was,' Rose agreed, 'but to me it looked a contrived thing, how rightly or wrongly I don't know.'

Joe shifted uncomfortably in his chair.

'But I felt when I saw her that she had been murdered. Initially when I saw the blood in the bathroom, I thought maybe she was in the shower, or getting out of the bath. But as soon as I looked beyond where the blood was in the bathroom, it was quite apparent that wasn't so. And I just knew, Pat, she had met a horrific death.'

'Did she have any enemies?' Pat asked her. 'Is there anyone she had a falling out with?'

Joe rubbed his hands together.

Rose threw Pat a look.

'I don't want you to mention any names,' Pat clarified quickly.

Rose nodded.

Pat turned to Joe. 'You said she was well liked by everyone?'

'Yeah,' Joe replied, then sowed some seeds of suspicion. 'I mean she was very straight and wonderfully innocent when it came to people. I mean she didn't have a lot of tact. You couldn't make an enemy of her from the things she'd say. She was very straight.'

'She also had done some self-defence,' Pat prompted. 'So she might not have made it easy for her attackers.'

Joe sucked air through his teeth and agreed wholeheartedly. 'Definitely not,' he answered. 'She was an accomplished athlete. As I say, swam for Western

Australia, threw discus and shotput for Leinster, she was an Irish softball player, a world record holder at softball. She did tae kwon do.

'Certainly if this was, depending on what theory you're reading in the papers, if this was two random burglars, they certainly didn't break into the house of a defenceless little old lady. This was . . . they would have really been surprised number one to find Rachel coming home, but they would have been equally surprised to get her down on the ground and kill her. I don't think it would have been easy at all.' Joe licked his lips.

'You know the way the Gardaí give you statistics,' Pat said, 'and say that in eight or nine out of ten murders the victim may be known to the murderer. Based on the situation you found in the house, did you get the sense that she'd been taken unawares, that this was someone that perhaps she trusted?'

Rose nodded deeply, closed her eyes and kept nodding.

'Yeah,' Joe cut in, 'I think so. Where the murder happened was in the bedroom, which is the very last room in the house, so it's the last place you're going to bring someone you don't know because you're cornered. Em, my view as well would be and again it's just my view, it's not a police theory, [it's a] personal belief, would be that she knew the person because why else would you kill her? If it was a violent robbery, why go to the extreme of murdering someone unless they can identify you? That's why we've talked about this and practically nothing else for the last three weeks . . .' He looked to Rose for affirmation but didn't get it, '. . . we just feel it's someone she would have known or could have identified.'

Pat turned to Rachel's family and friend in the audience.

Grief was etched raw on Ann Callaly's striking face as she described who Rachel was, her voice breaking, 'an amazing person, a natural nurturer, a super wife, a fantastic sister, everything, fantastic daughter'. The void left in their lives would never be filled, she said. 'There were children's toys all around the place,' she explained. 'Whoever did this has deprived those beautiful boys of a fantastic mother.'

'How much do the boys know of what's happened, Joe?' Pat resumed.

'We're staying in my mother's house in Dunleer,' Joe replied, adding, 'When I brought the boys back on Monday night, Adam, thankfully, is young and doesn't understand. Luke is that bit older and he'd ask questions in the car on the way back. He was asking me, "Who is dead?" . . . "What is the blood about?" . . . "Did Mammy hurt her head?"

'So Rachel's aunt Lucy died last year and Rachel explained Lucy was an angel who had gone to heaven. So I explained that Mammy had hurt her head and gone to heaven and was an angel and Luke didn't want to accept that he wasn't going to see Mammy again and said, "Holy God is bold," things four-year-olds would say.

'Since then he's asking more questions every day, you know, "Was there much blood?"; "Did we put a plaster on her head?"; I guess with Hallowe'en just around the corner he's hearing things. "Is she a ghost?"; "Is she a skeleton?"; "Is she under the ground?" Stuff like that.

We're just trying to keep the memories there for him and he's started to come around now.'

The camera showed Rose's reaction. Her composure was gone. Tears rolled down her face. Pat asked again how much Adam knew.

'He just knows there's something wrong. They've both been plucked out of their house, their room, their surroundings, from their mother, with no notice,' Joe explained. 'They're staying in my mother's house which thankfully is a place they know very well, but it's not home and Mammy hasn't come home yet. He's very clingy, especially at night time, but thankfully he's very young and he does seem to be getting through the worst of it although my view is, when we do bring them back to the house and they do see Mammy's things around again, that might be when it really hits them.'

'Have you been back to the house?' Pat asked.

'I went back to the house last Tuesday week with the gardaí to go over the crime scene and to see could I notice anything else missing. Em, since then I've been back pretty much every day, an hour here, an hour there and so I'm building up the time that I'm in the house. Obviously I've got to go through the bills and stuff.'

'Are you going to go back and live there?' Pat probed, sounding surprised, then quickly adding, 'The boys, will they feel happier to be in a place they know, even without their mother?'

'I don't know to be honest,' Joe replied. 'My goal now is to make the house habitable again and to clean away and paint away the bloodstains and stuff like that.'

Rose stared downwards.

'And then to, after school, to bring them back . . .'

The camera panned to the audience. Jim looked torn in two. He clutched Sarah's hand. Sarah was weeping.

'To see how it affects them,' Joe continued. 'If they can move in happily, great, because it is a great house, it is in a great area, neighbours and friends have been overwhelmingly generous. It's such a great place. The schools that they're both in are fantastic.'

The camera switched to Ann, who was wincing.

Rose shifted uncomfortably in her seat.

'But if they're not happy, I'll just move,' Joe reacted. 'I'm not going to put them through that.'

'Rose?' Pat asked. 'Have you been back?'

'I have,' she admitted, sorrowfully. 'The first day Joe went with the detectives. Then Jim and I went. I never thought I'd put my foot across the door, Pat, but Joe had been there the day before with the police and he said he felt a sense of peace and he asked Jim and I would we go so we went back the following day. And then Jim and myself and my son and brother, a team, went down last Saturday and cleaned up. My sister-in-law, you know, spent the day down there.'

'Terrible, terrible, gruesome job . . .' Pat sympathized. 'You're here to make an appeal. People are already familiar with your story. They've now heard you tell it first hand. If there was anyone in the area, in The Naul on the fourth, whatever help they give . . .'

'Well, I would appeal, we feel, Joe feels the same, there must be some evidence and maybe somebody they think they're shielding, they must have some suspicions,' Rose said, adding, 'and I would appeal to them to come forward, you know, even if it's the least important bit of evidence it might be the piece the police are looking for to put the puzzle together. And we feel that person or persons are out there and they could do the very same again and put families like ours, it's just absolute hell. You don't want to live the first few days, the first week you don't want to breathe, you just have to and we feel there won't be any closure until something comes and we know there's some breakthrough made.'

Pat relayed the telephone numbers for the incident room in Balbriggan. Just as he began to thank them, Joe piped up, 'We just feel that somebody somewhere must know something. Being to the house quite a bit, there was a lot of blood, and so therefore there would have been a lot of blood on this person, whether it was on their hair, or their face, or their hands, clothes. If they've got into a car, there would have to have been bloodstains in the car somewhere. If they lived in a built-up area, you know, if you took the Monday morning off sick, if you looked out your window, if you saw someone covered up getting out of their car, they look like they're in a hurry, more hurry than normal, if you were out, acting in any way suspicious. If you were out jogging in the area, walking your dog in the area, anything, no matter how in-significant, no matter how trivial it may sound to you. The Gardaí have put a huge amount of effort into this, it could just be the missing nugget they need to close this off because this person is still at large.'

'As time moves on it's off the front pages, people's memories are not as sharp, now's the time,' Pat wound up, thanking Rose and Joe. The camera cut their reaction off quickly.

6

Suspect

Nikki Pelley must have cringed watching *The Late Late Show* in front of her parents, Fraser and Margaret. Joe was playing the grieving husband on the telly but had been spending at least two nights a week with her in her parents' house on Ballyroan Road in Rathfarnham. Joe was even calling over tonight after the show ended; he'd declined *The Late Late Show*'s offer of a hotel room. She'd lied to gardaí who called to question her the day after the murder by telling them the affair was over.

At thirty-four years old, Pelley was tanned, slim, had shoulder-length blonde hair and, unlike the other women in Joe's life, was of average height. Her two sisters had places of their own, but Nikki conducted her relationship with Joe under her parents' roof. Joe had convinced them that his marriage to Rachel – the woman he still lived with – was over, and that he wanted a future with their daughter. He had even brought his children over to see them on several occasions.

In her career, Nikki was an independent, successful woman. She had been an advertising executive with Maiden Outdoor Company since 2003, having previously worked with Joe in Viacom. They got involved romantically after meeting at a function held by Poster Management Limited in The Barge pub, beside the Grand Canal in south Dublin in January 2004. Joe told her he had effectively split from Rachel a year and a half earlier, and that they slept in separate rooms. They kept in touch after the party by emailing each other jokes and texting. A few months later, she met him for lunch in the Templeogue Inn. Afterwards they went to the cinema in Liffey Valley. That was around April. By June, she was besotted and thought of him as her husband. They met and had sex three or four times a week. She wore a gold band on her wedding finger and had a Visa card with the name Nikki P. Reilly, made from clipping the names off each of their cards and sticking them together. She had seen Rachel once at a softball tournament but she didn't believe Joe's wife suspected anything was going on between her and Joe. She had even stayed in Joe and Rachel's house once when Rachel was down the country. They planned a 'permanent future' together, according to her.

Her friends did not buy Joe's 'wife doesn't understand me' story so easily. One girlfriend, 'D', found his attitude to Rachel disrespectful. Even if the marriage was over, Rachel was still the mother of Joe's two children. But he continued to slag Rachel off to such an extent that another of Nikki's friends joked that if Joe wanted Rachel 'bumped off' to give him a ring. Nikki confided in D that when she told Joe, his response was, 'If I thought I'd get away with it, I'd do it myself.'

As the affair grew in intensity, Nikki found it increasingly difficult to settle for stolen weekends at her parents' holiday home near Courtown, Co. Wexford, or for two nights a week. They usually met on Tuesdays after Joe finished softball practice and Saturdays when she would sometimes spend the afternoon with him and the boys, including one occasion on which they went for a day out to the zoo.

Nikki's expectations were rising. She told D that she had given Joe an ultimatum to end it with Rachel by November or she would finish with him. Joe claimed that he in turn had told Rachel she had two weeks to tell her family that the marriage was over.

Nikki fell out with D over Joe. D disliked Joe and thought Nikki had been taken in by him too easily and had changed as a person. She used to be bubbly before she hooked up with sullen, sulky Joe. D felt Nikki should be more sceptical of everything he told her about Rachel as it was only his side of the story.

After Rachel's murder, D got back in touch with Nikki. She assumed Joe was guilty. Nikki told her she thought he was innocent, but she sometimes had her doubts.

As Nikki watched *The Late Late Show* wind up with Joe's appeal for information, she must have wondered about the row he'd told her that he'd had with Rachel the night before her murder. Her recollection of what they spoke about on the day Rachel died would fade with time.

Joe must have still been on a high the morning after his TV debut when the phone rang and he agreed to give a follow-up interview to the crime reporter John Mooney on the other end of the line. In his answers to questions, he appeared once again to try to sow seeds of doubt, to create shadowy suspects and motives while exonerating himself.

Asked if there was any reason why anyone would want to murder his wife, he replied: 'No, there's no reason at all. Myself and her family, we've looked at it every which way we can. It makes no sense to us. She was very straight. If she had a problem with you, she would tell you.

'Unlike me, she was very forgiving in nature and wouldn't hold a grudge. No one who would have known her well could have done this. Possibly, as we said on TV and to the guards, it was someone who knew her well enough that she could get something for them from the bedroom or bring them [there] to do a bit of work.

'It doesn't add up to us, to be honest with you. We are not guards or detectives and we are not used to crime, so we just don't know, we are only guessing. If Rachel walked in on a robbery she would have got out and into the car, called the guards.

'The bravest thing she would have done would be to follow the car to see where they were going, or to get a good description. If she had walked into the kitchen and there was someone there looking for stuff – if they were teenagers or something – she may have grabbed them. Because you would really want to have been on your best day to take Rachel down in a fight. She swam and played softball for Australia.

'She was a strong woman. Many a guy even messing on the softball team would be surprised how strong she was. Her dad's a plumber and even he was surprised at how strong she was.'

Joe pushed his theory that Rachel had some vague link to her killers.

'I think they knew her enough that she would have [let them in]. She was an Avon lady. [Maybe] it was someone collecting his wife's Avon. [Maybe] someone knocking as a tradesman at the house, because we were getting a lot of work done. It might have been a guy coming in to do a job and she said, "Hey, I'll get you something in the bedroom," or "Will you do wardrobes?" or something.

'There's no way she would let a stranger into the house, none whatsoever. And if someone tried to barge their way in, the blood wouldn't have been in the bedroom, it would have been in the kitchen.

'I don't have names but I would know of people who have been to the house for one reason or another that may have done it. In fairness to them, I'm sure everyone, including myself, is still a suspect until everything is resolved. I was questioned the same as everyone else. Statistically . . . what's it . . . eight out of ten, nine out of ten . . . it's the husband, boyfriend, whatever. I'm sure if the gardaí thought it was me, I would have been questioned by now, arrested or something. Maybe I'm not the number one suspect now, but at the start I was.

'I have given the guards as much help as I possibly can. I'm still going through the house, looking for phone numbers that I don't recognize and giving them to the guards. And I'm saying to the neighbours, if there's any little thing, something too small that you don't want to say to the guards, tell me, I will say it to them.

'Having seen what violence can do, it has completely turned my stomach. I'm getting nightmares and I only saw her dead. I can't imagine what she went through. How scared she must have been. It's just horrible.'

Despite having come from Nikki Pelley's bed that very morning, Joe lied when asked if he had a mistress.

'No. Nothing like that at all,' he insisted. 'We are as normal a plain vanilla ordinary family as you will get. Two young kids, me working, Rach doing part-time stuff.

'The only plausible explanation is that she might have known someone, she might have brought them in for a cup of tea, they might have followed her into a room, they might have tried something on, she'd have said no and then rather than live with the shame, or [risk her] informing his wife, he said I can't leave her around to tell the story.'

Behaviour analyst Stan Waters rewound then played the videotape again, then hit the pause button to freeze-frame the image he wanted. A close-up of Joe O'Reilly appeared on the screen, cropped at the forehead.

The behavioural expert who had interpreted interviews for the FBI was searching for any verbal clues O'Reilly gave during his *Late Late Show* appearance.

'I mean, [we were] just carrying on life as normal,' Joe

told Pat Kenny in the clip, as Waters hit the play button. 'The last thing we expected was, em, what happened.'

In Waters's opinion, Joe was lying. 'The use of the pronoun, "we", means he's hiding in the crowd,' Waters stated, observing also how vague Joe was about his movements on the morning Rachel was killed. 'Unless you're a very good liar, the brain locks.' Waters searched for another clip, then hit playback.

On the screen, Joe was telling Pat: 'So what I usually do, was my normal routine as well, is I'd leave the house at five thirty, six o'clock. Em, travel across city, go to gym, do quick workout there, shower and a shave, and then into the office. So business as usual really.'

O'Reilly wasn't even forming complete sentences. He was talking in bullet points. The contrast with the detail he gave about what happened after the murder, when he had no difficulty in telling the truth, was startling. 'The sequence of the calls he made, the times, everything's spot on,' Waters speculated.

The investigation team didn't need a behavioural analyst to tell them what was going on in Rose's mind during the interview. Joe had described her daughter as 'plain, ordinary'; he had hinted that Rachel had brought somebody down to the bedroom, implying an affair; he had suggested she might have had enemies because she was a straight talker. No wonder Rose's eyes spoke volumes every time she looked at Joe. It wasn't hard to work out the message from the story she'd told about her daughter in the cot. Between the lines, Rose was telling the audience that Rachel was the kind of person who would try everything to make her marriage work. If she'd given up, she'd probably be still alive.

Joe O'Reilly was now suspect number one.

7

Breakthrough

The last pieces of the jigsaw began falling into place for the investigation team when they got confirmation that a signal from Joe's mobile phone had bounced off a mast near Murphy's Quarry. It pulled the rug from under the alibi, corroborated by Derek Quearney's recollection, that Joe had been in Broadstone near the city centre when Rachel was murdered. The signal could not have been rerouted through the mast at the rear of the O'Reilly home if the phone was over twenty miles away, the technical experts explained. It was impossible.

Joe's phone also revealed how a plot to kill Rachel coincided with the firming up of his intentions towards Nikki Pelley. He'd sent a series of extraordinary texts to his lover. In June, he texted his girlfriend, 'Hey I will only be your husband. I know my place.' By September, his fantasy about Nikki supplanting Rachel was fully fledged and he texted, 'Our boy had his first school day. He had fun but will have lots of homework tomorrow. Love you. XXX.' By now, he was also calling her 'my beautiful bride-to-be'. That same month, he also texted, 'Your three willies tucked up in bed. Lights out. Missing you.' And three days before he murdered Rachel, he texted Nikki,

'All the boys down on the beach, only thing missing is you. XXX.'

Through interviews with Rachel's friends, the detectives had discovered just how far removed the couple's life was from the 'plain vanilla ordinary family' Joe described. By September the marriage had hit rock bottom. Rachel had found out about Nikki that month. Joe had tried to deny the affair by making a skit out of it. The boys had been overheard referring to Nikki as 'dad's girlfriend' by a member of Rachel's family who warned him if he didn't tell Rachel, they would. He'd told his wife, 'Apparently I'm having an affair and I should tell you about it.' But Rachel gave him an ultimatum, either to start being a husband or to stop. He was in England at the time. Over the phone she told him she wouldn't tolerate his 'overnight inspections' excuse for staying out all night any more.

Trying to make his marriage work was never an option for Joe at this stage. He indicated he wanted to remain as a full-time father to his children when he sent his email to his sister Ann, back in June. He hadn't just fallen out of love with Rachel. Everything about her revolted him. And the detectives discovered another incentive for her demise. Joe had taken out an insurance policy on Rachel's life worth €194,000. Their mortgage of €240,000 would also be paid off in the event of her untimely death. Joe stood to become a wealthy independent father to his children and husband to the woman he loved, instead of a weekend McDonald's dad, living in a flat while financing the family home.

There was huge public pressure on the investigation team to make an arrest. They wanted every detail nailed down before they revealed their hand. They were also aware their suspect was starting to get jumpy, and hoped it was a sign he was feeling the pressure. Joe seemed agitated on 14 November when he learned from Paul Callaly that there was a CCTV camera in the quarry behind his house. Paul had gone to The Naul to watch a football match with Joe at Lambay View. Joe asked Paul if he had heard of any developments in the case. Paul told him what he knew. Joe reacted angrily. He said if he had been aware there was a camera then he would have objected to it being there.

He seemed to be trying to gather as much information as he could about the progress of the investigation. He contacted *Herald* journalist Mick McCaffrey to ask more questions and he pestered Rachel's friend Celine Keogh, who'd been due to call on the morning of the murder, to tell him everything the gardaí had asked her and what she had told them. He was getting carried away in his attempts to point the finger of blame in other directions. Joe remarked that Rachel's relationship with her birth family was 'not too hot', singling out his brother-in-law, Thomas, whose blood was discovered at the house – but for legitimate reasons, as he had cut himself building the deck.

Joe also created a fictitious fight between Rachel and the neighbours 'over land'. And he named several Viacom employees whom he had fired, including one who had thrown a fire extinguisher at him in a row. All were innocent of any involvement.

Joe was also trying to cover himself in the event of things going pear-shaped. He told Rose and Jim Callaly there would be rumours he was having an affair but they weren't true. He also told them there were rumours they had abused Rachel. He told Naomi Garrigan, whose daughter Alannah was in Adam's crèche, there were rumours they were having an affair.

But revealing as Joe's stone heart and strange behaviour appeared in the aftermath of the murder, they wouldn't make a convincing case in a court of law. The team used his actions as a reference point. The clinical ease with which they suspected him of having dispatched his wife tallied with the manner in which he was now moving on as if unaffected by the tragedy. Joe had gotten rid of Rachel's pet dogs and was getting stuck into the DIY – painting and putting up new curtains. Neighbours had nicknamed him 'the Robot' because of his striking lack of emotion when talking about Rachel.

Investigators feared arresting Joe before they had any hard evidence. He still hadn't shown a shred of remorse and they didn't anticipate he was likely to confess under interrogation.

The towering stack of 119 CCTV tapes seized from premises in Dublin City and in north County Dublin at last yielded the investigators the break they needed.

Joe O'Reilly's movements on the morning of 4 October blew his alibi out of the water. At 8.07am he was captured on the reception camera in Viacom, leaving the building. Another camera snatched him leaving the Bluebell

Industrial Estate at 8.12am in his distinctive navy Fiat Marea. Joe claimed he'd headed directly to the Phibsboro bus depot but at 8.55am he was filmed passing the Europrise premises in Blakes Cross, north of the airport. He was just eight kilometres from his home and headed towards The Naul.

They had snapshots of Rachel's last movements too. The image was unmistakable. Her Renault Scenic could be clearly seen heading away from her home at 9.03am. The CCTV camera overlooking Murphy's Quarry had captured her in the process of driving Luke and Adam to school. The tragedy was palpable for the detectives who witnessed her making her last journey with her boys. In the grainy images before them she had less than an hour left to live.

Then, the breakthrough. Five minutes after Rachel's car passed by, Joe O'Reilly's car came into view at Murphy's Quarry, blurry but recognizable. He was headed in the opposite direction from his wife, towards home. It was 9.08am, an almost synchronized time gap of five minutes since Rachel had passed. Had he hidden somewhere, watching, waiting for her to leave with their two sons in the car?

At 9.41am Rachel passed the quarry again, arriving back on the return leg of her journey, almost home.

Then eighteen minutes later, at 9.59am, Joe's Marea passed by again, heading south, away from his home. Footage picked him up again at Blakes Cross at 10.07am. The five-minute theory was bearing out. Why had it taken Joe thirteen minutes to get from Blakes Cross to Murphy's

Quarry on his way home and eight travelling the opposite way, leaving the crime scene?

Had he sat in wait, frightened Rachel would turn back to the house with the children, having forgotten something? Did he ensure she didn't see him so he could keep the element of surprise? It all sat perfectly with the other areas in which he had displayed a chilling single-mindedness in the execution of his plot. His clinical detachment from his emotions never ceased to amaze detectives. On the first month's anniversary of his wife's death, he left a message on her voicemail. 'Hi Rachy, it's Joe. I am really, really sorry for the early phone call. This time exactly a month ago you were probably doing what I am doing now, getting the kids ready for school. Now you are so cold and the sun was out, it was a normal day. You had less than two hours to live.'

The image of his car leaving the scene was blurred but visible. The distinctive damage to the front right fender of Joe's car was impossible to make out, but his roof rack was visible in some of the shots. As they strained to make out exactly what they were witnessing, several agreed it looked like a woman driving. Had Joe dressed in drag?

At 2.14pm, the Marea passed the quarry again. Joe was returning home with Adam but this time to a different world. Everything had changed. Rachel was dead. Joe had finally got what he wanted – sole custody of the boys and a new life with his lover. And the images revealed he was wearing different clothes from the ones he had worn to work.

The detectives had enough to arrest him now, but the

five thousand other owners of Fiat Mareas would have to be questioned and ruled out of their inquiries.

They were almost ready to bring him in. They would need to hit the people protecting him first, Nikki Pelley and Derek Quearney. At the forefront of their minds was also the realization that if Joe changed his story and admitted he had returned home on the morning of the murder, or denied having his mobile phone on him all day, their case against him would collapse.

Derek Quearney and Nikki Pelley were arrested on 16 November. Both were sticking to their stories. Derek continued to corroborate the alibi he had first provided on the night of the murder and again, two days later, on 6 October.

He agreed he had met Joe at the gym and then in the Viacom offices. Joe headed off for the depot ahead of him, and he followed at around nine. When he arrived in Phibsboro at about 9.30am, he rang Joe and asked him where he was.

'Joe said he was at the back of the pits,' Quearney told gardaí. 'I got out of the car. I said I'd find him there.' Derek first reported to the foreman that he was from Viacom and he was doing an inspection. After surveying some buses, he claimed to have met up with Joe at ten to ten, or ten o'clock. He said they then split up to inspect buses separately. He said he phoned Joe again and they hooked up again at 10.30am, inspected more buses together and left at around 11am.

The phone contact told detectives the two men were

actually in different places when they communicated. Over two days gardaí continued to ask Quearney to think hard about his memory of what exactly had happened. They showed him the calls he made to O'Reilly on the O_2 log that morning. His mobile phone was bouncing off a city centre mast while Joe's was bouncing off one in The Naul. Could he be wrong about his times?

Under pressure, Quearney admitted he might have got the times wrong, but he said he didn't understand how because he remembered that he and Joe had done an inspection together before splitting up for thirty to forty minutes. The gardaí also showed him a PowerPoint presentation of where the phones were in the city at the times of the calls. He continued to insist that while he must have been wrong in his recollections, that was the way he remembered it.

Nikki Pelley was also struggling with her memory. In her case the problem was the detail. She could not recall the specific details of what she and Joe talked about during their multiple conversations over the course of the day. Their first conversation was at 5.45am, made from the landline at her home in Rathfarnham to Joe's mobile. The call lasted almost twenty-eight minutes. It placed his mobile close to the O_2 mast at Finglas Garda station in Dublin.

Joe rang Rathfarnham from his mobile at 7.35am. The call lasted almost five minutes and placed Joe's mobile on the Nangor Road at the Riverview Business Park in southwest Dublin.

At 8.12am Nikki rang Joe's mobile and they chatted for

almost twenty-six minutes. Joe's mobile was located near the Chapelizod mast, near Phoenix Park. Nikki's phone was routed through the Rathfarnham mast.

At 8.46am Nikki texted Joe's mobile, located near Airways mast, close to the M50 at the airport. Nikki's phone was routed through the mast at Milltown, close to Dundrum.

At 11.02am Joe's mobile received a call from Maiden Outdoor, Nikki's work phone. The call lasted four seconds and was diverted to his mobile. No location was discovered for Joe's phone during this call.

At 11.05am Nikki's work phone contacted Joe's mobile and they spoke for three and a half minutes. Joe's phone was near Dominic Street in north inner city Dublin.

At 12.06pm Nikki called Joe's mobile. The call lasted twenty-seven seconds. Joe's phone was near Killeen Road ESB mast, which covers the Bluebell Industrial Estate, where he worked with Viacom. Nikki's phone was routed through Dundrum.

At 12.59pm Nikki texted Joe's mobile, which was still near the ESB mast.

At 15.21pm Joe's mobile was called from Nikki's work number. The call lasted seventy-four seconds. The phone was close to the mast at Murphy's Quarry a few hundred yards from his home. By this stage gardaí were already on the scene.

At 16.33pm Joe's mobile rang Nikki's home. The call lasted five minutes and was routed through Dunleer, Co. Louth, where Joe's mother, Ann, lived and where he went after Rachel's body was found.

At 17.22pm Joe's mobile rang Nikki's landline. They spoke for four and a half minutes. Routed through Dunleer.

At 17.51pm Nikki's mobile texted Joe's phone. Dunleer.

At 18.28pm Nikki texted Joe's mobile in Dunleer.

At 18.51pm Joe texted Nikki's landline.

At 18.56pm Nikki's landline texted Joe's mobile. He was still in Dunleer.

There were at least fifteen texts and calls. Under pressure, from the incredible detail gardaí had gathered, Nikki eventually admitted that Joe had told her he'd rowed with Rachel the night before and that she'd lied about the affair between them being over when first questioned.

On 17 November, Joe was arrested and brought to Drogheda. As anticipated, he was sticking to his original story. He woke at 5.20am and left for the gym. He claimed he didn't return home until a quarter past two in the afternoon. He left the gym at about half seven and headed to Viacom, based in the Bluebell Industrial Estate, arriving there at around 7.45am. He claimed he left the office to do the bus inspection at 8.15am, telling Derek he'd see him there. He said he arrived at the depot at nine. He said he spotted a Viacom van there, but didn't see the employee driving it, Damien Tully. He said he met up with Derek Quearney at around ten and left Phibsboro at 11.30am, arriving in Viacom at noon.

Joe's attempt to cover himself by giving the corroborating detail about Damien Tully's van backfired. It was clamped outside Pearse Street Dart station at the time. He had studied the work rosters before leaving Viacom to murder his wife, not factoring in a margin for human error.

But the team had scored the two biggest hits of all. Joe admitted that he had his mobile phone on him all day. And he never said he had returned home for any reason. Detectives could now place him in The Naul at the time of Rachel's death. Then an unexpected arrival at the station brought the interview to a sudden halt.

8

No Regrets

Hardened detectives could barely believe their eyes when frail Rose Callaly burst into Drogheda station demanding to see her son-in-law. Joe had been arrested that morning and taken in handcuffs to the station. His interview had formally begun at 11.40am.

'You're not denying killing Rachel?' Sergeant Sean Grennan had asked him.

'I deny killing Rachel,' Joe replied.

By 8.15pm Rose could not tolerate waiting any longer for news. She wanted to talk to him herself and she was not taking no for an answer. Her mind was in turmoil. The only thing that could make Rachel's murder worse was the prospect that Joe had murdered her. Rose had been suppressing that possibility and giving him the benefit of the doubt ever since day one, when she watched his reaction to finding Rachel's body and heard her daughter's voice say, 'Mam, it's him, he did it.' Now, she needed to look her son-in-law in the eye once and for all and either put her mind at rest or face the unimaginable.

Senior investigators could see the potential in facilitating contact between Rose and Joe. Their appeals to his conscience were falling on deaf ears. He refused to admit to killing Rachel; maybe Rose was just the catalyst they needed. They granted her unusual request, suspending Joe's formal interview. Sergeant Sean Grennan supervised a short meeting between the two.

The tension was palpable as the bereft Rose came face to face with Joe. He looked completely different to the immaculately groomed man who'd sat alongside her on *The Late Late Show*. The high-flying advertising executive was dressed in denims and a fleece jacket. He was ashen-faced, his head shaved, and he sported a dodgy goatee.

Rose had only one question for him. She wanted to know about Luke and Adam. Who was minding them now their mother was dead and their father was in a garda station, she asked. But not even her highly charged appeal caused his stony mask to slip. If anything, the cold fish just withdrew further into himself. Rose knew she was banging her head off a brick wall. But she could no longer deny what was staring her in the face. Joe had murdered Rachel.

With her departure, the official interview reconvened.

'Have you ever had a steel bar in the house?' Sergeant Grennan quizzed.

'No, I don't think so,' Joe replied.

'Are you sure?'

'No, I'm not sure.'

After twelve hours, he was released without charge. Outside the station, a crowd had gathered. It was the first real indication of just how much the Irish people had taken Rachel into their hearts. And if the heckling from the crowd was anything to go by, Joe was beginning to feel street justice.

Doorstepped by journalists at her home, Rose admitted her head was 'astray'. Holding back tears she said: 'You can just imagine what is going through my head at the moment. I'm just praying that we can get justice for Rachel. I can say nothing else.'

Joe's mother also spoke publicly. 'If I thought for a second that Joe had anything to do with Rachel's death I would disown him,' Ann said. 'He is a good and kind-natured son and it is not in his character to be violent to anyone. He would not be allowed under my roof. Anyone who knows Joe and the relationship he had with Rachel would know he positively had no involvement in her murder. People will say I am his mother and naturally I would stand by him, that is what mothers do. But no one knows Joe better than me. I reared him and brought him up, I know what I'm talking about. As far as I'm concerned he has been in a state of shock since day one.'

Christmas 2004 only served to emphasize the Callaly family's grief. It wasn't just that they were trying to cope without Rachel any more. Their contact with Luke and Adam had all but ceased. Relations with Joe were so strained that they could no longer bear to be around him and he punished them by restricting their access to their grandchildren. His arrest and release without charge in November had also caused a huge anticlimax. As long as Rachel's killer was still at large, a cloud was hanging over them.

Behind the scenes, the investigation had hit a major setback. The CCTV footage was deemed too poor in quality to enable a prosecution. The tapes were sent to a state-of-the-art lab in the UK but the process of enhancing would take time and there were no guarantees. The investigators were acutely aware that each passing day just added to the Callalys' agony. In January 2005, a tip-off came from out of the blue and gave an unexpected chink of fresh hope. Detectives were informed that some of Rachel's family and friends had left notes in her coffin before her burial. Joe had been seen placing his message under his wife's pillow. Was it possible he might have penned a confession? It was the longest shot yet, and if it backfired it would cause the family unnecessary and untold distress. But as ever, the Callalys were in support of whatever needed to be done.

An exhumation order, normally the preserve of suspected poisoning cases, was sought and granted by Fingal County Council on 9 February. It was a rare occurrence; only three such orders had occurred nation-wide since the body of John Gethings, an elderly patient at Naas General Hospital, was exhumed in July 2003. Rachel's case was making headlines again, by now to the fury of the Garda Commissioner who had ordered an investigation into leaks. The probe found the gardaí had no case to answer.

On 8 March 2005, Rachel was exhumed, then reinterred in a subdued ceremony that marked one of the lowest points in the ongoing tragedy for her friends and family. The detectives involved in the exhumation realized they were going to need a miracle. The five notes removed from the coffin were in a dire condition – damp and illegible. The documents were sent to the forensic science laboratory in the Phoenix Park for treatment with chemicals and an ESDA machine, which reads indentations with infra-red technology.

Remarkably, the scientists yielded the miracle nobody had dared to hope for. Not only could Joe's message be revealed, but it actually contained an apology. Folded around notes from his children which read 'Love you mammy, Luke xxx' and 'Love you mammy, Adam xxx,' Joe had written: 'Rachel, I love you so very, very much. I can't think of what to do without you. You're the best thing that ever happened to me. This is the hardest letter I've ever had to write for reasons only we know. Rachel, forgive me. Two words, one sentence. I'll say them forever.'

But as remarkable as it was to everyone involved in the case, the apology was still only circumstantial in the eyes of the law. The DPP's office wanted hard evidence if they were to recommend a prosecution of Joe O'Reilly for the murder of his wife. Joe's alibi, Derek Quearney, might have admitted that his recollections could be wrong but he had emigrated to Turkey. Ireland had no extradition treaty with Turkey.

The investigators appealed to the DPP's office for more time, keeping the office briefed of potential developments. In January 2006, detectives from the NBCI flew to Turkey to try to persuade Derek Quearney to return to Ireland. At his seaside home in Istanbul, he refused their requests.

*

The investigation team realized they were going to have to interrogate Joe and Nikki again. They went to the courts to get special warrants to give them new powers of arrest. A district court judge was persuaded, by the coffin letter, the results of the new CCTV analysis from the UK and the phone technology, that there was substantial new evidence for rearresting the pair.

Joe and Nikki were rearrested and questioned separately in Drogheda on 14 March 2006. The date could not have been more poignant. It was also the date scheduled for Rachel's inquest, which had been adjourned the previous September at Dublin County Coroners' Court in Tallaght. Superintendent Tom Gallagher had applied for the stay under Section 25 (1) of the Coroners Act, confirming to the coroner, Dr Kieran Geraghty, that no file had yet been submitted to the DPP. Dr Geraghty extended his sympathies to Rachel's family.

As news of the new arrests spread, Nikki's father, Fraser Pelley, hit the airwaves to defend her position on afternoon radio. He explained that Nikki thought she was being followed by photographers as she travelled to work. Instead she was arrested by gardaí who brought her to Drogheda for questioning on suspicion of withholding information about the murder.

'She one hundred per cent believes that Joe is innocent,' he explained. 'Nothing has altered her mind since [October] 2004 to today.'

He revealed how long he had known Joe. 'We met Joe

before his wife was murdered. There was, if you like, a relationship between Nikki and Joe before Rachel was murdered.'

He revealed how he and his wife had also been questioned by gardaí.

'They basically wanted to get our opinion on what we thought of Joe and the family. We told them the truth. We've known him for nearly eighteen months. We know his children very well. He's very, very good with them.

'We have seen nothing that would indicate that he was involved in the murder, but that is just our opinion.'

He said Nikki did not know Rachel and had never been in trouble before.

'It's an awful predicament we find ourselves in. We've had tremendous support from our friends and a lot of people.'

Nikki was once again released without charge.

Joe was put through the ringer. In custody, Garda Malachy Dunne said to him, 'At no stage have you said you did not kill Rachel. Can you look me in the eyes and say that?'

Joe then looked him in the eyes and said, 'I did not kill Rachel.'

Asked whether he had any regrets, Joe replied, 'For what?'

'For the murder of your wife?' Dunne probed.

Joe answered, 'I have regrets my wife was murdered.'

The interrogators ran the message he'd sent Nikki from his phone a few days before Rachel was killed. 'All the boys down the beach. The only thing missing is you. XXX'. What did he mean?

Joe didn't remember sending it. He continued to maintain his innocence throughout. 'I deny killing Rachel,' he said coolly.

The crowd had doubled since his previous interrogation. This time up to one hundred locals were waiting to catch a glimpse of him on his release. As he walked to a white Fiat Punto parked about two hundred yards behind the station, some took photographs of him using camera phones. They shouted, 'Burn the car' and 'Let the air out of the tyres.'

Detectives also searched his mother's home in Dunleer, Co. Louth, hoping against hope they might finally discover the murder weapon.

In the summer of 2006, the team accepted they were at the end of the road and the file finally landed in the DPP's office, where it seemed to stall. As the Callaly family neared the second anniversary of Rachel's death, the prospect of justice seemed as elusive as ever. By now the file had been with the DPP's office for over three months.

'The longer it is going on, you keep thinking every day that you will hear something – you are just living in hope,' Rachel's dad admitted. 'You are helpless – you can't do anything; you just have to wait for the decision. We haven't heard a whisper. There is a fierce amount of correspondence. It will be some time. We haven't got a time frame at all. We hope there will be a conclusion, we're nearly two years waiting now and it is a long time going on.'

But he said he understood the reason for the delay.

'The police have been very thorough,' he said. 'We're stuck in a living nightmare. In fact we're barely surviving and it takes all our effort just to get through the day. We can't bear the fact the killer is out there, getting on with his life as if nothing has happened, while our daughter is lying in her grave.'

Relations with Joe had hit rock bottom. No tombstone could be put on Rachel's grave because of a dispute over the name. The Callalys were using Rachel's maiden name in anniversary tributes in the paper and whenever they referred to her. Rose and Jim were even threatening to take Joe to court in a desperate bid to see their grandchildren.

On Rachel's second anniversary around four hundred friends and family gathered in a heart-rending vigil outside Lambay View. Joe had locked the gates, drawn the curtains and taken the boys to his mother's house. The well-wishers placed a framed photograph of Rachel with her sons at the small wooden gates with fresh flowers and candles. Joe, Luke and Adam were noticeably absent as the sound of sobbing carried through the chant of prayers.

Rose thanked everyone for their support. 'Rachel left this world on her own,' she told them. 'She had a very lonely departure, there was nobody around her. But she is among us today. We just let her know that we will never forget her. The number of people here is proof of how touched people are by this tragedy. We feel everybody is behind her, but what we want now is justice. Of course we want justice for her, that's the big thing.

'I just pray that there is justice for her. I ask everyone that is here today to pray the man who did this is caught. Hopefully he will [be]. It is now two years to the minute since I found Rachel in there. It is very hard to take. It has all come back to me . . . I just feel Rachel is here with us. She was a much-loved and well-known figure walking up and down these roads with the two little ones. She loved the area around here and I know she is here with us now.'

Rose said anyone who knew her daughter would remember her always singing. Changing the lyrics of the Irish ballad 'Grace', she sang, 'Rachel, you were the gift of life to me, and now you can no longer be. With pride we watched you grow up, you wanted so much to change the world for me. Rach, you gave our simple life its key. But Rach, you faced the truth and you stood tall, and we now face the hardest truth of all. For you had to say goodbye and we must go on living. But when our life is through, we will always be with you, together with your song.'

Rachel's sister, Ann, broke down as she described Rachel's love of life and of her two young sons, Adam and Luke. 'Yours is a life that cannot be replaced, a void that cannot be filled. Rachel, we know you are with us, stay near. You are always loved and never forgotten,' she said through her tears.

'She was not just a name in the newspaper,' Ann added. 'She was vivacious, and larger than life. She was a beautiful daughter to her heartbroken mam and dad, and a great sister to us.' She also described how Rachel lived for the boys and was always buying presents for them, and how Luke and Adam would practically knock her over when she came home from shopping, knowing she'd have something for them.

'She was a gust of wind, her presence filled everywhere she went. She was outgoing and sporty, and had no fear. She was never shy and was the life and soul of the party. She had a charisma that grew with her into adulthood. She was great at everything, and she did love a challenge and succeeded nine times out of ten.'

Fr Tom McGowan, who moved into the area on the day of Rachel's murder, said he hoped the family would draw comfort from the massive turnout that spilled down the rural lane.

By the end of the year, the prayers of everyone at the vigil were answered. The direction came back from the DPP that Joe O'Reilly was to be charged with murder. Due to the huge caseload in the legal diary, his trial could not be scheduled until June 2007.

9

The Trial

If Joe was experiencing any pre-trial nerves on Monday, 25 June 2007, he showed no sign of it. Wearing a sharp charcoal suit, dazzling white shirt and striped blue tie, his expression was that of a focused businessman as he jauntily strode into Court Number Two for his trial. It was a million miles from the casual attitude he displayed while chewing gum at Swords District Court when first charged on 20 October, dressed in combats and a shabby fleece.

He carried his paperwork under his arm, emulating the legal eagles around him. Avoiding eye contact with reporters, he entered the wood-panelled room flanked by his drawn-looking mother, his auburn-haired sister and his brother, Derek – a ringer for him, but a foot shorter. Joe's unflappable attitude was even more incredible in the wake of recent death threats and the level of anger shown at his Swords arraignment, when he was jostled by an angry mob and called a 'scumbag'.

The level of public interest had by now gone off the Richter scale. The trial was about to play out over twenty-one days to a packed public gallery, with queues of disappointed people turned away each day. From day one, there was no shortage of drama. The trial almost collapsed because the judge was forced to discharge a juror. It came after a member of the jury panel rang the jury office to say he had struck up a conversation with another juror during the selection process. He said the woman expressed the view that Joe was 'guilty anyway'. Three days later a portion of the book of evidence ended up in the jury room and almost collapsed the trial again.

Some 144 witnesses would be called for the prosecution, and only two for the defence. Throughout, a stony-faced Joe never lost his composure, spending his time taking studious notes. Occasionally, a crocodile tear ran down his cheek – when the note he left in Rachel's coffin was read out or when he heard how the devastating injuries had shattered his wife's head. But he was unmoved on day two and sat impassively when Rose Callaly wept in court as she described discovering her daughter's bloodied and lifeless body in the bedroom of her home.

There were gasps in the courtroom when Rachel's biological mother, Teresa Lowe, took the stand, as the onlookers were hit by the striking resemblance to her murdered daughter. She delivered heart-rending evidence of having given birth to a baby girl she named 'Teresa' whom she had been reunited with and had lost again.

After intense legal argument between Joe's barrister, Patrick Gageby SC, and Denis Vaughan Buckley SC, who led the prosecution, it seemed to all trained observers that the case was going Joe's way. Evidence about another of his extramarital affairs – with professional golfer Barbara

Hackett – was deemed by Judge Barry White to have no relevance to the trial. The Limerick sportswoman had been prepared to testify that Joe told her he had not split from his wife because he wanted full custody of his children. He was not happy to be a part-time dad. Joe's grisly reconstructions of Rachel's death and his 'tours' of the murder scene were also kept from the jury, even though his recreation bore a chilling similarity to what pathologist Dr Marie Cassidy said had happened.

On day fourteen, Thursday, 12 July, all eyes bar Joe's were on Nikki Pelley as she took the stand. The pair blanked each other throughout the sitting. She was dressed casually in a white flowing top, red floral skirt and black boots. But there was a hint of steel in her attitude. She was there as a witness for the prosecution, but in her omissions her heart was clearly siding with the defence. She grudgingly admitted that Joe sometimes called Rachel a 'wasp' or a 'cunt' and had suggested she should play down their relationship with gardaí in case it was construed as a motive for murdering Rachel.

There was another courtroom flutter when Joe's alibi witness, Derek Quearney, took the stand. Shaven-headed, he swore the oath in a strong but quiet Dublin accent. Joe's barrister, Patrick Gageby SC, led him through his evidence. The 46-year-old was brought up in Ballyfermot, had spent twenty-one years in the army and left in 1998 to go into advertising, joining the firm TDI (later taken over by Viacom). He was operations manager and later delivery manager. He had known Joe since 2002. Quearney might have been the reason it took so long for gardaí to bring charges against Joe O'Reilly, but in testimony he finally obliterated his friend's alibi, admitting to the jury that he must have been wrong in the times he recollected seeing him on the morning of the murder.

Hard-hearted Joe, despite the relish he took in numerous media interviews, did not take the stand to defend himself.

Prosecution counsel Dominic McGinn, in his closing speech, said that Joe was the only person with a motive to kill his wife. He said that the evidence against him was mostly circumstantial and advised the jury that if they had reasonable doubt about his guilt they had to acquit.

Mr McGinn added: 'Your role is to decide the case on the evidence. There has been considerable media interest in this case but you are to ignore it. You are also to ignore emotion, sympathy and prejudices. This will be difficult as you must be feeling that it can't be easy for Rachel O'Reilly's family sitting here listening to the evidence. It can't be easy for Joe O'Reilly, his family and friends but you can't allow that to affect your judgement. You must look at this in a cold and analytical way, using logic as a starting point.'

Mr McGinn said the jury should consider the evidence in this case as a rope with many individual strands. He added that while each strand in itself did not have any great consequence, when taken in its entirety the evidence was strong enough to convict beyond all reasonable doubt. He claimed there was no doubt that the killer had intended to murder or cause serious harm to the thirty-year-old mother.

Mr McGinn also asked the jury to consider whether a burglar had committed the murder. He questioned if a thief would have left behind €450 in cash in Rachel's handbag and a further €860 in a plastic container in the living room.

Mr McGinn claimed O'Reilly had attempted to make it look as if a robbery had taken place by disturbing CDs and taking a video camera and jewellery box. He said these items were placed one hundred yards away from the family home and also told the jury that O'Reilly could not take his wife's handbag before the murder as she would have missed it. He claimed the bag containing the video camera had been dumped before the murder, explaining the absence of blood on it.

He addressed the issue of motive, claiming that the series of emails between O'Reilly and his sister, Ann, showed his state of mind and how he really felt about his wife. He said that these messages contrasted dramatically with what Joe told gardaí in the aftermath of the murder. He compared them with the series of concerned messages that O'Reilly had left on the phone when he knew that his wife was already dead.

Turning to the CCTV and mobile phone evidence, he quoted O_2's expert who said it was impossible for a mobile phone signal to be picked up in The Naul if the handset was in Broadstone. Mr McGinn said: 'Mobile phones are useful for business but not so useful in this case as far as Mr O'Reilly is concerned.' He added that Cell Data Analysis was crucial in this case because it placed O'Reilly at the scene at the time of the murder. And

Mr McGinn asked whether it was a coincidence that a car similar to O'Reilly's had been spotted on camera four times with mobile phone records supporting this timeline.

He said O'Reilly lied consistently, particularly about his relationship with Nikki Pelley. Mr McGinn concluded: 'The only rational explanation is Mr O'Reilly killed his wife and you can have no reasonable doubts. If you have no reasonable doubts then he is guilty.'

It took the jury of nine men and two women nine hours and six minutes to reach their verdict.

The tension in the room as they returned to Court Two was unbearable. Yet Joe's stony mask didn't slip even as the word 'guilty' cut that tension in two like a knife and released a flood of emotion. There were whoops of joy from the public gallery and the Callaly family cried tears of happiness. Even the detectives who had stayed with the case from day one, several of whom had since retired – Chief Super Michael Finnegan, Superintendent Tom Gallagher and Detective Pat Marry – became emotional.

But as Justice Barry White handed down the mandatory life sentence, the blood drained from O'Reilly's face for the first time. He looked shocked as he nodded to his mother Ann, brother Derek and sister Ann at the back of the courtroom.

'This case has attracted more publicity than any other trial that I can remember in my forty years' experience as a judge and barrister,' the justice remarked.

Rose Callaly then made one of the most emotional speeches ever heard in an Irish court. She said: 'Rachel, I would have given my life to you. Three years ago Rachel kissed goodbye to her beloved Adam and Luke for the last time. For the next twenty minutes Rachel was subjected to a barbaric attack no human being should have to endure. Even though justice has been done our grief and distress will never diminish. Rachel was a truly beautiful, loving, caring and capable girl who has left so many memories and she meant so much to us and to our aunts, cousins, nieces and many friends. Each one of us has been traumatized by feelings of helplessness, shock, grief and the reality that we can do nothing to bring her back.

'That is the hardest part of our pain. Not only did Rachel leave without saying goodbye, she also left her beloved sons, Luke and Adam, confused, scared and angry and heartbroken. And the biggest damage will surely be left at their door as they live their lives without the guidance and counselling of their best friend. Rachel was never away from their side. Her harrowing loss has left a huge void in both the boys' lives and in our lives.

'Every day we find it so very difficult to accept the devastation of her death. We struggle to come to terms with the fact that she is now gone for ever. There are days we feel overwhelmed by grief. Sleepless nights, nightmares and panic attacks are the norm for us. We often wake traumatized with fear by the images of terror, violence, trauma and brutality and we wonder if we will ever return to some sense of a normal life.

'We lost Rachel at the young age of thirty years and we are devastated that we will never be able to share with her the milestones she was so looking forward to in her life and the possibility of one day sharing with her the enjoyment of seeing her own grandchildren.

'As a parent it is devastating to lose a child in these circumstances. At times it is unbearable. Rachel, if I could have given my life for you that awful day I would have. You were such a big part of our life. Thanks for the short time. It should have been so much longer and full of so much more happy memories. We treasure the memories and shared time with you. We miss and love you very much. We hope you can now rest in peace, my darling. Your loving mam and dad, brothers and sisters and sisters-in-law, Declan and Denise, Ann and Anthony and your two sons Luke and Adam.'

Joe O'Reilly remained impassive.

Meanwhile it emerged that O'Reilly would have got away with his brutal crime had he just peppered his story with a grain of truth. Senior gardaí said they would never have been able to bring the 35-year-old to trial had he just said he had gone back to his home in The Naul on the morning of Rachel's murder.

'Even if he just said he forgot something and had to go back but missed Rachel that would have been it. We would never have got him and he would have got away with murder,' a leading investigator said. 'He reckoned he was just so clever but he ended up tripping over himself by not altering a very small part of his story.'

O'Reilly was a cold and very calculating killer who planned his wife's murder with military precision, giving himself less than half an hour to stage a botched robbery at his home. In the days before the murder they believe he hid a camcorder and some jewellery and deposited the items in a ditch near the house so officers would look for a raider whom Rachel had disturbed. They also believe that he studied head injuries so he would know exactly how to kill her. They believe the murder weapon was still in his car boot when he drove Luke and Adam to stay with his mother just hours after murdering their mum. They believe he dumped the weapon, probably a dumbbell, in water on the way to Dunleer.

The O'Reilly house became a shrine to Rachel immediately after the verdict.

People left letters saying how much they despised Joe.

One said, 'Dear Rachel, your family never gave up on you and the whole of Ireland believed in you and the gardaí never gave up on you. Rest in peace and may that bastard burn in hell.'

Another read: 'To Rachel, rest in peace. I love you. I hate your husband for killing you. Lots of love from Anne. Rest in peace Rachel, justice was done.'

10

Weekend Dad

Prisoner number 42807 was moved out of Mountjoy on 22 July 2007 amid fears he would take his own life or be murdered by other prisoners. He was one day into his life sentence.

Transferred to his new home in the Midlands Prison, Joe O'Reilly was medically assessed by a prison doctor and deemed to be in good health. He was not considered to be a suicide risk as he showed no signs of stress about his new surroundings. His neighbours on the C1 segregation landing included James Martin Cahill, serving life for the murder of Limerick bouncer Brian Fitzgerald. Cahill is being kept apart from other prisoners after agreeing to turn state witness and help gardaí crack the vicious feuding gangs. Also on C1 was John Lynn, a Scottish-born drug dealer accused of slashing a prison officer while in Castlerea Prison. Wayne O'Donoghue, who killed his eleven-year-old neighbour Robert Holohan and callously dumped his body after duping Robert's parents by helping in the search for him, was also locked up in the Midlands for his own protection.

On being allocated a single cell, O'Reilly requested a Bible. It was only after his first visit from his children that he finally broke down. The 'robot' who had spent months plotting to kill his wife rather than ending up a McDonald's dad sobbed for fifteen minutes solid, and then returned to his cell to begin work on his appeal challenging the safety of his conviction. He was appealing on five grounds: that his right to silence when questioned by gardaí was abused; that the voluntary statement he gave to gardaí, in which he lied about his movements, should not have been used in the trial because he had not been cautioned properly; that mobile phone evidence which tracked his movements should not have been allowed; that CCTV imagery from Murphy's Quarry and Blakes Cross showing his Fiat Marea moving towards his home not long before 9am and away from his home not long before 10am was not clear enough; and that emails sent to his sister about Rachel citing 'Me + Rachel + marriage = Over!!!!' were sent four months before Rachel was murdered and irrelevant, prejudicing the jury against him.

He was backed by his family, who insisted he was not guilty. His brother, Derek, described the case as 'a miscarriage of justice', while his mother, Ann, claimed he was 'innocent'. As the months wore on, Joe stayed focused on his appeal, convinced he would be freed. His girlfriend Nikki Pelley would visit him twice a month. (He is entitled to one thirty-minute visit each week and up to three people can visit at a time.) When she was photographed bringing Joe's sons in to see him, it drew the ire of the Callalys. 'We were disgusted with that – his mistress bringing our grandchildren in to see him,' Rachel's father said, adding: 'We took it bad.'

To add insult to injury, Joe blocked their efforts to erect a headstone on Rachel's grave by insisting he wanted any memorial to bear her married name.

'I have no intention of asking that fella that killed my daughter for his permission to put a headstone on her grave,' Jim Callaly said.

The fact that Rachel's children are being reared by Joe's family has also been a source of contention between the two families.

When not preparing for his appeal, Joe studied a philosophy course through the Open University and began attending regular prayer sessions in the 'box' with a Jehovah's Witness pastor. He also took up painting and even gave Nikki Pelley a portrait of her on one visit. Joe then threw himself into holiday brochures to find the perfect honeymoon destination, absolutely convinced he'd be freed.

11

The Other Mother

I wanted to talk to the woman who'd lost Rachel twice, her birth mother, Teresa Lowe. I'd watched the way she always deferred to the Callalys in court, took her seat silently behind them and kept her head down. It was thanks to the Callaly family's constant public appeals that Joe O'Reilly finally ended up in court but what voice had the woman with the staggering resemblance to Rachel had? Could she throw any light on the daughter she'd been reunited with, and her relationship with the man who'd killed her?

Teresa Lowe was only seventeen when she gave golden-haired Rachel, whom she called Teresa, up for adoption in October 1973. 'I always knew I'd see her again,' the softly spoken, 49-year-old birth mother, who now has four other children, told me in her Clondalkin home. 'There wasn't a day that went by that I didn't think about her. Birthdays, Christmases, she was always on my mind. I hoped that one day she would get in touch and find me and she did. I had told the social workers that if she wanted to contact me that was OK and the minute she turned eighteen, she did. It was brilliant.'

Sitting in an armchair in her comfortable sitting room,

with her daughter, Sandra, aged twenty-six – Rachel's half-sister – sharing memories on the couch, Teresa glanced at a framed photograph of Rachel as she began to recall a time before the trial which turned her daughter into a household name.

'When she was eighteen, I went to meet Rachel and from the first minute we just got on. We had our talk and she understood everything about what happened. We became great friends. We were great pals.'

Teresa didn't want to go into the pressures she faced as a teenager that led to a decision that has haunted the rest of her life.

'That's between me and Rachel,' she says. 'This is not my way. I like to be in the background. But I understand that people have taken Rachel into their hearts and that's the only reason why I'm speaking about this. On the day I met her, my sister Rebecca came with me. It was very emotional. We met in town, there were social workers there. There was no awkwardness. We hugged and we cried and we made arrangements to see each other again.'

They were soon in regular contact, she explains. 'She loved her two mothers,' Teresa says, explaining that Rachel wrote everything she was feeling in a series of letters which she now treasures.

Teresa also told her other children that they had another sibling out there. 'We knew about Rachel when we were growing up . . . that we had another sister,' Sandra explains. 'We knew she was out there somewhere and we always wondered about her. We are a very close family and when she got in touch it was like the missing part of the jigsaw. She and Mam were so alike. They had the same mannerisms. And Rachel looked and sounded exactly like my auntie Rebecca!'

Over the next twelve years the family would grow closer and closer. Teresa denies there was any row surrounding Rachel's wedding to Joe, which she did not attend.

'I didn't go, but that was Rachel's decision. She was thinking of everyone's feelings on the day. There was no row over it whatsoever. We were fine about it afterwards.'

Teresa's son Thomas would grow particularly close to his sister, and built the deck for her in her dream house in The Naul where Rachel moved eighteen months before being murdered.

But in October 2004, thirty-one years to the month after losing her the first time, twelve after making her peace with her, Teresa would lose Rachel again, this time for good. 'I never got to say goodbye to her this time,' Teresa said. 'That was Joe's fault and his alone. I went to the trial every day. My motto was, if she can't talk, I'd be there for her.'

The hardest part was listening to the emails in which Joe referred to Rachel as a 'cunt' and a 'wasp'. 'The emails he wrote were so hurtful and cruel and cold,' Teresa said. 'That wasn't the Rachel we loved.'

Sandra, who christened her own baby daughter Sophie Rachel, described the devastation of losing the sister who first came into her life when she was ten.

'Rachel was just lovely. She was very intelligent; she was a legal executive and very smart. But she was deep and bubbly and a laugh at the same time. She was childish too. She loved her girlie nights and she loved her Disney characters. She used to travel up to Newry to get her Disney stuff. Tinkerbell was her favourite. I used to ring her voicemail all the time after she died so I could listen to the sound of her voice. I miss her so much.'

The impact of her loss was so overpowering that Sandra had to be hospitalized during the trial.

'Everyone's life is devastated,' Rachel's half-sister told me. 'Before the trial we were preoccupied with trying to get the case to court. Then during the trial we were kept busy wondering if there would be a conviction. Now everything has stopped and we have to deal with our grief. It's a very, very hard time for us.'

For the Lowe family, the nightmare was compounded because they were taken in by Joe. As they've known him almost as long as they have known Rachel, they feel they have been duped by him exactly the way she was.

'I believed him,' Teresa said. 'He looked me in the eye after her funeral and he said, "You'll read in the papers I was having an affair. I swear to you it's not true." He stood face to face with me when he said that.'

Sandra added: 'We felt foolish at how much we were taken in by him. A nicer guy you couldn't have met. To try and explain . . . Rachel was beautiful, very feminine. She could have had her pick of men. She loved her family and her friends. People wanted to be around her. And we thought about Joe, she couldn't have picked better. He took us all in. We all thought he was good to her.

'I met him in the gym and built up a strong bond with him. He used to say to me, "You're a mini Rachel," and I loved that. He used to want to meet to go to lunch.'

Sandra also described how she was still haunted by a text Joe sent her the day before he slaughtered her sister. 'This evil thing happened,' she said. 'I still can't get my head around it. Joe texted me the day before the murder to say he was in Liffey Valley with Rachel and did I want to come down and meet them for a coffee. I'm convinced that because he knew how attached to her I was, he thought he was giving me a chance to say goodbye.'

Teresa says she cannot understand how he could have tried to frame her son Thomas for the murder. On one job in the O'Reillys' home, Thomas had cut himself and bled. Joe lied to gardaí when he told them that this had happened during a struggle with Rachel. 'What was very hurtful was the way Joe tried to blame Thomas,' Teresa says. 'Joe and Thomas were great friends. Thomas still hasn't got over that.'

The family say they draw great strength from the fact that Rachel could not have had better adoptive parents in Rose and Jim Callaly or a nicer bunch of friends. 'They were great people and she loved them. She loved her two mothers and her two families. When I saw that her friends brought wine and sneaky cigarettes to her grave, I thought it was hilarious. That was Rachel all over. She was great fun.' But the court victory still feels 'bitter-sweet', she says.

'All we have left of Rachel is her Velcro boys, Luke and Adam. They were always stuck to her. We want to have contact with them again,' Teresa says. 'We will support any battle to get them back.'

'They're all we have of Rachel,' Sandra explains. 'The last time I met Lukey, he asked did I want to see the treasures he had in a little box he was holding. When he opened it up it was full of spiders. So many lives have been ruined by Rachel's death but Luke and Adam are the real tragedy in all this. The mother they loved is gone. That is their legacy.'

Rachel's mother and sister have a special message to other families experiencing the 'nightmare' of the court system.

'To the families of other women out there who are going through the same thing we want to say that this case is your beacon of light. We hope this case gives people strength,' Teresa said. Sandra added: 'Stay strong and keep your loved one's memory alive. There is such a thing as justice. Having people come up to us, touch and hug us after the trial meant so much. But it's been two and a half years of intense media pressure. On the one hand seeing her in the papers makes you flinch. But on the other you're grateful that her real memory is being kept alive and not the one Joe tried to paint.'

Rachel's downfall was her giant heart.

'She didn't even realize the marriage was over,' Sandra says. 'He must have been some kind of psycho to have been able to convince everyone he was something else and do that to her.'

Epilogue

Joe O'Reilly's efforts to get out of prison were rejected by the Court of Criminal Appeal in March 2009.

He showed no emotion in court. Crossing his long legs, he reached into the inside jacket pocket of his suit for his glasses which he calmly put on, then licked a finger before leafing through the thirty-four-page judgment. The former advertising executive could have been flicking through the minutes of a board meeting for all the sentiment he showed.

In his direct line of vision, the family of his murdered wife, the stalwart Callalys, began to hug, give little victory clenches of their fists, and to cry. Rachel's mother, Rose, was flanked by her frail husband, Jim, who'd aged immeasurably since Joe was convicted of murder. Their other daughter, Ann, with movie-star good looks, wearing long black gloves and a Jackie Onassis-style suit, shook violently and shot bewildered looks at her three brothers as the family's protracted road to justice wound to a close.

Rachel's biological mother, Teresa Lowe, sat quietly behind them on a bench marked 'Family 2', completely removed from their celebrations but the only one to have lost Rachel twice.

In the third row, marked 'Family 3', Joe's younger brother, Derek, at whom Joe had winked when he arrived, stood up and moved towards a prison officer and asked if he could have a word. The prison officer told him to wait.

Joe, dressed in a dark, charcoal-coloured suit, light blue shirt and dark blue tie, with his hair cropped tight, was busy sliding into the solicitor's bench to discuss the case.

If the crime had occurred five years earlier, the *Star Wars* fanatic would probably have pulled it off. But advances in technology meant his private emails revealed his motive – he wanted full custody of his two sons. Meanwhile, CCTV footage and mobile phone evidence rubbished the alibi given to him by a Viacom work colleague, locating him in the vicinity of the murder and not on a job inspecting billboards in Broadstone as alleged. The grounds of Joe's appeal read like a sulky realization of just how close he'd got – his lawyers arguing the guilty verdict should be overturned because the trial judge, Barry White, had erred in law on five grounds.

In complete contrast to Joe's cold-hearted, clinical analysis of the case, outside the court Rose Callaly read a heartfelt statement on behalf of the family: 'Joe O'Reilly is not the only one serving a life sentence – he gave our whole family a life sentence the day he murdered Rachel,' she said.

Retired Assistant Commissioner Martin Donnellan remarked: 'He thought he was a clever man, but maybe he was too clever for his own good. . . . He sent a text message to his wife, who was deceased shortly after 9am, and the message started at one mast and finished at another closer to the city, which indicated he was on his way back from Balbriggan.'

Evidence such as this revealed that Joe O'Reilly – the ordinary Joe who flicked a pathological switch and turned off all emotion so he could callously murder the mother of his two young sons – was even more terrifying than he had seemed. He was now facing an average life sentence of fifteen years behind bars.

Lyin' Eyes

I thought that the country would never again see the likes of 'Black Widow' Catherine Nevin, who plotted so elaborately to murder her husband, Tom – out of sheer greed.

But when Sharon Collins, a mother of two from Ennis, googled the word 'hitman', she schemed with equal dedication to have her property magnate partner, PJ Howard, bumped off. And Sharon also wanted PJ's two sons assassinated, as she believed this was necessary to ring-fence her inheritance rights.

Like Nevin before her, Collins would end up convicted of soliciting to kill. But there was a further twist in the tail. Incredibly, once both were behind bars, I discovered that the pair already knew each other . . .

Niamh O'Connor
August 2009

Prologue

5.20pm, Tuesday, 4 April 2006

Sharon Collins typed the words 'Dear Gerry', then stared at the computer screen. Her email needed to grab the attention of the housewives' favourite DJ, Gerry Ryan, if he were going to read it out in that way he had – all blustering indignation. But where to start? The swingers' clubs; the sex with transvestites; the constant pestering to go on the game, to be intimate with another man? She typed 'Sleeping with the enemy' in the subject line, and stalled again. This must be what writer's block felt like. It was her life's dream to one day write a bestseller.

At least the house was quiet. Her partner, PJ, spent most of his time in Spain; his two sons, Robert and Niall, had moved out; her own boys, also in their twenties, had their own lives too. Gary now lived in Dublin, and David was in college. Not that space had ever been an issue. Aside from the lakeside mansion in Ennis, Co. Clare, PJ had a holiday home in Kilkee, a two-storey apartment in Fuengirola in Spain, and *Heartbeat* – the boat he'd bought after recovering from a quadruple bypass – was moored in the Costa del Sol.

The first rule of her creative writing class was to 'write what you know'. Suddenly the next line began to flow: she was writing because she was in an 'unbearable situation . . . with few real options' and she hoped the letter would be 'aired' to 'clarify things' and push her into 'making the move' that frightened her so much. What Sharon needed from the women of Ireland, with the help of RTÉ's shock jock, was a steer, a little moral support. It was an ideal time to find out what they thought, because 'my partner is away at the moment'.

The hardest part was living a lie. Nobody who knew him suspected PJ could be 'like that', she wrote. They all considered him an upstanding member of the community. But she, on the other hand, was under immense strain from being constantly told she was 'boring' and a 'stick-in-the-mud' for not partaking in perverse sex acts that made her want to be sick.

The email was beginning to write itself . . .

She was being constantly 'pestered' for 'strange sex'. 'Nothing I do is ever enough. His black moods are unbearable. Tantrums can be thrown at any time. He has even told me he would love it if I would work as a prostitute . . . pick up a stranger and have sex with him,' or 'have a threesome with a male escort' . . . 'Every time I have sex with him I have to describe in detail what I would do if I were with another man. This it seems is necessary for him to keep an erection.' PJ 'enjoyed sex with transvestites' . . . that was the 'main attraction' of the holiday home in Spain. She had been taken to swingers' clubs 'on many occasions' and she had seen things 'I sincerely wish I never had to see'. 'I am no prude' but what is so wrong with wanting a 'monogamous' relationship? Her fingers hovered over the keyboard. There was only one thing left to say – why she didn't just walk away: 'He is a very, very wealthy man and is always showering . . .'

Sharon, startled by the sound of somebody else moving about the house, quickly saved the draft email, and switched the computer off.

1

Ring of Fire

Two years, three months later – 2.40pm, Tuesday,
1 July 2008

Barrister Úna Ní Raifeartaigh was in no mood for the
runaround. The dynamic state prosecutor with the razor-
sharp tongue was nearing the end of another sweltering
afternoon in an epic conspiracy-to-murder trial that had
been dominating Dublin's Central Criminal Court. She
placed her hands on her hips and watched with scepticism
as the petite defendant stood up and sauntered towards
the witness stand for the first time.

Sharon Collins was forty-five but could have passed for
a lot younger. Her pale skin sported only a hint of make-
up; her short hair was dyed a cheap blonde and cut
expensively – Princess Diana-style. She was dressed in a
black, pinstriped trouser suit – shiny from regular wear,
and ironed to within an inch of its life. Making her way
past her co-accused, the alleged hitman, Essam Eid, she
climbed the steps to the dock without so much as a sidelong glance in his direction.

The wood-panelled court was packed with gardaí,
lawyers, journalists and members of the public. But as

Collins reached for the Bible, seasoned detectives began shooting each other worried looks. The state had taken a big gamble pitching two such different women against each other. What if the plan backfired and the jury felt sorry for the underdog? The women were of a similar age, but Ní Raifeartaigh was a hotshot lawyer with a lightning mind, and a reputation for winning every case she turned her hand to. She was a former Professor of Criminal Law at Trinity College – and both of her immediate predecessors, Mary Robinson and Mary McAleese, had gone on to Áras an Uachtaráin.

Sharon Collins, on the other hand, was a single mother of two who'd dabbled in get-rich-quick pyramid schemes, worked as an aerobics instructor, and sold fitted kitchens in her native Ennis, Co. Clare. Her climb up the social ladder had come only after she moved in with a wealthy man, PJ Howard – fourteen years her senior – whom she stood accused of trying to have assassinated, along with his two sons.

Ní Raifeartaigh was not about to make any allowances. Strands of her long brown hair escaped the sparkling tooth-grip pinning it at the back as she bounced stacks of paperwork on the desk in front of her impatiently. This was the seventh week of a trial that had been expected to last only four. Some of the country's most distinguished barristers were involved in the case – Collins's legal team included Paul O'Higgins SC and Michael Bowman JC. Essam Eid's barrister was David Sutton SC.

On the prosecution side, Ní Raifeartaigh was guided by the legendary Tom O'Connell SC – the craggy state lawyer, instrumental in convicting the woman once considered the most notorious female killer, Catherine Nevin. O'Connell's opening statement to the jury back in May had described the defences put forward by Sharon Collins and Essam Eid as 'confabulations and lies'.

With the atmosphere between the three teams of legal eagles tetchy at best, it fell to the genial judge, Roderick Murphy, to keep the peace. And with the 'star' of the show about to speak, anything could happen.

After swearing to tell the truth, Collins took a sip from her bottle of Ballygowan and settled herself comfortably in the chair. She nodded at the judge, threw her baby-blue eyes at the jury, fidgeted with the diamond-encrusted crucifix around her neck, and leaned in close to the mike to ask in a lilting Clare accent, 'Can you hear me now?'

Ní Raifeartaigh laid out the case in no uncertain terms. Collins had attempted to have her partner, the property magnate PJ Howard, and his two sons killed so she could inherit the Howard family's fortune.

Collins looked mystified.

After googling the word 'hitman' on the internet, Collins had contacted Essam Eid – who ran the internet website *Hitmanforhire.us* – and solicited him to bump off the Howards.

Collins flapped her hands, shook her head and smiled wanly. It simply wasn't true.

The defendant had agreed to pay Eid the bargain-basement price of $90,000, with the third 'mark' having been thrown in for free because, as Eid had put it, 'this is three birds with one stone'.

Collins was appalled. The plot was 'horrific', and 'appalling'. And it had absolutely nothing to do with her.

Ní Raifeartaigh took a long look at the defendant's cool demeanour and changed tack. 'PJ Howard is also a man of secrets?' she goaded, referring to two emails Collins admitted penning to *The Gerry Ryan Show*. 'You let the secret out of the bag,' Ní Raifeartaigh pushed . . . Were the allegations true?

For the first time, Collins began to look uncomfortable. 'It certainly was a topic that PJ and I had discussed.'

'He wanted you to go up to strangers and pick them up for sex?' Ní Raifeartaigh said.

'That was discussed . . . I'm not sure how serious he was about that.'

Was it true? Did PJ frequent transvestites?

'Yes,' Collins said reluctantly.

Did he ask her to work as a prostitute?

'It was mentioned . . . I most certainly didn't like it. After that, it was no longer an issue . . . This is a private matter between two people that should not be aired in public . . . To be honest I don't want to discuss this at all.'

Ní Raifeartaigh was not about to let the defendant set the terms. 'It was your motive for trying to have him killed,' the barrister said, because 'he was asking you to do things that were disgusting to you?'

'And that was a motive to kill three people?' Collins exclaimed. 'I know you need a motive to kill somebody, but that sort of thing is a motive to leave somebody, it isn't a motive to kill somebody.' The prosecution should not have entered the email as evidence, since not all of it had been recovered by Garda computer experts, she said. She regretted the humiliation it had caused PJ. 'I think I may have exaggerated,' Collins concluded.

'The email to Gerry Ryan said life was "unbearable",' Ní Raifeartaigh reminded her. PJ Howard had made never-ending sexual demands . . .

'I imagine there are very few couples out there where everything is perfect. I don't know what is normal.'

'You despise PJ Howard,' the lawyer suggested.

Collins looked appalled. 'I don't hate PJ! . . . Anybody who knows me knows that I don't . . . I think sometimes a person might actually hate or dislike a quality or an action but still love the person.'

But not 'the package', Ní Raifeartaigh said drolly, adding: 'Well, I suggest the bit of the package you liked was his money.'

'Oh God, no!' Collins reacted.

Ní Raifeartaigh claimed that the defendant had set up an email address, *lyingeyes98@yahoo.com*, so she could contact her co-accused – Essam Eid, who adopted the alias 'Tony Luciano' on his website. Collins had solicited him to murder PJ and his two sons, and conspired with him as to how the deaths should occur to establish their best chance of success. The lawyer paused for breath.

'You're mistaken,' Collins stated categorically. She looked directly at the jury of eight men and four women and declared, 'I am not Lying Eyes.'

One year, eleven months previously – 2 August 2006
It was business as usual at the office of Downes &

Howard, a house-rental company situated at the Westgate Business Park on the Kilrush Road in Ennis, Co. Clare. But the person working behind the reception desk on the Advent desktop computer was throwing regular nervous glances at the entrance. It was lunchtime and the coast was clear. The person typed the word 'hitman' into the Google search engine and hit return.

The six letters returned twenty-nine million hits. The person behind reception in the office of Downes & Howard clicked on *Hitmanforhire.us* and stared at the picture of a square-jawed guy in a trench coat, wearing a trilby on his head. There was a Thompson machine gun, the kind favoured by Al Capone, in the background. The text read:

```
Hitman is the perfect solution to your
killing needs. We offer a variety of
professional assassination services
worldwide. We are a privately owned
independent enterprise that specializes
in reliable contract killings. We take
our business very seriously and are the
best at what we do.
  Assassinations are the most practical
solutions to common problems. Thanks to
the Internet, ordering a hit has never
been easier. We manage a network of
freelance assassins, available to kill at
a moment's notice. All you have to do is
send us an email, along with the
```

details, and wait for further instructions. All the correspondence is done through our secure online forms.

We offer several options to suit the specific needs of our clients.

Each case is analyzed and designed for maximum protection and satisfaction.

Basic contracts start at base cost plus expenses. We require a photograph, bio, and address of the target, along with a deposit. The balance is due no later than 72 hours after the job is done.

HOW TO ORDER A CONTRACT KILL:

1) Send us an encrypted email through our secure contact form with basic information — who, where, and when.

2) You will then receive a set of instructions telling you how to send a deposit. Follow these instructions EXACTLY.

3) Once the deposit is received you will get another set of instructions. This is when you will give us specific information about your target.

4) Once we fulfill our contract you will receive a final set of instructions for the final payment. You will have 72 hours to pay the balance due.

The contact was one Tony Luciano. He sounded like a cross between Tony in the Sopranos and Lucky Luciano, a key player in the New York mafia scene in the thirties, the kind of person who tied bodies to blocks and dumped them in the Hudson. Perfect. He could be contacted at *hire_hitman@yahoo.com*.

A special email address was needed to get in touch with him – something that couldn't be traced back. The alias 'Lying Eyes' seemed appropriate given the circumstances, but *lyingeyes@yahoo.ie* was already taken. However, *lyingeyes98@yahoo.com*, using the year Sharon Collins had met PJ Howard, was not . . .

2

Crazy

The prosecution barrister had a personality as big as her intellect – a contagious laugh and a terrific sense of humour. But on the flip side, Úna Ní Raifeartaigh did not suffer fools gladly. And the accused, Sharon Collins, was clearly trying her patience by insisting the phrase 'lying eyes' didn't even ring any bells. 'You've never heard of the song, "Lyin' Eyes", by the Eagles?' Ní Raifeartaigh reiterated. '. . . Did you know it's a song about a beautiful young woman moving in with an older man and cheating on him?'

'. . . If somebody actually composed that email address that was quite a bad-minded thing to do,' Collins replied.

Standing room in Court Number Two was by now at a premium as lawyers attached to other cases dropped in to check out Ní Raifeartaigh's blitzkrieg style. Collins's two sons, Gary, aged twenty-four, and David, twenty-two, watched anxiously, along with their father, Noel, a handsome man with Mediterranean looks from whom Sharon Collins had split eighteen years previously. His new wife, Fiona, stayed close by his side.

'Come on,' Ní Raifeartaigh coaxed. 'This was a very familiar song in the seventies, which is around the time you and I grew up, Miss Collins. Were you not listening to music then?'

'A friend of mine pointed it out to me recently,' Collins admitted '. . . sent me the first verse of it . . . It's Robert Howard who likes old music; I'm more into Justin Timberlake.'

So if Collins wasn't Lying Eyes, how did she explain the fact that minutes later the mystery user who'd created Lying Eyes' email address in the office of Downes & Howard had also opened Sharon Collins's personal email account – *sharon.collins@eircom.net*.

Collins could not comment because 'I wasn't there.'

Was that her personal email account?

'Yes,' Collins agreed readily.

The mystery person who'd also set up the Lying Eyes address and hacked into Collins's own email account had been 'rather considerate'. They had deleted her unwanted messages. Lying Eyes had coincidentally used three computers – the Advent desktop and a Toshiba laptop in the Downes & Howard office; and an Iridium laptop in Ballybeg House. Sharon Collins worked as a part-time receptionist in Downes & Howard, and lived in Ballybeg House.

The traffic on the computers also indicated that Lying Eyes had been looking at Sharon Collins's bank account; checking flights to Malaga where PJ had an apartment; researching single mortgages, loans, domestic violence, inheritance rights, astrology, revenue repayments, and Tesco diets. An email to Lying Eyes had also been sent from Sharon Collins's Eircom account.

Collins looked baffled. She had been 'shocked' when she'd learned about it from gardaí, she said. Her password for her email address was saved on all the computers Lying Eyes used. She had written to the DPP asking him to investigate the 'theft of my life'.

If it wasn't Collins, who was it, Ní Raifeartaigh asked.

'I wasn't there so I don't know.'

So you believe you are being framed, Ní Raifeartaigh concluded, 'because either it's you, or it's someone setting you up by initiating the kind of searches that you would have, and then going into Lying Eyes to make it look like you'.

'It's not me anyway,' Collins answered.

'Who has a motive for setting you up? You might as well say it . . . Who else had access to those three computers?'

'I had, Robert, Niall and PJ and my lads . . .' Collins looked down at her sons and quickly clarified that her own sons 'would have access to anything in my house, but not in the office'. She had also given the names of the people who had keys to the office to gardaí. But: 'Not everything was actually transcribed the way it was said. If my counsel put everything to the guards that I asked them to, we'd be here till Christmas and people want to get away.'

'Tesco diets is an odd place to go if you are a mystery man setting you up for conspiracy to murder,' Ní Raifeartaigh said. Lying Eyes must have been 'devious' in the extreme – 'telepathic' even – in setting up such an 'elaborate plot' to impersonate Collins, visiting her favourite websites and even using her mother's maiden name in one email, all to make it look like she was the one using the computer. But how did Collins explain Lying Eyes' purchase of Reductil – a weight-loss drug that Collins admitted using in the past, which was bought during Lying Eyes' intense internet activity?

Collins pulled a face. She couldn't explain it because she hadn't bought it on that occasion. She gave a half-smile. 'I took it in the past but I wouldn't recommend it, I can assure you,' she said.

Ní Raifeartaigh knocked the jaunty attitude on the head by quoting from some of the 'callous' emails Lying Eyes had sent to the hitman's website. One email joked it mightn't be necessary to kill PJ, because he'd 'probably have a heart attack when he got the news' about his sons' deaths.

'I nursed PJ through a lot of his illness,' Collins replied, voice quivering as she recalled his cardiac problems in 2000.

The information in the emails from Lying Eyes to the hitman calling himself Tony Luciano was very detailed, Ní Raifeartaigh said. Wasn't it remarkable that the language used in one of Lying Eyes' emails should mirror another that Collins admitted sending to *The Gerry Ryan Show*? Lying Eyes had also said PJ had 'black moods', and had also described Collins as being in 'a vulnerable' situation.

'It's a common word,' Collins said.

Ní Raifeartaigh quoted another email, in which Lying Eyes asked Tony Luciano, 'In your experience when you show up here to take care of someone . . . do they ask who sent you?' The barrister was full of scorn. 'Picturing the assassination?' she enquired.

'. . . I will never get over the shock of this but I certainly didn't write that. It's terrible,' Collins responded. What had happened was 'horrendous'. She'd been accused of plotting to kill the people she cared most about in the world. '. . . My life and my sons' lives have been destroyed.' Anyone who knew her would know how much she cared about PJ and his sons and that 'I couldn't hurt a fly'. The idea that anyone would want PJ pushed from a balcony after learning about the deaths of his two sons was 'horrific'. '. . . I did foolish things. I did stupid things. I should never have written that letter about PJ to *The Gerry Ryan Show*. But certainly I did not and I would never attempt to kill anyone . . . Who do you think sent them?' she asked the barrister.

'You, Miss Collins, you,' Ní Raifeartaigh reacted, pressing her again to name the mystery person or persons Collins believed was trying to frame her.

But Collins would not be drawn. She couldn't say. '. . . I have been brought down to the Garda station, I have been questioned at length, I have been charged with crimes that I most certainly did not commit. I have been put into prison; you cannot imagine the effect that has had on my life. I am not going to accuse anybody of anything when I don't know . . .'

Ní Raifeartaigh could not hide her irritation. Collins had as good as named the people she was pointing the finger of suspicion at, she said. The only other people who would have had access to the computers used by Lying

Eyes were PJ Howard's sons. The implication was that they, and specifically the eldest, Robert, who had as good as taken over the family business, had set her up. And their motive was to get Collins out of their father's life to protect their inheritance, Ní Raifeartaigh presumed.

'You should have asked them when they were giving evidence,' Collins answered.

But the barrister needed Collins to spell out the name of her suspect to enable her to rubbish Collins's theory. Did PJ's sons have the opportunity to use the same computers as Lying Eyes, so as to hack into her account to set her up, she quizzed.

'It's possible,' Collins said.

3

Money, Money, Money

Lying Eyes kept the first email to Tony Luciano strictly businesslike, typing: '2 male marks in Ireland. ASAP. Usually together. Make it look like an accident. Then possibly a third one 24 hours later. Prefer a suicide. Would appreciate a call by return.'

But after Tony called back to introduce himself, Lying Eyes felt a lot more comfortable about opening up, and began emailing with much more of a flourish:

```
Hi,
  We were just talking. As you can
imagine, I am extremely nervous about
sending this message and even talking on
the phone.
  There are actually three, but two of
them would probably be together and the
third would not be in Ireland, he would
be in Spain. I don't want to give you
the names of the people involved just
yet, but, I will give you the location,
```

293

and tell you what I want — ideally . . .

The first two live in Ireland, as I said. The town they live in is Ennis, Co. Clare in the west of the country. They are brothers, one aged 27 (big guy) and 23 (not so big). They share a house, at present, but there are two others living in the house as well.

They work in the same place, and spend a lot of time together. I do not want it to look like a hit. This is important. I want it to look like an accident — perhaps travelling in a car together or in a boat (they do a lot of boating) off the west coast. Or maybe you have some ideas of your own.

The third is an older man — aged 57 and not very fit or strong. He would probably be in mainland Spain, if not in Ireland. His location would depend on when the job could be done. Again, it is imperative that it does not look like a hit. I would prefer suicide — or is it possible to look like natural causes? He's got a lot of health problems.

What I need to know is: How soon could the above be done? Days? Weeks? Months? If the first job is done in Ireland, is it possible for the second job to be done within 12 to 24 hours in Spain if that's where he is?

How much would it cost and how much of a deposit would be needed up front? I ask this because, I would have no problem getting my hands on the money immediately afterwards, but it certainly would be very tricky beforehand.

Can it be done in the manner I've stated, without causing suspicion?

Most importantly, if a deposit must be paid, how do I know that you would not disappear with the money and not do the job? After all, who could I complain to?

Where are you located? Just curious about that.

It might be easier to email back for now. I'm not comfortable talking about it on the phone — even though this phone is unregistered and not used for anything else. I may get a chance to email you again within the next hour . . .

Lying Eyes almost couldn't believe it when Tony Luciano replied. And Lying Eyes was starting to feel they had a connection. He'd explained that ordinarily his fee was $50,000 per target but 'because this is three birds with one stone, we will do it for $90,000'. He wanted half the fee upfront – a down payment of $45,000.

Lying Eyes replied immediately:

Hi Tony,

 . . . I know it must seem terrible of
me, but my back is to the wall and I
don't have much choice. I would prefer
if it was just my husband, but because
of the way he has arranged his affairs,
it would be way too complicated if his
sons were still around and I'd still be
in much the same situation as I am now.

Regarding payment. The price you quoted
seems very fair, and I would gladly pay
it, but I will have to give some thought
on how to come up with the deposit. I
could put my hands on it, in cash
immediately, but the two sons would see
it gone and would know it was me and
that would cause too many problems for
me. I'll have to try to borrow it and
that will take a little time. I'm not
even sure that I will get it — I don't
have any assets of my own to borrow
against, but I'll certainly give it a
go.

Now, you said in your message that
you'd leave a cooling-off period between
the first two and my husband. How long
are you thinking of? I'll tell you the
way I was thinking. My husband is in
Spain and lives on the top floor of a
tall building while he's there. If he

were to hear that his sons had a fatal
accident, he might suddenly feel suicidal
and just jump off the building. Is that
too far-fetched do you think? Otherwise,
he would find out about the missing
money (if I try using that) and if I
borrow it from the local bank (the only
place I'd have a chance of getting it)
he'd hear that too and put two and two
together. It's very parochial here. My
husband is friendly with the bank manager
and they talk a lot. Another thing, I'll
have to look into is the cashier's
cheque or bank draft. There's a record
kept here of anything over a certain
amount, I'm not sure if it's 5K or 10K,
but I assume I could send a few drafts.
I'd be worried that if the cops got
suspicious though, and looked into it, I
wouldn't have answers. Do you know if
cash can be parcelled up and FedExed
safely?

I have to go to Spain next week — my
husband is putting me under pressure to
join him and I must try to keep him
happy for now, while I figure things
out.

You quoted in dollars, so I assume the
money goes to the US and then the guy or
guys doing the job get their cut from

there. I'm saying this just in case it
would be possible to give you the
location of the cash to be picked up
after each job is done. Is there any
chance of that do you think? It would be
very uncomplicated for me in that
situation. I could go ahead with it
straight away.

  The other thing I need to know is, if
it's possible for it to look like an
accident and not a hit?

  I look forward to hearing from you.

  S

Tony replied, saying nothing was going to happen without a deposit. But Lying Eyes now thought of him as the
character played by Pierce Brosnan in *The Matador*, and
the haggling over the price was a minor detail:

Wow. I'm a bit scared to be honest. The
two guys here usually go to a place
called Kilkee on the west coast of
Clare, each weekend. They've got a
holiday home there. They usually have
friends with them and the younger one
usually has his girlfriend with him. The
older guy broke up with his girlfriend a
couple of months ago and might be open
to being chatted up etc. I think he has
been dating lately, but I don't know yet

if he might bring that girl with him. I
can find out, but it will be Monday
before I will see him — it would be too
suspicious for me to ring him over the
weekend to ask.

They drink in a bar called the
Greyhound Bar on the Main Street in
Kilkee. It's easy to find. What do you
plan — putting poison in their drinks? I
have to ask you what poison it would be
— autopsies would be done and I need to
know what would be concluded from the
autopsies. I think it might be easier
for your people to stay in a hotel in
Kilkee and get talking to them in the
bar, but then you know your business, I
don't.

I would be in Spain with my husband
when the above job would be done, if
it's arranged for next weekend or even
after that. What would you do about him?
Especially with me around. You say you
will take care of him yourself. You'd be
coming a long way from the US to Spain.
I could get the keys of his apartment to
you and arrange a time to be out, I
would be a suspect, if anything looks
suspicious, especially when I would be
the one to inherit. Many people think
I'm with him for his money anyway, he's

a bit older than me etc. and that would also look suspicious.

Please realize that I may not be ready to go ahead as soon as next week. I'm leaving here to go to Spain on Wednesday and it will take a lot longer than that for me to arrange a loan. I won't be back in Ireland until some time in September, it may be towards the end of the month before I'm back.

You see, as I said, I could use cash that I have here and buy a cashier's cheque, or a number of them with it, but the sons might notice the money gone after I leave on Wednesday and ring my husband and tell him. And he would know that I took it . . . And then what? This is my problem and I will have to work it out. But as I say it might not be as soon as I hoped, I'd really like to see an end to all of this soon though.

I can't talk on the phone right now and I will be away from the computer for the next few hours. You could always send a text to my mobile phone but it would be better for now to send an email.

I appreciate all your help and we will definitely do business. I've no conscience about my husband, he's a real asshole and makes my life hell, but I do

```
feel bad about the others, however, I
thought about it long and hard and I
realize that it is necessary or there is
no advantage to getting rid of my
husband other than not having to look at
his miserable face again. But I must
be sure that I will be ok financially
etc.
    S
```

Lying Eyes could tell Tony was growing impatient when he answered: '... Sorry we have to have the deposit before we proceed ...'

'I suppose you're right,' Lying Eyes replied:

```
I should just leave it to you and not
worry. But I do worry.
  I could send the keys of the apartment
to you or leave them somewhere in Spain
near the apartment for you to collect.
There is a further complication about
Spain though — he has a boat and could
arrange to be away on it at any time.
It's impossible for me to say where he
will be until much closer to the time.
In any case, I suppose we could stay in
touch by text if he and I are on the
boat. But if I'm on the boat I wouldn't
want anything to happen to him there. I
guess if he were to get news about his
```

sons, he would immediately return to the
apartment to pack anyway.

I definitely have photos of my husband
and I think I have one of the guys, but
I will have to look tomorrow and email
them to you.

I know you say not to worry about the
cash and that they won't have time to
find out, but I have to consider what
would happen next if you couldn't get
near the guys here in Ireland next
weekend. There is a major concern for
me. I can't get them suspicious of me in
any way. I'm already walking a very fine
line here. Believe me, if it would do
you, I think I could get approximately
13,000 euro without too many problems
before Wednesday (not money that would be
missed). How would it be if I sent that
and paid a little more than the quoted
fee after the job is done? I'm not sure
how much cash there is in Spain, but I
think it is a considerable amount and
would go a long way towards paying the
total fee. Once my husband is taken care
of, I'd be 'bringing him home' and any
balance can be sent immediately once I'm
back here (a matter of days). Whatcha
think?

If this is totally unacceptable to you

please confirm that you will be willing
to do this job at a later date when I've
had a chance to get the money together.
  Kind regards,
  S

Lying Eyes must have been delighted when Tony gave in
and dropped the money he wanted posted by $30,000:

Here's the deal, you can send $15,000 by
Wed and after we arrive we can have the
$30,000 which is the balance of the
deposit it will be the 18 of Aug . . .
and . . . $45,000 no later than 72 hours
after the job done . . . this is our
contract or you will be our target.
Sorry to say that but this is our
policy. Now we need pics, names, and
address for all of them.
  . . . Let us do our job and just relax
cause if you make a mistake and we both
gonna be in trouble. Is that a deal?

Lying Eyes replied:

Sorry for taking so long getting back to
you.
  Tony, I'm not trying to be difficult
about the money. If you can get me out
of the unbearable situation that I'm in

and I don't get into trouble for it,
then it's money very well spent as far
as I'm concerned.

What you suggested in your last email
is very fair, but as I said before, I'm
going to Spain on Wednesday and I'd have
to take the cash and leave it somewhere
for you. But if I do, the sons could
notice it gone after I leave and tell
him — my husband. Then the shit would
hit the fan for me. I know you'd be
taking care of him on Sunday, but I'm
afraid he would say it to someone. He's
got close friends with him in Spain (in
the apartment next door) he might tell
them.

I have to tell you I have absolutely no
intention of being your next target by
not paying the balance of any money I
owe you after the jobs are done. You
most definitely will be paid within 72
hours.

I've got children of my own and I
intend on being around for them. That's
another reason why I want to be as
careful as possible that I don't end up
in jail. I want to be absolutely sure
that when I start this thing by paying
you the 'booking deposit', I'll be in a
position to finish it by paying you what

I owe. In addition, there may possibly be one more person I might add to the list a little later, but I'll get this job done first.

I've been thinking about it all earlier today and I wonder if you wouldn't mind giving me some advice. Tell me honestly, would it look more believable if one of the sons were to go first, followed by a few months later the other and then immediately by the father (as planned this time). The reason why I wanted to get it all done together was I thought I could take all the money to pay afterwards and no one would be around to notice, but maybe it's the wrong way. I know it would be a more expensive way to do it, but please let me know if it would be better.

What I'm thinking is, maybe I could borrow the $50,000 to pay for the others. I'm not very brave, am I? But then again, you do this all the time, I've never in my life considered anything like this.

Another thing I need advice with is this. I used the computer at work (we all work together) to surf the net for a hitman. If the cops seize the computer, could they find evidence of my search?

As this is the weekend, I won't be able
to talk to the bank about a loan until
Monday, so there's no way I can confirm
if this thing will be on for next
weekend until the bank sanctions a loan,
but I will keep you informed all the way
of my progress.

I'm hoping I will be able to talk to
you later, but in the meantime would you
email me back and let me know what you
think about the above.

Tony replied: '. . . I said we need $15,000 by Wed and I will get the rest after the 2 son is gone . . . So 15,000 by Wed and 30,000 by Sun the 20 Aug and the rest after the husband . . . the last thing what's your name?'

Lying Eyes decided, since he had made a hotel reservation in Limerick for 18 August, to send him the money.

4

Walk the Line

There was a collective intake of air in the Central Criminal Court when Sharon Collins suggested she'd been framed. Úna Ní Raifeartaigh now set about pointing the finger of suspicion right back at her, by using three letters Collins had written to explain her innocence – written to the DPP.

Collins had contacted the highest legal officer in the state, James Hamilton, in March, April and May 2007, telling him that she had learned from his website that she had the right to state her case. Describing herself as 'an ordinary woman living an ordinary life with which I was happy before this happened', she tried to paint a picture of herself.

Sharon Coote was one of three sisters who had grown up in a broken home, in an estate off the Kilrush Road in Ennis. At seventeen she began a computer course in the National Institute for Higher Education in Limerick, which she never finished, choosing at nineteen to marry a local man, Noel Collins, instead. The couple lived in an estate near her mother's – Maiville – and had two sons, Gary and David, but they split after five years.

PJ Howard was the son of a wealthy car dealer, Jack

Howard, who'd started the family business with Denny Downes on the Mill Road in Ennis in the fifties. The family expanded into the property market two decades later, and PJ is thought to have amassed a personal portfolio of seventy properties, with estimates of his personal wealth ranging between €12 and €60 million. His marriage to Teresa Conboy, from Leitrim, broke up after eighteen years, and they parted in 1992. He moved from the family home on the Kilrush Road into a modern mansion, Ballybeg House, on the outskirts of Ennis, which featured an imposing second-storey bay window overlooking a lake.

Sharon Collins met him in 1998, when PJ came into the shop where she worked selling fitted kitchens. She already knew of him, and remembered first seeing him when she was a young girl of nine or ten and he was a grown man of around twenty-five. When their paths crossed again in the kitchen shop, the moment was a kind of epiphany for her. She told the DPP that she'd experienced an instant feeling they were meant to be together. 'I knew he was coming for me. It was almost like a recollection.' She could tell he was suffering and needed someone 'to look after him'. PJ's partner, Bernie Lyons, had died of cancer that same year.

After PJ invited Sharon and her boys, then aged twelve and fifteen (PJ's sons were fifteen and nineteen), to join him at his home in Ennis over Christmas, the Collins clan relocated there permanently. 'I didn't take the move lightly,' Collins told the DPP. 'A very short time after we met, PJ asked me if I thought we could make a life together and I agreed to do so and so the decision was made to stay together.' Sharon moved out temporarily in 1999, around the first anniversary of Bernie's death because 'he wanted to be alone'.

Collins's address wasn't the only thing to change when she met PJ. She also began working for Downes & Howard as a part-time receptionist, earning €850 a month, with €1,000 in personal expenses. She was renting out the house she'd lived in with her ex-husband, Noel, and also had an apartment in Ennis and a retail outlet in Tullamore.

Collins's first letter to the DPP was written 'in my own words, what I do know and trust that you will consider it in conjunction with the evidence submitted to you by the gardaí' and returned to the theme that she'd been stitched up. 'No one would go to this trouble for nothing. I feel totally lost and can't understand why the gardaí won't investigate the theft and complete destruction of my life, to which, I have to say, they are contributing. I have so many questions as to what could have happened and as time goes on, so many theories too. But that is all they are and I have no way of knowing the truth. However, one truth I do know is that I didn't and wouldn't do what I was arrested for.'

She said her solicitor had told her writing the letter 'was a complete waste of time, but this is my life and that of my family and I must do what I feel is right. My solicitor's argument is that I will be giving away whatever my defence might be if charged, but I feel that the truth is the truth and I can only tell you what I know and I feel that now is the time as I would rather be dead than subject my family – both my immediate family and extended family – to the embarrassment of such a case. My life is in a shambles.'

Collins found the idea of being charged 'so unbearable . . . I can't just sit here and do nothing while our lives are torn to shreds'. She wanted the DPP to consider how farcical the case against her was. Even if she had wanted to have PJ bumped off, 'Wouldn't it be daft to try to hire someone from a website? Sure, you wouldn't know where or who they were. They could be your next door neighbours or connected with the police in any given country.'

She rubbished her own supposed motive, writing:

I have nothing to inherit in the event of their [the Howards'] deaths. If they all died, then PJ's brother and sister would inherit anything he has. I would be throwing myself on their mercy and they have their own families to look after. If I was legally married to PJ and he and his two sons were murdered, I'm quite sure I would be arrested within minutes of their deaths. The question would be asked 'Who is to gain here?' and I'd be hauled down to the station and charged immediately.

. . . In addition, who in their right mind, would want to have everyone in a family killed in one go? Wouldn't that raise numerous questions and suspicions? Another thing here is that I have been aware that my marital status gives me no protection if the relationship breaks down, or God forbid, if anything was to happen to PJ. Like most women, security is important to me and PJ has often mentioned that he wants to make provision for me in case anything were to happen to him, but that hasn't been done yet. I know the law regarding co-habiting couples is under review and is expected to change at some stage in the future which would give a dependant or a co-habitee some rights, but at the moment there is no protection for someone like me. Therefore, even if I hated PJ, which I don't, why would I want him dead at this stage? It doesn't make sense.

. . . I don't have many unusual transactions on my bank account. Rental income goes into it and mortgages, loans and bills are paid out of it. That is the bulk of what goes on in my account. Any big withdrawal would stand out a mile. I imagine if someone was plotting to kill someone, and would be a potential suspect . . . they would surely withdraw it little by little, put it aside over a period of time and wait until they had enough.

. . . I feel there are just too many paths leading to me. I know I did some stupid things . . . If I was plotting such a dreadful crime, surely I would try to cover my tracks and not leave so many trails back to me. It all seems so far-fetched. PJ and my son both think it does and so does PJ's son, Robert, even though he does blame me now for all this hassle . . . I had a fantastic relationship with Robert. He confided everything in me and is like a cross between a son and a good friend to me. I love him. I also get on very well with PJ's other son, Niall, but if I was to be honest, Robert is my favourite. He is an exceptional young man . . . But now I doubt that our relationship will ever be rebuilt again. Bad enough that they have lost a mother, now they've been told that their surrogate mother wants them dead.

... Anyone who knows PJ Howard would never believe that he would commit suicide. He is just not that type of man. If something happened to his sons while he was in Spain, he would be home on the next available flight, making arrangements and getting to the bottom of what happened. He is a very capable, astute businessman.

I think I remember the Gardaí mentioning during questioning that death by natural causes would also be a way for PJ to die. How could anyone believe that this would be possible in this day and age?

... If by writing to you in this way, I have overstepped the boundaries – and I strongly suspect that I have – then please accept my apologies and realize that it is only because I am at the end of my tether and I am desperate to be heard and to see an end to this.

Collins's second letter was only a third of the length of the first, and it was faxed 'for the sake of speed', after an article about the case appeared in a newspaper.

PJ rang me after speaking to the Gardaí and said the situation looks extremely serious. He said that the Gardaí are adamant that I am involved in hiring this man to kill him and his sons, Robert and Niall.

Recently I have been thinking that there's more to it than that and that someone thought they had something to gain by setting me up in this way, by discrediting me in this way, and perhaps, had hired someone to frame me.

This was a theory that only began to dawn on me in the past few weeks, as various things came to mind and I have very, very strong suspicions regarding it, but I know I could be completely wrong. I know what it's like to be accused in the wrong and I wouldn't wish it on another soul.

All along, I didn't think that anyone had any intention of killing anybody, and I told myself it would all come to light, but now, it turns out this man, Eid, actually did have serious means of killing someone. Terrifying stuff, and, even more terrifying to me, that the Gardaí believe that I employed him to use it on PJ and worse.

. . . I'd do anything for PJ and this is breaking my heart. I'm worried he won't be well and I won't be able to take care of him. Do you know that when PJ had his by-pass, I would arrive at the hospital at 8am every morning and I wouldn't leave until they kicked me out each night at midnight? . . . It upsets me that someone would even think that I would want to harm a hair on his head. Then I read in the paper today that the poison that was found would bring about a slow and agonizing death, and the Gardaí are telling him that I hired someone to give him this and I just can't tell you how sickened I feel by that . . . everything is adding up and it's like joining the dots but the problem is, I didn't hire anyone to kill anybody . . . you are the only person who can decide if our lives are to be destroyed or not. I know what I did – I was an ass for giving away information about myself . . . I am guilty of that and I am most certainly paying the price of that stupidity. Apart from that, I have lived my life to the best of my ability. I am family orientated, maternal, and PJ tells me, quite domesticated. I am outspoken, direct and can be a bit abrasive, but I am very soft behind it and feel very deeply for people. I also have very definite views on crime, and dare I say it, believe that the death penalty should have its place in certain circumstances. Perhaps I should change my mind about that now given the present situation I find myself in.

Sharon offered the DPP her views on other matters of jurisprudence. She believed in 'assisted suicide . . .' and 'I'll stick my neck out, but I believe abortion is necessary in some circumstances . . .' Euthanasia was acceptable when someone had 'no hope of recovery from illness and was in unbearable pain'; PJ had not agreed with the execution of Saddam Hussein, she wrote, but she had believed it 'the right thing to do'. 'With the exception of self defence the above are the only circumstances in which I believe it is acceptable to take another human being's life. I want to be 100pc clear about that. To me there are no excuses for it and I certainly wouldn't do it or want it to be done – to anybody.'

Having now moved out of Ballybeg House, she was worried PJ would eat junk food every day and end up dying young.

. . . My mother is 73, still very active, but beginning to show her age, she is very attached to PJ. News like this would kill her. My sister Catherine and her husband are secondary school teachers in Waterford. They are good,

314

decent people and I know that a scandal like this would cause them great distress. My other sister, Suzette, is some kind of psychologist with the Department of Education and is married to the managing director of a large pharmaceutical company near us. Being associated with something like this would affect them very badly indeed. For myself, being charged would be a very severe punishment indeed for something I did not do. Not alone would I lose my relationship and my home, but I am also totally financially dependent on PJ and that would be gone too. Can you imagine how heartbreaking it is for me to listen to my 21-year-old son David, crying on the phone as he feels so helpless? His life is falling apart now. He is making arrangements to move out of his home and it's killing him. He loves PJ like a father. He works in retail and was sent home from work today as he kept breaking down.

I can't imagine how badly the news will affect my older son, Gary. As I've said he is in Australia at the moment and I don't want to worry him, but if I am charged or if it is in the papers, he would hear it immediately and I know he just wouldn't be able to cope with the news. He would be completely devastated. I am not exaggerating when I say to you that I am afraid that one or both of them would take their own lives, as you hear of young men doing all the time these days.

. . . So, Mr Hamilton, if you were me, what would you do? I admit I have seriously considered suicide myself on the basis that it would save my family all the embarrassment and stigma of being associated with me if I were charged and it would stop the not knowing. I would have something to leave my boys and I have three rented properties that are mortgaged to the hilt but are covered by life assurance policies. I wouldn't have to face the prospect of a very high profile trial where every aspect of our lives would be examined and reported in the papers and TV. That, too, would save PJ on many different levels and I would like to do that for him. As well as that, we all die sometime, so why not now for me? I've recently had a mammogram done that shows a small mass on one breast and the doctor wants me to undergo further examination – he says it's probably non-malignant – but what if it isn't, that could get me anyway? So I've certainly thought why not take this option. This is all way too much for any one person to bear and I'm not sure I'm strong enough. The only problem here is, I didn't do this thing and if I take this option I won't be able to defend myself and my good name and my family will have to live with the stigma of it anyway. The spiritual implications weigh heavily on me too should I take this option.

. . . I have very strong suspicions these days as to who could be behind this and I could point this out – it's a theory that makes a lot of sense to me but I could be wrong. Anyway, hopefully I'd be found not guilty, but what kind of life would be left for everyone after that? I can't even bear to imagine what would happen if I was to be found guilty. This would destroy my family completely . . . I did not hire any-one to kill PJ, Robert and Niall. I did not hire anyone, full stop . . . I have never experienced such depths of despair in my life. I am by no means a saint, but I am not a bad person. I am not a dangerous person.

. . . Charging me with this horrendous crime will only serve to feed a media frenzy and will probably not get to the bottom of what really happened and if it does, too much damage will have been done to innocent parties, namely myself, PJ and my family. As it stands, miraculously, no one has been injured, thank God, and any hurt that does exist is not physical and can be healed with time . . . Lastly Mr Hamilton I want to ask you to please not to have me charged in relation to this matter. Please let us get on with our lives. They are ordinary lives, but we were happy in them and could be happy again. I have told the truth about everything I know and I pray that you will see that. The lives and happiness of many people are in your hands.

Collins's third and final letter was the shortest. She said that there were times when she had felt like 'killing' PJ ('and I don't mean literally!'). 'Perhaps throttling would be a better word – but those times had passed and we had reached a deeper understanding of each other and we had mellowed too which was really good for both of us.'

She said if she was plotting a murder she wouldn't have used a computer that she used day to day to set up an email address because the IP address could be traced back; she said she didn't have inheritance rights and if she'd been doing it 'just for the hell of it' why would she risk everything for that? She would not have given personal information about herself to a dangerous stranger over the internet – 'That would be lunacy. I'd stay anonymous.'

She would not have withdrawn money from her bank account.

> If I was unhappy with my relationship with PJ why not just have him killed [and not his sons]. I would have thought that Robert would have looked after me if anything happened to PJ.
>
> . . . Then there's the question of timing, why then? Why the rush? Why not wait until a dependent co-habitee had some inheritance rights? Or why not wait until PJ had something in place for me? My son David had just bought a house for investment purposes with PJ's help. PJ had guaranteed the mortgage and I was delighted for David. He said he would do the same for my other son, Gary. Why would I want to prevent that from happening? PJ had also just helped me to buy an apartment in Limerick and had told me that he intended buying a commercial property for me, which would be mortgaged, but which would be paid out of his estate if anything happened to him so that I would have an income. If you wanted to kill someone, wouldn't you wait for that first so that you would have security.

She also told the DPP, 'I'll write a book yet.'

Standing in the belly of the Central Criminal Court, Ní Raifeartaigh ratcheted up the tension by reacting with disdain instead of pity to Collins's writing skills. She summed up the letters as, 'My son is at risk, my mother is at risk, various people may commit suicide . . . PJ may

get a heart attack . . . And whose fault would that be?'
Collins's eyes filled.

Counsel for the state also annihilated the idea of a
happy, ordinary couple. The only reason PJ Howard still
believed Collins was innocent was because his 'pride' simply
would not allow him to accept that 'a very attractive,
younger woman' with whom he had lived for eight years
had set out to have him killed, the barrister said. 'Wouldn't
that be frighteningly humiliating for him?' she asked Collins.

'I think if I'd heard someone was planning to kill my
two sons, I'd get over the humiliation, wouldn't you?'
Collins retorted. '. . . I wouldn't let pride get in my way.'

'You wrote to the DPP against the advice of your
solicitor at the time,' Ní Raifeartaigh continued. '. . . In
the arrogance we have come to expect of you, you decided
you are different to everyone else and trying to use what
you have always done now and in your life – emotional
manipulation . . .

'You got in here not to give useful facts but to sit there
smiling at the jury and to manipulate them into thinking
a woman who smiled like that couldn't plot to kill her
[partner's] two sons,' Ní Raifeartaigh said.

'I'm not smiling,' Collins said.

'No, but you were smiling.'

'I'm not trying to manipulate the jury. I was extremely
nervous and sometimes I'm smiling when I'm nervous. I'm
here to tell the truth. I've always, always told the truth.
I'm not trying to manipulate anybody,' Collins said. And
what she was saying had to have some substance, because
PJ Howard believed her.

August 2006

The big problem with working as a professional poker dealer was no matter how many cards you flipped, it was always someone else's life that changed.

At fifty years of age, Essam Ahmed Eid had seen it all – big winners, big losers, every stunt in the book – and he still needed tips to survive on a pay packet of $6.50 an hour. But every time 'Sam' arrived for work at the Bellagio Hotel in Las Vegas, the heavy-featured card player with round, rimless glasses and a moustache turning white was reminded just how far he had come from his impoverished upbringing in Egypt.

The Sin City strip was a shrine to unfathomable excess. Directly outside the Bellagio, an eight-acre, man-made lake – bang, smack in the middle of the Nevada Desert – featured choreographed fountains that danced to songs like 'Luck Be A Lady Tonight' and 'Hey Big Spender'. Inside, the hotel's conservatory and botanical gardens displayed all four seasons all year round; there was also a gallery of fine art.

And last but not least, Sam had to rub shoulders with the casino's 'special' customers, the ones chaperoned into the Bobby Baldwin Room – named after the 1978 World Series player – who could throw enough good money after bad to turn their luck around. If there was one thing Sam had learned from watching gamblers converge on Vegas from every corner of the world, it was that you needed money to begin with if you were going to make real money. Otherwise you took your seat alongside the other losers on the slots.

Sam knew he was good at what he did; only the best in the business got to deal cards here. Apart from the obvious skills, a specific personality was required. You had to be calm, tactful and presentable; someone who was good at diffusing tension and welcoming but firm. But stacking cards in the 7,000-square-foot poker room alongside thirty-nine other card dealers was no longer viable. Not now he was returning home to two wives living in his four-bed detached home in 6108 Camden Cove.

When he got home to the quiet, residential, newly built street in north Las Vegas, the reality was a sudden immersion in day and night; no oxygen supplies being pumped into the air to keep him pepped; a mortgage of $308,135 taken out with his ex-wife – Lisa Eid – and having to live up to the expectations of his new one, Teresa Engel.

Sam had met Teresa in a casino in Detroit, Michigan, where she'd worked. Like Sam, she'd been married numerous times previously, but to the same person – Todd Engel. Sam's wife prior to Lisa was Linda Moir. They'd split in 1999, after only four years. Linda now lived in Detroit, with their eleven-year-old daughter, Emily. And there was another wife and daughter back in Egypt. But his current situation – living with two wives at the same time – was unsustainable. Normally, he could get around Lisa, but the tension in the house was near breaking point. His only hope of resolving the impasse was with real money, and in January 2006 he set about making it by taking the biggest gamble of his life.

He'd set up an internet-based contract killing company, *Hitmanforhire.us*, using the administration password 'Casino' and an alias he'd been using on and off for the last five years – Tony Luciano. The future for the business looked bright. He'd had enquiries from a customer in California called Marisa Mark, who wanted one Anny Lauren Royston, the new woman in her ex-boyfriend's life, 'neutralized' – and in Ireland from a Sharon Collins who wanted her partner, PJ Howard, and his two sons dead. At this rate, he could buy Lisa out of the property outright within a year.

Having equipped himself with the tools necessary for his new trade – a Browning 9mm pistol, a Taser stun gun, silencer parts, two semi-automatic handgun magazines and a box of 9mm Luger ammunition – he prioritized the Irish job. The client wanted the two younger men poisoned. After some basic research on the web, Sam decided to use ricin, one of the deadliest substances known to man but hard to detect during a post mortem. It had made headlines in the case of the so-called 'Umbrella Murder' in 1978 when a Bulgarian writer, Georgi Markov, who had defected to Britain, was killed on Waterloo Bridge by being pricked in the leg with an umbrella spike doused in ricin. Could it be any simpler?

5

Stairway to Heaven

15 August 2006

Lying Eyes had just FedExed Tony Luciano his deposit of $15,000 along with a pair of goggles, described as having been 'left behind on holiday in Ireland'. In the run-up to the decision to advance beyond 'Go', Lying Eyes had barely been able to contain the enthusiasm in emails to Tony:

> Gee you got back to me fast. Thanks.
> Let me get this straight. Are you
> saying that if I FedEx $15,000 to you on
> Monday to pay three people in Ireland,
> that you will do the rest and wait for
> the balance till after my husband is
> done? This is possible for me. But maybe
> I misunderstand. Please confirm. You
> didn't say whether you think it is the
> best way to do it . . . all of them like
> this or one first and the other two
> later.
> About the boat. I must explain. The

boat is not in close proximity to the
apartment and when you leave the
apartment block there are lots of shops
and vendors all around. They are open
until very late and they know him well.
I think it would be difficult to get him
out without raising suspicion and
remember, I need it to look like he has
committed suicide after hearing about his
sons. Also, the boat is quite big and
perhaps difficult for you to handle, if
you are on your own.

I think it is important that I tell you
exactly the way it is there. And also
point out any complications that might
arise. OK?

The apartment is on the top floor of a
14-storey apartment block. It has a
private terrace and plunge pool on the
roof. An Irish couple, with whom he is
very friendly, own the apartment next
door. They are in Spain now too, but I
think they have tenants in it for the
summer — I'm not sure, but I can find
out later. This couple also have a boat
here, near his boat and if they are not
in their apartment, they will be living
aboard their boat — another reason why
you might find it difficult to get away
with taking him out on it.

My husband is planning to go on a boat
trip for a few days when I get there —
but I don't know when this is or where.
I really don't know that until we are
going. But I think, wherever it is, when
he gets a phone call about his sons, he
will immediately return to his apartment
to pack to come home. Unless he decides
to go directly to the airport from the
marina. If he does this, then I don't
know how you would get him.

I will be there, as you know. How do
you suggest we stay in touch, so I'm not
there when you get there? Also I will
need to let you know when he gets the
news about his sons and what he is doing
then.

My husband has a bad heart — maybe when
he gets the news about his sons you
won't need to do anything at all (except
get your money!) but I feel I should
point out all the pitfalls to you
beforehand. Another complication could be
his friends — they might come back to
the apartment with us to sympathize with
him. The Irish are like that! And there
are lots of Irish friends of his out
there.

In your experience when you show up to
take care of someone, do they ask you

who sent you? Do they offer to pay you
to kill that person instead of them?
Just wondering . . .
  S

But there was so much to worry about, as Lying Eyes
explained:

I was told by a guy in the computer
company that services our computers that
even if you delete stuff, it can be
still accessed. I'd have to take the
computer from the office before I go. I
better think of an excuse to do that.
  I'm just wondering now, if it might be
easier to wait until we return from
Spain to do my husband. After all, you
plan to do his sons on Sat 19th, right?
He'll get a call about it immediately
and go home as soon as he gets a flight.
Even if you hit him on Mon 21st, I still
have time to pay you, don't I?
  Just an idea. The only thing is, one of
my sons lives here with us and will be
here, as will I. Not sure how that would
work. Again, Tony, it must look like
suicide for him. Or natural causes. This
is vital. And the body can't disappear.
It must be there.
  S

Lying Eyes had been obsessing about the finer details:

OK, so do you intend for us to talk on
the phone in Spain or meet face to face?
 The money. Am I to give it to you in
cash? It's all going to happen within a
few hours, right? As far as I know, my
husband has enough cash there for me to
give you the equivalent of $30,000 in
euro. I'll be able to check how much
cash he has when I get there on Wed and
let you know. I won't be able to take it
while he is there, but if you are going
to be in the apartment, I can give you
the combination to the safe and you can
help yourself. Is that OK? He always
likes to have a lot of cash with him, so
I'm not sure if he would take the cash
from the apartment while we are gone and
you can check the money to satisfy
yourself that it is there. But I would
ask you not to touch it until he is
gone, we can talk about it anyway. With
everything going on, he will be upset,
therefore, I don't see a problem. I
could FedEx the keys of the apartment
with $15,000 on Monday.
 Do you have any idea how long it would
take for the authorities to release his
body from Spain? I'll need to get home

asap after you've done your bit to send
the rest of the money to you. Will I
have to stay there until they release
the body or do you think I could leave
without causing too much suspicion and
let them forward the body to Ireland
afterwards? Perhaps you would know how
this works?

Photos, I don't have a scanner here to
send the photos. I'll have to source one
tomorrow and send them to you then.

My name . . . Tony, if you knew me, I
wouldn't harm a fly, seriously. I've just
been put in such an impossible situation
that I feel I really have to take
drastic action. There's no point in going
into the details of it with you unless
you need to know. Anyway I want to sleep
on it tonight and decide for once and
for all if I will be able to live with
myself afterwards. I'm a real softy and
there was a time when I really loved my
husband, but he has truly killed that.
But even though I can't stand him now
and have been wishing him dead for a
long, long time, I found it really
upsetting when I read your emails and
saw it there in black and white. The
reality is fairly startling, especially
for an un-violent person like me. I know

```
he has asked for it and would do the
same himself, if he was in my position,
but that doesn't make it easy for me.
   I will let you know tomorrow for sure
and will give you my name then, if I
must! My son is around at the moment, so
I won't be able to talk on the phone
tonight as I had hoped, but we will have
a talk tomorrow. Is that OK?
```

Tony assured Lying Eyes that he was a 'professional' and even if PJ offered ten million euro, he would honour the contract. He recommended Lying Eyes stay with PJ's body, as leaving to go home after the murder would be too suspicious. Lying Eyes liked the way he thought and had been bouncing everything off him:

```
I've been trying to think of an excuse
for removing the computer from the
office. It's my husband's business and
his sons work there too. I think it
would be a good idea to leave it there
in case anyone decides to check it out.
   I also have been thinking about getting
the cashier's cheque. Here in Ireland,
any time you buy a bank draft or
cashier's cheque, the bank keeps a record
of who you are and you have to do it at
your own bank. It's regulation. Anyway,
if there is any question of it at a
```

later date, I can say that I got it from
my husband, that he told me to. And if
I'm asked what he wanted it for, I can
say he didn't appreciate being asked
questions. He always told me not to
question him, just do what I was told
(which is true actually). In addition if
there's a FedEx record of the envelope,
I will say that I was asked at work to
send it. I don't know what it was. What
do you think?

Might never come to that anyway.
Hopefully not anyway . . .

OK then, I'm 90pc decided to go ahead
with it. I know you want me to leave it
to you and not question you, but I can't
help it.

I'm still caught here with my sister
and her husband. I was hoping that you
could ring me tonight, but I don't want
them to see me checking emails and I
don't want to seem impatient with them.
As you said, I want to act normal. Can
you email me your telephone number and I
will ring you when I can?

If you're going to Spain, you will have
to fly to Malaga. I forgot to tell you
that.

Anyway, I was just talking to my
husband. The couple with the apartment

next door to ours will not be in their
apartment. They will either be on their
own boat or gone home to Ireland. I'll
know when I get there on Wed night.

My husband plans for us to take a boat
trip to Puerto Banus on Friday and stay
there until Sunday or Monday. In any
case, he will surely have to return to
his apartment after he gets the 'sad'
news of his sons!

I will be able to give you my Spanish
mobile number and if you get yourself a
Spanish phone when you get there you
will be able to text me and then I'd be
able to tell you what we are doing. I
probably wouldn't have access to the
internet most of the time.

I'm still not in a position to talk on
the phone, but hopefully in a while. I
have visitors staying in the house and I
need total privacy to talk.

I'm assuming your people will put that
substance in the guys' drink. Is that
it?

Tony, as I said before, nearly every
weekend, those guys go to Kilkee, on the
west of County Clare. They spend a lot
of time in a bar there and they also go
boating. But there is absolutely no
guarantee that they will be there next

```
weekend. Occasionally they go to visit
cousins of theirs at the other side of
the country. I can't think of the name
of the place right now, but it will come
to me. The country is small, so no
matter where they are, it's only a few
hours away. I assume this will not be a
problem? I will do my best this week to
find out what they intend doing and will
email you as soon as I can, so your
people can make alternative hotel
reservations.
   Do you still intend travelling to Spain
yourself? It's quite a distance for you
to have to travel. I don't think there
are any direct flights between the US
and Malaga.
```

But by August 14, Tony was getting tired of the small talk. He wrote: 'Time is running out, we have to know where we at . . . If you can't send the money today forget about it . . . it will be too late. My people not wait . . . plus I will pay them the rest from my pocket till you pay me after the job done . . . now it's up to you . . . sorry but I have to give them the green light and I can't if no money sorry the pressure on me.

'By the way you have a nice voice . . . sorry to say that.'

Lying Eyes tried to reassure him:

```
I will be sending the money later today.
```

332

It's 11am here now so once I get the
envelope to FedEx by 5pm today, we're
OK.

Will you email the address for
delivery?

I'm at work right now — have to behave
as normal and when I'm sent to the bank
later, I will sort out the money. Don't
worry I'm going to do it. I've decided.

I also need to spend some time here
with one of the sons to find out what he
will be doing next weekend. Will let you
know as soon as I do.

Thanks for your phone number — will you
email me the correct prefix.

Tony was placated. He wanted to be told if the money
was FedExed or lodged: 'I want know what we are
looking for . . . I will talk to you later sweetie.'
Lying Eyes replied:

I've decided to parcel up the money and
send it that way. I will probably put
something else in with it to make it
look like a present.

I'll also put in the photos and the
keys.

I'll email you the address, combination
and directions etc.

Just busy at work right now and under

```
pressure to get everything done so I can
get away early to send off the parcel.
   Will email you later and let you know
the tracking number etc.
```

Tony was back to his old charming self: 'I guess from your voice no one can touch you and I guess you are beautiful too . . . sorry to say there is no way to me or anyone killing you . . . I hope we receive by Thursday . . . I will try to email you my pic but don't make fun of me.'
Lying Eyes couldn't wait to respond:

```
Finally I have a chance to email with no
one breathing down my neck. Again, I
must apologize for not being able to
take your calls tonight. I thought I'd
be on my own, but my son who is 20 came
home much earlier than I expected. He's
a good kid and said he wanted to spend
some quality time with me, as I'm going
away on Wednesday. We were watching a
movie and chatting, and at the same
time, I was trying to email you, but as
I said, we are always having problems
with internet connections at the house,
so I lost the very long email that I had
hoped to send you.
   Anyway, what I was saying was, thank
you for the photos. Your daughter is
beautiful and clearly loves her dad and
```

you're very handsome yourself. Italian of course!

I had to smile when I saw your photos — for as long as I can remember I've been saying that I would love a sexy, yellow sports car . . . and as I've always wanted to visit Las Vegas . . . maybe, you'll take me for a ride in yours, if I ever get there! Now, that's cheeky isn't it?!

Anyway I was sitting with my son last night and thinking if he only knew what his mother was planning. He would definitely wonder if he ever knew me at all. My boys would be devastated, if they thought I would do such a thing. My other son is nearly 23 and works in Dublin. I miss him a lot. We are very close. In fact my boys are everything. I got married (for the first time) when I was 19. It was a disaster. There was no divorce in Ireland at the time, but I got an annulment from the Church and when divorce was introduced I got one. I didn't have to resort to extreme measures at the time . . . I can get on quite well with my ex-husband now. I think it's important for children that parents try to get along, even when the relationship breaks down. Otherwise, the children question their own worth.

335

I suppose you think I want to be rid of
my husband so I can get what he has?
Well, I do want to inherit — I want my
house and an income, of course I do. But
there's a lot more to it than that. For
one thing, he resents any time I spend
with my boys and tried to keep me away
from them. That's a reason why my son
wanted to take advantage of being with
me last night, while my husband's in
Spain. My husband wants to control every
moment of my life and has a dreadful
temper. And he makes sure I have no
money of my own. But the main reason I'm
doing this is because he is continually
trying to force me to go out and pick up
a stranger for sex. He finds the idea of
it exciting and insists I must do it or
I'm out and he will make sure that I
have absolutely nothing. Well I will not
do that. No way! The mother of my boys
is not a slut. I think it's disgusting
that a man would want his woman to be
with another man. He never, ever stops
pushing for it. Frankly, I don't care
what he does. I don't mind if he has sex
with hookers or transvestites (of which
he is particularly fond) every day, but
leave me out of it. He has gone so far
that I'm at the stage now, when I would

be happy if I never had to hear of sex
again. I would be perfectly content on
my own now with no man. I certainly will
never marry or live with someone again.

You might ask yourself why I don't just
leave and sue him, but it wouldn't work,
believe me. I'm in a very vulnerable
situation. And because of the way he has
things tied up, I'm afraid his boys are
going to suffer now — and I really
regret that. I wish so much that it
didn't have to be like this, but then
again, I know that if my husband was
dead and they were still here, they'd
screw me anyway. In fact I'm sure of it.
So now I want to protect myself and my
boys.

Gee, Tony, I must be boring you out of
your mind. It's the last thing you need
to know. Sorry — I do go on.

To get back to business. I still
haven't found out where the guys will be
this weekend. They probably don't know
themselves yet. More than likely though,
it will be Kilkee.

Tony's replies were getting more and more flirtatious: 'I
bet you look so beautiful too. Maybe after we done the
business . . . maybe it will be my pleasure to have dinner
with you . . . you gonna pay for it? Hahahaha.'

337

Lying Eyes was flirting back:

Tony,
   As I said, I'm not sure which photos
were which while I was sending them.
   You'll be able to tell which one is my
husband . . . And I'm the devil in the
red dress!
   The photo with the guy on the left is
the younger one and the one on the right
is the older.
   I'm with them now so email later.
   Sharon

But without the money in hand, Tony was still edgy:

Hello Sharon
   You look so great I can't wait to see
you. OK, let's talk business . . . we
agreed before 50pc which is 45,000 and
we went down to 15,000 and now you tell
me after all done . . . sorry Sharon we
don't know each other yet to do that and
I'm sorry.
   I did trust you for the 30,000 and now
I feel you take advantage . . . that's
what I feel.
   So if I didn't receive the money or
some of them by Thursday forget about it
well! Email me the tracking number or

```
let me know within one hour what you
gonna do.
    Thanks.
```

But Lying Eyes knew it was only a question of time
before the money arrived and emailed:

```
Now I know for sure you sleep as I've
just been ringing you. Well, I'm glad,
I'll need you at your best . . .
    What I really need to know urgently is
where to leave the keys of the office
for your people and what name to put on
the envelope.
    I will not put the address in the
envelope with the keys, I will give it
out to you after you receive the money
and confirm the job is still on.
    But I will give you some details for
getting into the office:
    If they leave it until late, there will
be no one around (there is a cleaner who
comes on her own time, but not at
night).
    There is an alarm, so they must do the
following — two locks on the outside
door. It's not a very secure door
anyway. Light switch to the right of the
door. Straight up the stairs and into
reception. Sometimes the door at the top
```

of the stairs is locked, but the key is
always in the door lock. Light switch to
the left of the reception door just
inside reception area. Walk behind
reception. There are two doors behind the
desk and also an opening to a small area
behind the desk. The alarm is just
inside this opening on the wall . . . The
code is 5584. This turns the alarm on
and off. The computer that I am concerned about is the one at the reception
desk. No need to take the monitor or
keyboard, just the hardware left on the
floor under the desk.

It would be a good idea if the alarm
was turned on when they leave, same code
5584. And leave the door locked as
before.

There's a safe in the office, but there
is never much money in it. Just a few
hundred euro. I don't want it touched. I
just want it to look like one of the
sons took the computer themselves for
repair or something.

I've just saved everything important
for work on a CD and have it with me. If
I don't hear from you, in time I will
decide myself where to leave the key and
let you know.

There is something else I want done — I

want an email sent to my husband's email
address. I will give you the details
tomorrow.
 No time now. Trying to get ready for
this trip.

6

Stand By Your Man

PJ Howard had taken the stand more than a month before Sharon Collins stepped into the dock. The diminutive 59-year-old was impeccably dressed in a tailored, single-breasted grey suit, a blue-and-white pinstripe shirt, and a tastefully chunky blue tie. Sharon Collins's eyes widened as she took him in. PJ's grey hair was receding, his blue eyes hooded, and it was instantly clear from the way his chin was sinking even further into his fleshy thrapple that the whole ordeal was excruciating for him.

'You are a comparatively wealthy man?' the colourful state barrister Tom O'Connell asked.

'You'd wonder,' PJ replied, agreeing that there was no mortgage on his Ennis home or his Spanish retreat. He spent about half the year in Spain, he said, and Sharon was with him for three quarters of that time. But when he declared, 'It doesn't make sense to me at all,' tears began rolling down Collins's face.

'It's totally out of character and to be quite honest I find it very, very, very hard to believe . . .' PJ went on. Sharon was a 'far from greedy person. In the eight years that we've been together, Sharon has never asked for anything. I have often offered her things and she said no. If she is given €300 or €400 for herself, she would see if her two lads had enough. She would spend it on clothes and not save it.'

The character reference continued to glow. 'When I wasn't well she gave us a very good life.' She had looked after his medication 'for years'. 'We didn't feel there were any serious problems between us until this particular situation arose here. Up to that we were living quite normally.'

A flush began rising in Collins's face. Rooting a crumpled tissue out of her handbag, she began dabbing away the tears. She threw him a tragic look. PJ was playing a blinder. He had also written to the DPP for her, appealing to him not to charge her. Sharon's own letters confided how PJ 'keeps telling me that we will sort it out, but I'm frightened that we won't. We are desperate to figure out who and why someone would want to set me up in this way.'

He had been 'fantastic and . . . extremely supportive, but he has been told by the Gardaí that I have paid money to have him and his sons murdered. He does not believe it. I love PJ Howard dearly. He looks after my every need. We have a great life together . . . He is fantastic to my two sons . . . I would depend my life on him [*sic*]. I need him . . . I loved him and still do, very much. He is extremely good to me and I have always been impressed with the way he took in two teenage boys and looked after them.'

Sharon also wrote that she'd moved out of the 'family home' to protect PJ, who'd been getting pains in his left arm again.

PJ's solicitor, Michael Houlihan, and his sons have been putting him under enormous pressure to cut his ties with me. His solicitor even told him that he would stop representing him if he continued his relationship with me and Robert and Niall have argued with him several times. He told me that he never thought his sons would fall out with him until now. I can't allow this to happen to him. He has been so, so good to me and my boys for all these years. I have asked a friend if I can stay with her for the time being when I go home, to try and alleviate the stress for PJ and I have told him so. At the end of the day, if I am charged in relation to any of this, he will need his sons for support . . .

. . . If I am charged my relationship with PJ will be over – how could it possibly survive? As it is, I feel I must now move out so that he is not compromised and his sons will stop arguing with him.

But the relationship wasn't over. Here he was standing by her again, in the most public way possible – telling a jury that he did not believe she would have tried to kill him or his boys.

PJ also said that he had fully intended to marry Sharon, and the only reason he had not was to protect his sons' interest. They were running the family business now that PJ was increasingly taking a back seat. 'They were expecting to be left the business,' he explained. 'The business is too small to have it divided up.'

He said the only computer he had seen her use was a Compaq in Ballybeg House, and that he'd never seen her use the Iridium laptop, which had been stolen from the house after a party. He said after Sharon's son, David, had left for college he had never seen it again.

Having done his utmost to save her, PJ now left the dock. Sharon locked eyes with him as he shuffled back down the length of the courtroom and gave him a look of intense gratitude. But PJ's performance wasn't over. When he reached Sharon, he leaned forward to kiss her tenderly on the lips.

With the image sealed indelibly in the mind of the jury sitting directly opposite, only one other witness could create a 'checkmate' situation – and she was married to Sharon's co-accused, Essam Eid. Her name was Teresa Engel.

19 August 2006
Tony's latest email was not exactly inspiring Lying Eyes' confidence:

```
Hello Sharon . . . here's the deal please
don't call me a lot. We will call you
when the job is done . . . we can't find
the guys at all so we gonna do it at
their office . . . sorry it take [more]
time than we thought but the job will be
done just relax . . . we will let you
know as soon we done it.
    We change our reservation at the hotel
in Malaga to El Puerto, Costa del Sol I
don't know how but we don't care . . .
```

```
other hotel we will stay at Clare Inn
Newmarket on Fergus Dromoland in Ireland
I don't know how far from office.
  But we don't care either . . . Just let
you know where we stay at . . . After the
job done like we agree that we gone get
pay max the 3rd of August . . . I will
let you know where and how 110,000 euro
and $74,000. If we need info we will
call you . . . just relax be yourself and
lets do our job.
  Thanks
  Tony
```

Unlike PJ Howard, when Teresa Engel took the stand on 12 June 2008, she hung her other half, Essam Eid, out to dry.

In her late forties, the bushy-brown-haired American with large hooped earrings had nothing to lose by spilling the beans, having been guaranteed immunity from prosecution to tell what she knew.

When Tom O'Connell SC asked Engel if she had ever been in Ireland before, she explained that at the end of August or start of September, 'I was here to meet Ash [Ashraf Gharbeiah]. He was supposed to kill PJ and Robert . . . no, Robert and Niall, the two sons . . . Essam had a website, *www.hitmanforhire.us*. He got an email from Sharon to do a contract to kill PJ and his two sons, Howard, no, Robert and Niall. They corresponded. She sent him a down payment of like

$15,000. That would have been in August 2006.'

Engel said Sharon's email address was Lying Eyes and that she had heard Sharon speaking on the phone. 'I heard her voice. It was a very strong Irish accent. She spoke very fast. He kept telling her to slow down so he could understand her accent.' Engel was even at home when Sharon Collins's deposit arrived. She couldn't believe it, she said. 'The next stage was Essam getting hold of Ash and going through with it.' She and Ash had travelled to Ireland separately, she said. She came first to do a recce of the locations. She knew how to find Downes & Howard from 'directions from Sharon'. Ash met her there and had 'several medications that was supposed to cause a heart attack'.

But as the day wore on, Ash became convinced the plan wouldn't work, she said, and he went home the next day. She had stayed on in Ireland for a couple of days, before travelling to Spain where she collected a key to PJ's apartment left in her name at her hotel. Teresa was planning to check out PJ's apartment and to locate his boat and an internet café frequented by Sharon Collins, but she got sick and decided to go home. Essam was 'furious' and emailed the Irish embassy about getting a visa to travel to Ireland himself in a month's time.

On that occasion they'd brought ricin, a poison they'd learned how to make from an internet recipe, she said. But when they were actually in the country, they couldn't contact Sharon; she wouldn't respond to either phone calls or emails. Essam was beginning to suspect that Collins was trying to get out of paying the balance.

Sharon had left keys to Downes & Howard under a brick behind her son's house in Ennis, Engel said, and she and Essam collected them and entered the office to steal the incriminating computers, as per Sharon's instructions. They brought them back to their hotel – the Two Mile Inn, she said – hiding what they'd robbed in the wood behind the hotel.

Collins's and Eid's lawyers tried to undermine Engel's devastating information by ridiculing her. There were impersonations of her mid-American twang, which had been described as a deep, rasping, smoker's voice in the FBI files.

'Am I putting on my voice? No, this is my voice,' Engel replied to one question, looking confused. She leaned towards the mike, apparently unable to hear.

Engel denied that she had agreed to 'perform' in the witness box as part of her plea bargain with the US attorney, although she had pleaded guilty to separate fraud charges in the States.

'I know we don't make a lot of good television in this country,' Collins's lawyer said. 'But we often look at a lot of US television where we see lawyers making plea bargains and the like all the time, so we know exactly what they are.'

Engel described how she had been working in a Detroit casino in 2003 or 2004 when she met Essam Eid. At the time she was separated from Todd Engel. After marrying Eid, she had moved into his home with his ex-wife, Lisa.

'Isn't that a rather odd domestic arrangement or would it be considered normal in Las Vegas?' she was asked.

'It's quite bizarre,' Engel agreed.

It was put to her that *Hitmanforhire.us* was a scam to extort money from gullible customers, and never a real contract killing firm. The site was a piece of 'daftness' that would only attract 'a fool'.

'Who wrote the recipe [for ricin] as a matter of interest?' she was asked.

Engel couldn't recall, but she explained the process – boiling and peeling castor beans, then mixing them with acetone. They collected the powder in a contact lens case.

'You didn't test it on a passing mouse, or a porcupine?' the lawyer asked. 'You're not very good at your job, Miss Engel, are you? You've been caught every time . . .'

The courtroom erupted with a ripple of laughter. Essam Eid seemed to enjoy having his wife belittled more than anyone. But Sharon Collins was not smiling. She was scribbling notes and passing them up to her lawyers.

Monday, 28 August 2006

Private Brian Buckley stared open-mouthed at the email he had just received from Tony Luciano: 'Please help us out for this. I need some strong poison. One of us will be in Shannon. We cannot shift this stuff for security reasons – you know that – so please help us out. Will pay and I will owe you favour. Thanks brother. Tony.'

A month previously, on 29 July, the well-built, blue-eyed, 21-year-old soldier, who had only been in the Irish

Army for two years and was stationed in the Phoenix Park, had filled in a job application form for *Hitmanforhire.us* on a computer in his mother's house in Ennis. He'd been looking for cheat codes for his computer game Hitman, but he ended up typing, 'If you got work, I will do it.' He'd listed his skills as: 'Handgun, submachine gun, shotgun, rifle, sniper, heavy machine gun, grenades, limited poisons'. He'd given a false name, 'Will Buckimer', with his mobile number and a contact email address – *Judas69@gmail.com*.

On 10 August, Tony Luciano had first replied by email: 'I have a job for you if you are interested. Two males in Ireland. One in Spain. ASAP. Let us know. We will try to call you. Thanks. Tony Luciano.'

When Brian Buckley didn't respond, Tony had started ringing Buckley's phone. He'd answered once, telling Tony he had a wrong number. Tony kept ringing. Buckley kept ignoring the calls – seven in all.

And now Tony was on his way to Ireland and trying to rope him in to help execute three people . . .

Unbeknown to Buckley, two days after Tony's email asking about poison, Essam's pal Ash – Ashraf Fathy Gharbeiah, a part-time police officer in the Northville Township Police Department in Michigan – arrived in Ireland and hooked up with Teresa, planning to poison Robert and Niall Howard.

Essam, or Sam as friends called him, had known Ash for about ten years. They'd both worked in the tourism industry in Michigan. Ash had worked for a travel agency at a time when Sam was employed as a wholesale representative for Swissair. They were now close friends. It wasn't the first time Sam had approached Ash asking him to commit murder. He'd wanted to have his new wife's former lover knocked off at the end of 2005. Ash said he'd think about it but when he got back to him about it, Sam said not to worry, he'd found someone else to do it.

In the hotel bar in Shannon, Sam's latest plan was also going belly up, as the two personalities brought together clashed. Ash didn't like Teresa. He thought she was 'foul-mouthed', and 'vulgar', and ethically 'not right'. She had 'no respect for anyone, or anything'. He thought she wore the trousers in the marriage, and had more influence over Sam than the other way around. Before Sam had met Teresa, he could 'talk the talk, but not walk the walk'. After she came into his life, Sam had realized his dream of purchasing a Corvette.

Sam's previous wife, Lisa, was completely different. Ash believed her problem was low self-esteem, because Sam treated her like a doormat. He'd had a string of other girl-friends during the marriage, forced Lisa to partake in 'rough sex' and even in threesomes with Teresa. And Lisa had had enough. Ash had only visited the house once when the two wives were living there, and he found the situation extremely 'uncomfortable'.

Back in Shannon, Ash, who was a qualified emergency medical technician and worked for a medical company, had decided he could not go through with it. He found the whole situation too 'eerie'. Teresa believed he had brought several poisons for the job, but Ash travelled home the next day.

When Teresa got home, Sam was livid. He'd had the deposit for almost two weeks, and Lying Eyes was incensed he was not living up to his side of the deal, and growing increasingly impatient.

7

Achy Breaky Heart

Monday, 26 September 2006

A black-gloved hand turned the key and pushed open the office door of Downes & Howard, keyed in the alarm code '5584', and sealed the door gently shut. Only seven people had keys to the premises after hours: the owner, PJ Howard; his partner, Sharon; PJ's two sons; a cleaner; a handyman; and the firm's accountant. And now someone else . . .

The office was empty as predicted, so there was no need to wear the balaclava or wig. The intruder headed straight to the reception desk and bundled the Advent desktop computer, its keyboard and cable into a black canvas bag. Robert Howard's blue Toshiba laptop was on the desk as predicted, and it was fired into the bag too, along with a digital clock out of the wall. One last-minute glance around before a quick doubling back to lift a poster of old Irish currency off the wall, which might have some value – money having a particular place in the burglar's heart.

Tony Luciano tried to contact Lying Eyes to tell her everything was going according to plan. But Lying Eyes wasn't answering the phone. Nobody double-crossed Tony Luciano.

In the witness box, Sharon Collins's composure had finally cracked. Tears rolled down her face as she began to crumble under Ní Raifeartaigh's relentless cross-examination. The suggestion that the letters she had so painstakingly written to the DPP were not heartfelt but an exercise in manipulation had proved the last straw. 'I had been hauled out of my home,' she sobbed, indignantly. 'I was questioned at length at the Garda station. I was kept overnight. All kinds of allegations were thrown at me about things I would never do. I was out of my home, my family was in bits, I was absolutely shattered. I was not trying to be manipulative; I was trying to explain the damage that was done to me.'

Perched under his wine-coloured canopy, Judge Roderick Murphy looked over the top of his round spectacles and enquired if the defendant needed a break. Sharon Collins shook her head. She pointed to the stenographer's tissues and asked weakly, 'Can I have one of those?' The young female stenographer gave a quick nod, but kept her hands poised over her keys and her head craned away from Sharon towards the lawyers. After a prolonged pause, Collins stretched across the bench herself, pulled a tissue free, and began to blow her nose miserably.

Gary and David looked on rigidly, their young faces taut with the instinct to protect her. Ní Raifeartaigh's body language, as she swung at the waist and glanced around the court, suggested she was singularly unimpressed by the latest hold-up.

Collins wiped her eyes.

Ní Raifeartaigh believed them crocodile tears. Sharon Collins had FedExed $15,000 to 'T Engel', at Essam Eid's address, somewhere Collins believed Tony Luciano lived, on 15 August 2006.

Yes, Collins admitted, she had sent the money.

The money that secured the deal to execute the three Howard men, the barrister stated.

No! Collins replied. She had had no idea she was sending the money to a hitman, or to a Tony Luciano for that matter. She thought she was paying off a blackmailer. That woman's name was Maria Marconi.

10.35pm, 26 September 2006
'Hello, I'm Tony, I'm here to kill you.'

Twenty-seven-year-old Robert Howard stared at the swarthy-faced man with a bushy moustache and glasses in disbelief. Just five minutes earlier, the heavy-set Clare man had answered his phone to someone calling himself Tony Luciano, who'd said, 'I heard you lost a few computers,' and that he was about to drop by. Robert had thought there was something funny about the robbery at the office because the Chubb lock on the front door had not been forced and the alarm had been off.

Now, as promised, there was a middle-aged, foreign man on Robert's doorstep, dressed in a tracksuit and a navy baseball cap with the logo 'US Open 2000' pulled low over his eyes. But he wasn't talking about the burglary that had occurred at the office yesterday. He was talking about a contract to kill Robert, his father, PJ, and brother, Niall. Blood drained from Robert's face, as Tony informed him he'd been offered €130,000 to wipe out his family.

'Well, if you give me €100,000 I won't do it because I don't want to do it,' Tony said.

Twenty-three-year-old Niall Howard, just back from the pub, pulled the curtain aside to peer out the sitting-room window and see who was at the door. The brothers shared the house in Ballaghboy, Doora, in Ennis, with two friends. Their cars – a jeep and a BMW – were parked outside.

Niall could see his brother in the driveway talking to a man with a laptop on the bonnet of his jeep. He went out to the hall and listened from behind the front door.

Tony was babbling away to Robert in the manner of someone negotiating the sale of a used car. He was Algerian, he informed him. Tony had proof – Robert's Toshiba laptop stolen from the office, which he had in his hand. Tony said the other one – taken from reception – was back in the hotel. Both had been used to send emails, arranging the hits. Tony had photographs of the targets, which Robert managed to grab for a closer look. One was of PJ and Sharon, in which she was wearing a red dress, taken at a Christmas party in Dromoland Castle; the other was of PJ on his boat in Spain. Tony tried to wrestle them back. Robert retreated behind the front door and told Niall to ring the Gardaí before returning outside to Tony.

He was insisting the money be paid over by tomorrow.

He showed Robert the paperwork giving the directions to his house, without saying who had ordered the contracts. Robert took his time reading it, hoping the Gardaí would arrive shortly.

Lying Eyes had written:

The people you want information about are as follows: The family name is Howard. There is PJ Howard (57) and his two sons Robert (27) and Niall (23).

PJ Howard spends most of his time in the Costa del Sol in Spain. He has an apartment in Fuengirola, approximately 20 minutes from Malaga airport on the motorway. The address is the 14th floor, Torre III, Las Palmeras. This is a hotel and apartment complex. The entrance to which is beside the bus station and then ask the taxi driver to continue straight on to Calle Jac into Benevente. There is an entrance between Coyote Dance and Karaoke Video Café. There are a lot of shops in the entrance, with their merchandise on display as you walk through. When you go past approx 3 shops, turn left and the door to the apartment block is in the right. Any of the shop owners can direct you to Torre III.

PJ Howard also has a boat in

Benalmadena and spends most weekends
there on the boat.

Robert Howard and Niall Howard live in
Ballaghboy, Doora, Ennis, Co. Clare. To
reach their house, drive out the Doora
Road (beside the bus and railway
station). Turn left at the first
crossroads. The house is the 3rd or 4th
on the right. It is painted yellow with
a dark green trim. Robert lives in the
house, and Niall lives in the apartment
accessible from the back of the house
(basement). His girlfriend lives there
most of the time with them. They own a
Doberman dog. There are two other people
living in the house with Robert. They
rent a room from him.

Niall drives a BMW (small one) and
Robert drives a Land Rover. They also
have a house in Kilkee on the west coast
of Co. Clare. The address is 9 Byrnes
Cove, Kilkee. They usually go there at
weekends and often have cousins and
friends stay with them. There is a
possibility that they might go to a
seaside resort called Ballybunion in Co.
Kerry this weekend. Will find out and
let you know.

The Howards have a company called
Downes & Howard Ltd. The office address

is 7A Westgate Business Park, Kilrush
Road, Ennis, Co. Clare. Driving from
Ennis town in the Kilrush direction, go
through traffic lights at a co-op called
Coote, go past Seat Car sales on the
left. Then turn right into Westgate
Business Park — it is opposite another
car dealer (not sure of the name of the
dealer). There is a sign for John
O'Dwyer Hardware and other businesses in
the Business Park. Then turn right.
Various shop units there on left — go as
far as Aids to Independence, which is
the last shop in the first block and
there is a gap. The door for Downes &
Howard office is to the side of Aids to
Independence. It is not marked — no
sign. Just a timber double door.

There is a house on the Clare Road
(Limerick Road) in Ennis. Leaving Ennis
town, heading in the Limerick direction,
there is a filling station and car sales
called Estuary (Francie Daly is the
proprietor and his name is on a sign).
Immediately after this there is a turn
right — don't take it. Immediately after
that there is a blue house, then a
yellow house with a 'Sale agreed' sign
on it. The seller is Era Leyden
auctioneers. No one lives in the house.

```
Behind the house, beside the central
heating boiler, there is a concrete block
and keys under it.
  I will forward any further information
that you need as soon as I have it.
```

Robert looked at Tony differently after he'd finished reading it.

Tony seemed pleased. He said the Advent computer from the office reception, which contained email exchanges proving what he was saying was true, would be handed over once the money was dropped off. Call the police, and the contracts would go ahead . . . Robert tried to keep him talking, hoping the Gardaí would show, but twenty minutes had passed and Tony was beginning to smell a rat. He climbed into the car and sped off. Robert jumped into his own, Niall joined him and they took off after him, following successfully until it occurred to Tony to switch his headlights off. They lost him at the crossroads described in the directions.

The minute they got home, they rang their father in Spain to tell him what had happened. PJ was in the apartment with Sharon.

Maria Marconi was 'attractive, taller than me, about 5ft 7 inches, straight blonde, shoulder-length hair, sallow clear skin, brown eyes, little make-up, about 47, well-groomed . . . drove a yellow sports car . . . she had an American accent,' Sharon Collins recalled in one letter to the DPP.

'Your imaginary friend?' Úna Ní Raifeartaigh pronounced in the Central Criminal Court.

Collins was unfazed. The pair had struck up a friendship in January 2006, she claimed, after she'd received an unsolicited pop-up on her computer asking if she thought she had the talent to become a writer. Collins had filled in a form, and Maria Marconi emailed her to say she'd been assigned her literary mentor. 'Maria was a writer herself and had written several books under a pseudonym.' Collins did not know what they were.

Ní Raifeartaigh looked bored.

At first theirs was an internet-based relationship – Marconi would set Collins writing exercises, assess her work, and advise her how to improve. She became Collins's writing coach, teaching her how to write a novel, but over time the two became friendly – 'kind of like a pen-pal situation'.

After Collins's best friend had a baby born with Down's syndrome and 'too many problems of her own to be listening to my woes', she increasingly turned to Marconi for personal advice and trusted her as a confidante – telling her all about PJ's predilection for kinky sex. Following a row with PJ in April 2006, Collins wrote to Maria complaining about him. Later she told the DPP this email 'attacked him on every possible level as a man . . . I really don't want to expand more and I don't see the need, suffice to say that the last thing I would want would be for him to ever see what I had written.

'He said at this stage of his life he wasn't going to change. I suggested there was help to be got. It was an addiction and he would be a happier person if he dealt with it.' PJ said 'he was perfectly normal and that was that'.

Six months after the initial cyberspace introduction, Marconi communicated her intention to visit Ireland, and she dropped in to see Collins at PJ's business on 16 June, where they 'got on well', Collins claimed. When Collins offered to make coffee, Marconi asked to check her emails, and was left alone on the Advent computer in reception to do so. She stayed about an hour and afterwards Collins drove her around Clare, showing her the sights – Kilkee, Quilty and stopping at Lahinch for an ice cream – before bringing her home to Ballybeg House.

As soon as Marconi laid eyes on the property, 'She remarked that I should do well in a divorce or in the event of my husband's death and I replied that I would never divorce my husband and that I was only interested in my home and a reasonable income if anything were to happen to him. I told her that anything more would be too much like hard work for me.'

Collins brought Marconi inside, where she also asked to use the computer.

Some time after returning home, Marconi emailed to say her apartment had been robbed and her computer had been stolen. Collins worried that 'personal things' she had written to Maria, that she did not wish PJ to see, things she 'did not mean – exaggerated', written while 'pre-menstrual', were now out there.

On 8 August 2006 the blackmail plot started, Collins

said. She got an email offering to make her 'free and rich' for €100,000.

'I was abhorred [*sic*]. There were a number of these. I emailed Maria and told her about these messages. I wondered how someone could know my details or that of my husband. There was more than just the offer to kill my husband, there was an offer to kill his sons too. Then there were threats to kill my sons, or PJ and his sons if I did not pay. There were lots of these messages. I was very frightened by it.'

She didn't want to tell PJ at the time because he'd had a fall on his boat and was recovering.

Then another email arrived, Collins claimed, this one saying she should send $20,000 to prevent an email attachment being sent to PJ. It was the letter she'd sent to Marconi that April. She'd nearly 'died of shock'.

And she'd started getting unidentified phone calls from a man, Collins maintained. He'd demanded $20,000 to stop sending an email attachment to PJ containing identical extracts of what she had written to Maria Marconi about his sexual preferences. 'It was a copy of the email I had sent to Maria in about April. The contents concerned things which I had said to Maria about PJ which I didn't necessarily mean and which were exaggerated, but which I wouldn't wish PJ to see.' There was a reference to Collins's mother, described as 'a lively broad in pink', which she found intimidating.

Collins explained how she'd told the blackmailer she didn't have any money. She was told in no uncertain terms to pay up, or PJ would receive the email.

Collins went to Lough Derg on 8 or 9 August 2006, to 'pray about it and I naively hoped it would all be stopped by the time I got back'. But when she checked her emails on return, one said PJ would be contacted immediately if she didn't answer the mobile. Collins said she'd been 'stupid' because she'd agreed to send €15,000 by FedEx to 'T Engel, Camden Cove, Las Vegas, Nevada, USA,' to get the blackmailer out of her life. That's how her money had ended up in Essam Eid's house, she claimed. 'I should never have written that letter about PJ. I certainly never tried to kill PJ.'

She withdrew €15,000 and sent it to 'T Engel' as per the blackmailer's instructions.

On 19 September 2006, Collins claimed she'd received another email from the extortionist that said: 'You stupid bitch. Why don't you answer your phone? Do you think €15,000 will get rid of this?'

She tried to contact Marconi but discovered all her emails incoming and outgoing and her address book had been deleted. She never heard from Maria Marconi after that.

'I know it really seems crazy now to divulge so much of your life to someone that you don't know,' Collins had written to the DPP. 'But at the time, I didn't see the harm. I was glad of someone to talk to. I liked it that no one knew about her. I can't explain why.'

In the Central Criminal Court, Ní Raifeartaigh declared that Collins had realized the plan had gone wrong because 'T Engel' was Essam Eid's wife and the money she had sent her could be traced, so she invented Maria Marconi.

Nobody remembered meeting Marconi when she came to Ireland; there were no copies of the material Collins had produced in writing exercises; neither the Gardaí nor the FBI could find any trace of Maria Marconi in either country, or arriving and leaving by flight; and Collins had no contact details.

She exists, Collins insisted. 'The woman I met in June could well live in Ireland and I don't think her name was Maria Marconi . . . an American accent means nothing. She could have been local.'

So how did Collins explain the forty-seven calls from her phone to that of her co-accused, Essam Eid, aka Tony Luciano, in August 2006?

It was the same number Maria Marconi used . . . Eid and Marconi must have been in cahoots.

Ní Raifeartaigh reminded Collins that the secret FedEx number she'd received when she dispatched the money allowed only her to track its location en route to the Las Vegas destination. Whoever had input that number into the computer was also logging on to Lying Eyes' email, making them the same person. How did Collins explain that?

'I gave the FedEx number to the blackmailer,' Collins replied, so they could keep track of the money's arrival too.

But the Iridium laptop computer used by Lying Eyes to check the FedEx number at 8.10am on 16 August was in Ballybeg House, where Collins lived.

'The computer was missing from the house at the time,' Collins said.

'The internet dial-up times in Ballybeg House corresponded exactly with the times the FedEx number was checked,' Ní Raifeartaigh reacted.

'. . . It wasn't me anyway,' Collins said.

'Did anyone tell you there was a strange lady with an American accent in the house sitting beside the laptop? Was the mystery blackmailer walking around the house at the time?' Ní Raifeartaigh asked.

'I honestly don't know what happened,' Collins said. 'I have no explanation.'

'You are trying to ride two different horses,' Ní Raifeartaigh declared. 'When you realized the claim you'd been set up didn't cover all your bases, you created Maria Marconi.'

What happened 'has destroyed my life and my boys' life', Collins replied. Only once previously in her life had she experienced something equally devastating . . .

8

Rose Garden

When PJ cupped his hand over Sharon's to slice the wedding cake in Admiralty Lodge in Spanish Point, he'd grinned like the cat who'd got the cream. It was November 2005, and all the guests assembled believed they'd been invited to the five-star seaside resort to celebrate the happy couple's having exchanged vows in Rome the previous month. Nobody could have guessed that everything – the reception, the celebration, the toasts to each other's longevity – was all a front, designed to save Sharon face. She was still single.

Up until her trial, PJ calling off their big day was the worst thing that had ever happened to Sharon. She'd known he wasn't exactly jumping up and down at the prospect of tying the knot, but she'd never believed him capable of doing that to her, not after she'd told her friends and family that he'd proposed in January 2004; planned the reception in Dromoland Castle, where they'd celebrated her fortieth birthday just two years previously; and even planned a honeymoon in Sorrento, Italy.

Before they'd got engaged, PJ had always used the same old excuse for not wanting to tie the knot – it was im- possible because he was technically still married to his

367

ex-wife, Theresa Conboy. Although he was legally separated from Theresa, he didn't want to divorce his sons' mother, for Robert and Niall's sakes, and no amount of pleading or cajoling could make him budge on the matter. He hadn't even married Sharon's predecessor, Bernie Lyons, who'd died just before Sharon came on the scene. But when in 2003 Theresa also died, of a brain haemorrhage, Sharon believed things had changed and the way was now clear. She couldn't help feeling happy that Theresa was gone. She admitted to the DPP: 'I know that sounds terrible but it's true.'

When PJ proposed, 'I was over the moon, so was he,' she wrote. She craved 'security' and 'to belong'. But her happiness was short-lived when he changed his mind. She suggested another route. 'It was really the church side of marriage that concerned me, if the truth be told.' But as PJ learned from his solicitor that any form of marriage would affect his assets, and that a prenuptial agreement had no legal standing whatsoever in Irish law, the wedding Sharon had planned for 2005 was off.

PJ agreed to go to Sorrento but on holiday instead of a honeymoon, from 6 to 13 October. He agreed to go with her to the church where they were supposed to have exchanged their vows, to 'say a few prayers' instead. He allowed her to continue to wear her engagement ring, and he didn't object when she told friends and family that the marriage had gone ahead. He even went along with her wish for a wedding reception in Ireland, as planned, and didn't object when she issued formal, printed invites.

On 5 October 2005, just before they left for Italy,

Sharon did one thing in return – signing two legally worded documents, saying they were not and would never get married. One was for his solicitor, and the other she was to give to hers. Sharon signed, but didn't hand the document to her brief until after she'd been charged.

'I was as happy with this arrangement as I could have been had we been legally married, and he had nothing to fear with regard to his business,' she would tell the DPP. And since as far as everyone else was concerned they were now married, Sharon began treating the truth as if it were a minor detail, and PJ the one in denial. She tried to have her surname changed by deed poll to Howard, and when that failed because the form was not processed properly, she took a different route. A website, *Proxymarriages.com*, boasted it could supply a Mexican marriage certificate for $1,295.

She contacted the Irish embassy in Mexico to see how valid the marriage was, and got a curt email throwing a damper on her hopes: 'I have never come across a proxy marriage in Mexico and I strongly doubt it's possible.'

She learned she would need an apostille – a legal device that was a certification system for overseas officials unable to authenticate documents. *Proxymarriages* replied that they processed twenty to fifty marriages for Irish couples, and never had anyone been asked to produce an apostille.

Sharon emailed *Leonard@proxymarriages.com* to ask: 'What about inheritance? If one of us were to die, we are worried about our respective children arguing over whether the marriage existed?' However, despite her fears, she proceeded with the plan, sending emails from PJ's email account *P.J_Howard@eircom.net*, signing off his consent on his behalf, unbeknown to him.

Leonard@proxymarriages.com emailed PJ: 'We have tried several times over the past couple of weeks to ring you, but the calls were diverted to an answering machine. Sharon left a message over a week ago and again last night. I have to be honest, I am very worried and getting more sceptical as each day goes by.'

In any event, in November 2005 Sharon was married by proxy and received the marriage certificate, which was sent to her accountant, Matt Heslin, in Kilrush, because she claimed she didn't want PJ's sons to see the document.

And contrary to what the Irish embassy in Mexico had advised, Sharon was able to use her proxy marriage certificate to apply for a new passport in the Cork office, claiming her own had been water-damaged. A new one in the name 'Sharon Howard' was issued in February 2006, at which point she began using the name at every opportunity.

'It was a gesture,' she later told investigating gardaí. She wanted PJ to know she was happy to take his name.

Although PJ originally told gardaí he had not given his consent to Sharon to organize a Mexican marriage certificate, or known that she had used a copy of his birth certificate that he kept in the safe, he later relented. Sharon had rung him and reminded him that they had discussed the proxy marriage at the time, he said in court. But 'it was so long ago, I had forgotten about it'.

*

Tony Luciano rang Robert at 12.15pm in work the following day, 27 September 2006, to ask: 'What time are you finished work?'

Robert mumbled, 'The usual time,' still stunned.

'Have you got the money?' Tony demanded.

Robert said he had. Tony said he'd be in touch.

The next call was at 4.45pm. Tony wanted the handover to take place at the bus station in Ennis.

Robert said, 'No way,' and agreed to meet in the Queens Hotel. Tony told Robert to wait for a call.

At 5.40pm Robert was in situ in the hotel, when Tony told him to go to the ladies toilet where he was to hand the cash over to a woman who would count it.

Robert said no and hung up. He was very jumpy. Even with an attachment of gardaí forming a human shield around the hotel, the situation was still terrifying. He had no idea who wanted him dead. He didn't know what the hell would be waiting at the ladies toilet, even if the hotel was under surveillance.

Garda Beatrice Ryan and Garda Michelle Holian were sitting undercover at the bar, keeping a close eye on him. Outside, Garda Kieran Kelleher and Garda Albert Hardiman were watching who was coming and going in the car park. Detective Sergeant Michael Moloney and Garda Jarlath Fahy were also heavily involved.

Robert made a call and, after some reassurance that the hotel was heavily staked out, changed his mind and headed towards the ladies toilet. He needed to get to the bottom of what was going on.

A woman in her forties in a leather jacket and gloves, who turned out to be Teresa Engel, was also in the bar and made to follow.

Ten seconds later, Garda Ryan got up off her stool and headed in the same direction. Robert and Engel were talking in the hall outside the ladies.

'Have you got the envelope?' Engel asked him.

'Have you got the computer?' Robert asked, about the second one taken from the company's reception.

Engel spotted the plain-clothed Garda Ryan, got immediately suspicious and headed for the exit.

Essam Eid had been hanging around the car park outside, dressed in an anorak. Just before Engel emerged, he headed up the street towards a phone box.

Engel emerged from the hotel, saw him going up towards the phone box and began to follow.

The gardaí closed in.

During her stint in the witness box, Sharon Collins stole regular upward glances at the jury. Had the claim she was being blackmailed been enough to stir up some reasonable doubt? Did they believe PJ Howard? Were they aware of the significance of the evidence that backed up her version of events?

Collins must have been wondering how much regard the jury were giving to the alibi she had provided for 16 August 2006, the day the State claimed was crucial to the case – the day that marked the height of email and phone contact between Lying Eyes and Essam Eid; the day the money changed hands and the deal was sealed to kill the three men. For on 16 August, Collins had a witness to her movements.

Her builder, John Keating, dropped a bombshell in the court when he announced he'd called to see her at Ballybeg House at 10.30am on 16 August 2006, and that he spent the morning with her. After a cup of tea, they'd gone on some rounds – dropping into Brian Pyne's tile shop in Ennis, and to Collins's mother's house. Collins wanted Keating's advice about building a bathroom on to the house. She had been sketchy about the times but remembered he'd wanted to get away by lunchtime, saying, 'I'm not too sure if he wanted to get away so I wouldn't have him doing too many jobs.'

They'd also called to Downes & Howard but, as Collins was anxious to clarify, not for long enough to send any emails. 'As far as I know I went in there to pick up PJ's medicine,' Collins said. They'd travelled back to Ballybeg House together just before 1pm, and gone their separate ways.

John Keating recalled how they'd discussed the various jobs that needed to be done at Ballybeg House – there was a leak in the roof, and there was talk of adding on a conservatory. He said they'd then gone to Collins's mother's terraced house on the Kilrush Road, and spent about half an hour there discussing the building on of a toilet. In his opinion, it would be easier to buy a different house than to get the planning permission needed. They also went to Collins's old house, where she'd once lived with her ex-husband and which she now rented out, he said. Collins was considering adding two self-contained apartments to the site, and wanted Keating's opinion. The next stop was the tile shop, so she could check out some tiles for Niall Howard, who was building a house. Keating said the stop at the offices of Downes & Howard had lasted only ten to fifteen minutes. He concurred with Collins about the time they arrived back in Ballybeg House, just before lunch, claiming he left immediately and was home in Limerick by around 1.30pm.

The state lawyers reacted furiously to the suggestion that Collins was driving around Ennis with Keating at the exact times they were suggesting she was sending Lying Eyes emails to Tony Luciano. Keating's alibi had appeared out of nowhere; it was not included in the book of evidence.

Keating claimed he only remembered the meeting when he was contacted by Sharon's son Gary shortly before the start of the trial. Gary asked him specifically about 16 August 2006. Keating said he was absolutely certain that he had met Sharon Collins on 16 August as he had just returned from a holiday in England. Keating agreed to meet Sharon's solicitor, Eugene O'Kelly, in Bewley's on Grafton Street in Dublin, to provide a statement. Keating agreed that Collins had turned up too, and that she'd introduced him to the solicitor but had then left.

'Without notice to the prosecution, the defence has produced evidence seeking an alibi for Miss Collins,' Úna Ní Raifeartaigh complained.

The case against Collins was in danger of falling apart, and the prosecution applied to have the witness stood down until the Gardaí investigated the information further, and the judge agreed. The state had tried to rubbish Keating's story, claiming three different pens had been used in Keating's diary for 16 August 2006, but backed down on its assertion there was no evidence he had taken a ferry from the UK on the 14th.

Back in the witness box, Keating caused more mayhem, claiming the Gardaí had tried to intimidate him after he'd given the alibi. He said a female garda claimed she would have to handcuff him after he provided a partial alibi for Sharon. He said that he had been interviewed for over three hours and was asked a lot of questions.

The garda in question, Therese Flannery, denied the accusations. She told the court that it was her responsibility to marshal witnesses called to give evidence in the trial and bring them to lunch. She said she had gestured, holding her hands up as if bound, to indicate that they should keep together but had never said the name 'John' or used the word 'handcuffs'.

As she mulled over the way the jury was leaning, Sharon Collins might also have been wondering if they'd been impressed by the other witness she'd called in her defence – the one and only Gerry Ryan.

After being arrested on suspicion of handling stolen goods, Essam Eid aka Tony Luciano was picked out of an identity parade by Robert and Niall Howard in Ennis Garda Station on 27 September 2006. He would describe what happened next as 'the longest holiday of my life'.

9

Working Nine to Five

There was no mistaking broadcaster Gerry Ryan when he arrived in the Central Criminal Court to give evidence for Sharon Collins, on 1 July.

With his early background in law, Ryan was as at home in the Four Courts as in any radio studio, and he strutted into the witness box – hair slicked back and face set in the familiar fat-lipped pout – dressed in a suit befitting the sharpest of legal eagles, and a pair of glinting designer glasses that looked more like a rock star's shades. The enfant terrible of 2FM for the last twenty years reacted to the registrar's request to identify himself by stating his name dryly.

Everyone may have known who he was. But the big question was, what was he doing there? The shock jock had been parachuted in to give evidence while the prosecution was still delivering its case, meaning he had effectively skipped the queue, just because he had to catch a flight to London.

Collins's legal team fawned over him, describing him as 'the man who needs no introduction', and making great play of the fact that he would not be seeking any financial reimbursement for having turned up in court. But when he was asked if he remembered reading or receiving either of Collins's two emails sent to *grs@rte.ie* on 4 and 7 April 2006 detailing PJ Howard's predilection for kinky sex, Ryan replied, 'To the best of my recollection, no.'

Úna Ní Raifeartaigh was scathing. 'Why on earth was Gerry Ryan brought into the court to say he didn't see [Sharon's email]?' she later asked. 'Does it matter whether it made its way to Gerry Ryan or not? What matters is she wrote it.' Ryan had been summoned to court purely to 'feed the ego of Sharon Collins', the State's barrister lashed. 'She likes to be the centre of attention. She wants Gerry Ryan in there giving evidence, even though it bears no relevance.'

April 2007
Gardaí finally discovered the Advent desktop robbed from the reception area of Downes & Howard – in the boiler room of the Two Mile Inn in Limerick. The hotel caretaker, Christie Tobin, explained how he had found the computer in the bushes, wrapped in a black canvas bag, but hadn't told anyone because he was hoping to be able to bring it home as obviously no one wanted it. He'd put it in the boiler room to dry out.

In the witness box, Sharon Collins had done her best to portray just how far removed her life was from casinos, hitmen and poisonous plots to snuff out the lives of three people. During her evidence, she'd dropped mention of the constant caring calls she made to her elderly mother; how she'd nursed PJ through his illness; the fact that her boys, and PJ's, were the centre of her universe. 'I had a really good relationship with PJ's boys, they were like sons to me, I tried to be like a mother to them,' she said.

But the prosecution barrister had managed to turn even that around. 'Which makes it all the worse,' Úna Ní Raifeartaigh said. 'They trusted you, you're writing this about them,' she said, about Lying Eyes' emails.

Collins was now trying to fall back on the one single aspect of her life that could best explain to the jury who she was, and why she was such a fish out of water in this court; something she believed even Ní Raifeartaigh could not twist into something it was not – her annual pilgrimage to Lough Derg. Every year, without fail, Sharon travelled to the small island in Donegal, as confirmed by Monsignor Richard Mohan, who said he recognized her as a familiar face.

While her co-accused Essam Eid, and his wife who'd admitted complicity, were living a life of debauchery in Sin City, Sharon Collins believed fasting, walking barefoot and staying awake for twenty-four hours was a form of penance and atonement. Between 9 and 11 August 2006, she was throwing herself wholeheartedly into the most exacting of exercises in a place that the Catholic devout associate with purgatory. Eid and Engel may have been touting for assassinations on the internet, but Sharon was making the stony trek to the Stations of the Cross, barefoot. While Eid and Engel were debasing ricin from castor beans, she was praying with the other pilgrims at the first station – where Jesus stands before Pontius Pilate, who judged him for things he didn't do, and is shouted at by angry crowds who hiss and hurl abuse.

Collins did not need to spell it out. The look she was giving Úna Ní Raifeartaigh said it all. Did someone who could stay up all night, starving themselves and praying for good intentions, sound like the same person who could plot to murder three people?

As Collins put it herself to the DPP, 'I have always tried to ensure that I prayed daily – much more than that these days, mind you, as it gives me comfort and hope. I'm sure that there are a lot of good things I could have done and didn't do in my life, and also a lot of things I could have done better, but I never did anyone any harm, and never would, nor would I wish anyone any harm. I firmly believe that you reap what you sow in life and I am at a loss to understand why I'm being punished so severely at the moment with the threat of what might happen hanging over me.'

The state barrister was spectacularly unimpressed by Collins's attempt to brand herself purer than the driven snow. She looked at the jury as she reminded them that on the dates Sharon Collins was in Lough Derg, all phone calls and emails between Lying Eyes and Tony Luciano completely ceased. But as soon as Sharon Collins got back, communication recommenced and the cash deposit was FedExed shortly afterwards. And if Sharon Collins was such a selfless do-gooder, the kind of woman who put others first, where were all her friends now she needed them? Where were her two sisters, Maura and Cáit, a psychologist and a teacher, who had given evidence just before her? Why had they changed their names to Irish for court, if not to distance themselves from her?

'Oh, they're really into Irish,' Collins replied.

'I'd suggest that your sister, who was named here yesterday as Uí Liduihigh, is known locally as Liddy . . .' said counsel.

Where for that matter was PJ Howard, who was supposed to be standing by her? Ní Raifeartaigh asked. This was the most serious time of Collins's life.

He had been humiliated when the contents of an email she wrote to *The Gerry Ryan Show* had been read out in court, Collins said angrily.

The fact of the matter was the only people in court supporting Collins were her two sons, Gary and David. She and Eid, alone in court, were not so different after all.

Even the Lough Derg spin had not worked for Collins. Perhaps the jury twigged that her self-professed love of *The Da Vinci Code*, the book about the love child born to Jesus Christ and the prostitute Mary Magdalene, didn't tally with the image she was trying to portray of an old-school Catholic.

But if Collins learned anything from her trial, it was that the breaks were never of her own making. The biggest threat to the prosecution's case had come from within.

25 April 2007

A former UN weapons inspector in Iraq, Commandant Peter Daly of the Army Ordnance Corps, looked like a spaceman, kitted out in a biohazard suit, surgical gloves and breathing apparatus, when he appeared in Limerick

Prison. After he removed a contact lens case from under the bed of the evacuated cell of Essam Eid and organized a field test, the lens case tested positive for the presence of the deadly ricin poison. The tiny plastic container was then transported under escort to a military jet in Baldonnel, where it was flown to the LGC laboratory in Teddington, Middlesex, in England, which had a proven track record of testing substances for the Home Office. The lab was also developing the world's first chemical test for ricin.

Further tests on Essam Eid's contact lens case would confirm the positive reaction. He had brought the deadly ricin into the country, just as his wife Teresa Engel alleged.

The trial was well under way when Judge Roderick Murphy agreed with a submission by the defence that the discovery of traces of the deadly poison in Essam Eid's contact lens case could not be used. Collins's legal team had argued that they too should have been allowed independently to test a sample of the traces found. But now it was too late. The judge agreed this was not fair, and ruled the ricin evidence inadmissible. And as the State had already referred to the ricin poison in its opening speech, the jury would have to be discharged. The trial was on the verge of collapsing.

Sharon Collins became almost giddy and smiled brightly at her sons. The trial was adjourned until the next morning, for the State to establish if there was any of the original sample left that the defence could now analyse.

The next day one of the State's barristers, Tom

O'Connell SC, called to the bar almost thirty-five years previously, asked that Superintendent John Scanlan, who had headed the case, be called to give evidence. The superintendent told Collins's barrister, Paul O'Higgins, that the reason he had not preserved an extra swab in Ireland for the defence was because of concerns about the danger of the substance in question. The scientists who had analysed the ricin in the UK were then called to verify independently that they had established the nature of the poison.

In a dramatic change of heart, Justice Murphy then reversed his original ruling and declared the ricin evidence was admissible and the trial would go ahead.

Collins had come within a hair's breadth of walking free on a technicality. But as the trial neared an end, she was still convinced she had enough evidence to create reasonable doubt in the minds of the jury.

10

Sympathy for the Devil

The State's big worry as the trial drew to a close was that the one thing missing in a case chock-a-block with evidence was a body. What if the jury shared the mood in the public gallery? It was summed up by one middle-aged Dublin woman who came every day. 'I believe Sharon's guilty,' she said, passing around a bag of sucky sweets. 'But nobody's dead, and she has two young sons.'

David and Gary flanked their mother on the bench opposite the jury, day in, day out. The heavy-featured Essam Eid sat at the far end of the same bench, at the end nearest the judge. Normally reporters pack into the space where Collins and her sons were sitting. But in this case, a chasm of space yawned between the two accused.

Eid – alone in court and in the country – wore the same black Levi's, runners, Nike tracksuit top, and one of two shirts (with a preference for a pink one, sometimes worn with a blue striped tie). He low-fived prison officers who agreed to bring him outside for a smoke at breaks in proceedings, and tried stealing cheeky glances at Sharon, but she never acknowledged him. His reaction when he'd first laid eyes on her in Kilkee District Court just over a year previously had been 'I was cheated'. He'd spent much of her evidence with his head in his hands, looking completely and utterly defeated.

As she left the witness box and returned to her seat, Collins sank into her sons' arms and cried her eyes out, nuzzling their faces and nodding her head meekly at their whispered morale-boosters. Any journalist who tried to look in their direction was met with a steely glare that she held until they looked away.

'We are dealing with fools,' Úna Ní Raifeartaigh said in her closing address to the jury. 'But we are dealing with dangerous fools.

'Outside court, people are saying, "From a distance, this may look like a cheap thriller." There's a saying that the truth can be stranger than fiction . . . but this is a tragedy. It may not be a tragedy about dead bodies. It is a ridiculous plot between two people whose lives should never have intersected. That plot has managed to destroy lives. That's what's tragic.'

It had been an 'extraordinary' and 'bizarre' trial . . . with a 'mountain of evidence'. At times it had seemed 'incredible' and 'laughable' but 'underneath there is greed, callousness, deceit, dishonesty, hatred, love degenerating, corrupting into hatred . . . and manipulation, and arrogance'. If there was at times 'a feeling of triviality to it', or a 'bewilderment' because there were no bodies, 'remember that ricin was found in the cell of Essam Eid, and that takes this case out of fantasy and speculation. The case against him is overwhelming. It is open and shut . . . If this was a shakedown he would have come to Ireland without ricin.'

Contrary to what Sharon Collins had said ('it is your job to get a conviction, but I am not Lying Eyes'), 'that's not how the system works'. It's about 'hard facts'. Sharon Collins's 'vicious' emails showed 'the level of callousness' involved. She presumed PJ would never find out about the flights and hotel accommodation she'd booked for the hitman, because he'd be dead.

Collins's plot to have him killed appeared to have begun in the winter of 2005, when she organized a proxy marriage certificate. Sharon Collins 'wants to marry PJ Howard. PJ Howard doesn't want to marry Sharon Collins.' She tested out her 'con-job' marriage cert on the Cork Passport Office, and it worked. Collins's extra-ordinary sense of self-importance could be seen in her decision to call Gerry Ryan as a witness on her behalf, even though Ryan had nothing to say to advance her case. He hadn't even seen the email.

Three dates were crucial to the plot. On 2 August 2006, Collins had set up the Lying Eyes Yahoo address so she could try to hire a hitman anonymously, and at the same time she'd run searches for things she was interested in – travel plans, dieting, Reductil. The second important date was 8 August 2006, when Collins first contacted Essam Eid, aka Tony Luciano, and told him she wanted three men dead. And then there was 16 August 2006, the day after she sent the money to Las Vegas, when she checked the FedEx number, charting the progress of the package.

This third date was 'the smoking gun'. 'She can talk and talk but she can't explain that.' The computer in Ballybeg House 'is being accessed at midnight and at 8am', though

Collins said she didn't 'recall anyone being in the house'. Lying Eyes is also on the computer because 'Lying Eyes is checking the tracking number.' She'd been caught 'red-handed'. As the two plotters worked out the fine details in a 'very cold, very calculated and very businesslike' way, even 'haggling' over the price, a 'disgusting' flirtation began between them.

Dismissing Collins's alibi for 16 August, Ní Raifeartaigh said: 'Maybe [John Keating] is trying to do the best for someone in a tight spot. He likes her. They are friends. She has put a lot of work his way.'

Teresa Engel said she had travelled to Ireland with Eid at the end of September and brought ricin. But Eid couldn't contact Sharon Collins. He was 'furious'. 'The first mission had failed. Teresa and Ashraf called at the end of August ... Mission two: Essam Eid has to come himself in August and do the job himself.' But Sharon Collins isn't answering the phone. 'That's the turning point ... If she had answered, these two boys wouldn't be here right now and this would be a murder trial, not a conspiracy to murder trial, but thankfully Mr Eid has a short fuse.'

After Eid tried to get Robert Howard to buy out the contracts, Sharon Collins had to start covering her tracks. For the first time she told PJ about Maria Marconi, Ní Raifeartaigh said.

Fourteen points proved Sharon Collins and Lying Eyes were one and the same. The main ones were: Lying Eyes had used the Advent, Toshiba and Iridium computers in Downes & Howard and in Ballybeg House, where

Sharon Collins worked and lived; Lying Eyes called herself 'Sharon', used her mother's maiden name – Cronin – and knew the fine details about the Howards' movements; the phrases used in the Gerry Ryan emails, which Collins admitted writing, mirrored Lying Eyes' emails to Tony Luciano; Maria Marconi could not be found through the computers Lying Eyes used; Lying Eyes was in and out of Collins's personal Yahoo email account, and visited the sites she frequented; Lying Eyes had checked the FedEx tracking number for the money sent to Tony Luciano; phone calls to and from Sharon Collins's number and Lying Eyes emails corresponded with the key dates in the plot. Then there were the seventy phone calls showing contact between Sharon Collins's number and Essam Eid's number in August and September 2006. Eid's phone number was also called from the apartment in Spain. When Collins was on pilgrimage in Lough Derg, all phone calls and emails from Lying Eyes to Eid stopped.

The Howards' lives would never be the same, Ní Raifeartaigh said, because 'they got in the way of Miss Collins's greed'. And Sharon Collins's two sons' lives were also changed for good. They sat there every day 'looking crushed, angry that these things be said about their mother. She has betrayed her own sons,' Ní Raifeartaigh said. What she was asking the jury 'to do no more or less', she said, was to 'bring in a verdict according to the evidence'. She finished her closing argument quoting the infamous Eagles song about being unable to hide one's lying eyes, and that a smile is just a thin disguise; and from *Hamlet*, 'One may smile, and smile, and be a villain.'

Barrister Michael Bowman BL closed the case for Sharon Collins. He also brought up the phone records. Nobody took the time to pay any regard to parts of his client's story by going through the phone records, he said. On 14 July 2006, when Sharon Collins was in Spain, somebody made a phone call to Ballybeg House. On 13 July 2006, when Sharon Collins was in Spain with her entire family, somebody made phone calls from Ballybeg House to PJ Howard's mobile, Sharon Collins's Spanish mobile, Gary Collins's mobile and David Collins's mobile. 'Clearly somebody had access to the house.'

Essam Eid had called the Howards' family business from Ennis on 23 August 2006. Sharon was not there, but the call lasted seven minutes. On 2 August 2006, when the Lying Eyes email account was set up, Sharon Collins received a phone call on her mobile from the Downes & Howard office at 10.50am. If she was in the office, why was she being called on her mobile? There was another call on her mobile at 12.35pm from her mother. The State could have provided mobile phone cell-site analysis to establish exactly where she was, analysis which had been used in the Joe O'Reilly murder case, and which helped to find the decomposing body of missing schoolboy Robert Holohan in Cork, but this had not been done. If analysis had been done, it would also have proved whether or not Collins and Maria Marconi had travelled around Clare on the day Collins claimed Marconi had visited.

'Like a dog with a bone they picked up the idea [that Marconi was a fiction] and ran with it. Maybe they were delighted to be going back and forth to the US, working with the FBI. Nobody considered the alternative.'

The ricin evidence was automatically flawed, he said, because the FBI had not taken any photographs of what was believed to be ricin.

He said PJ Howard knew Sharon Collins a lot better than Úna Ní Raifeartaigh, and he'd said she couldn't have done it. He had written to the DPP on 23 March 2007 and said, 'I firmly believe Sharon should not be prosecuted. This was a scam by Essam Eid, Teresa Engel and Maria Marconi to extort money from Sharon.'

John Keating had provided an alibi. He 'is a man you can believe, a man who you can trust . . . He has been treated appallingly.' And once again, no cell-site analysis corroborating his and Sharon's movements had been done for 16 August 2006.

'She has been through hell and back. Her family has been torn asunder, she's been pilloried in the community, ridiculed in the media. There's a momentum in this case almost freewheeling to a conviction . . . Put the brakes on,' he appealed to the jury.

Essam Eid's barrister closed his client's case by describing him as a 'clown' and a fraudster but not a killer, in a plot 'worthy of the Coen brothers'. The bizarre scheme to kill a businessman and his sons was 'nothing but an internet scam run by clowns solely to extort money', David Sutton SC said. '. . . No one was killed here but no one was ever intended to be killed . . . They were there to do a shakedown, nothing else.' Eid had been used as a 'prop' in the State's bid to 'get' Sharon Collins. He had been made a 'patsy' by the prosecution. Sharon

Collins was 'the Great White Defendant', while Eid was 'the patsy being dragged along in the wake'.

Eid's involvement in the alleged demand for money from Robert Howard was questionable, Sutton said, thanks to Robert Howard's description of the man who had called to his door on 26 September 2006.

The State's case was based on identification, he said. Yet, when Robert Howard reported the incident to gardaí, he described a man who was 'clean-shaven and pale-skinned'. This did not tie in with Eid in the identification parade at Ennis Garda Station, where he was described as being sallow-skinned, with a moustache. Eid had stood out like a sore thumb in the parade because he was the only one with a moustache.

The lawyer also highlighted the discrepancy in the registration number of Eid's car in Ennis, which did not match the one given by the car rental company.

He poured similar scorn on the evidence provided by Eid's wife, Teresa Engel, the State's star witness. He questioned how anyone could believe a convicted fraudster, especially considering that she had sat in the witness box armed with immunity from the DPP, and a plea bargain in relation to her conviction in the US. He said Teresa Engel had produced 'what can only be described as one of the most self-serving and conniving pieces of perjury', adding that she had been caught 'like a rat in a trap'.

Engel sat here, Sutton said, with the 'stone face of a liar and is the person the State relies upon to tie together the whole case'. She was 'the shaky plank' on which the

State's case rested. The couple's hitman-for-hire website was simply a 'clownish operation, run by clowns in the hope of hooking fools'. Sharon Collins had sent $15,000 by FedEx to Mr Eid's address in Las Vegas, claiming that she was doing so because she was being blackmailed by a mysterious woman named Maria Marconi.

Sutton even imitated Teresa Engel's Mid-western twang as he mimicked her response when the money arrived. She 'couldn't believe it', he said, provoking laughter from the courtroom. He also told the jury that they should be cautious about the evidence of an accomplice. He said that the charges she had pleaded guilty to in the States were for extortion, not for murder.

The prosecution had never attempted to say that Mr Eid was the only person who had access to computers seized from his home and who used the *Hitmanforhire.us* website, he said. Insisting the case was based on this shaky premise, Mr Sutton accused the State of dressing up the murder conspiracy trial as the most important case on earth. The trial had more documents, more witnesses and more rows than any other case.

He insisted Eid had never intended to carry out any killings. He found it difficult to believe that in a country as 'paranoid' as America, FBI agents would not test a substance which they believed to be ricin poison. The FBI had contacted gardaí here after discovering a coffee carafe containing a white powder in Mr Eid's home. Yet it was not confiscated and the powder was never confirmed to be poisonous.

He said the main evidence the prosecution had that Mr

Eid was involved in a murder plot was the empty contact lens case found in his cell in Limerick Prison that had tested positive for ricin. Sutton told the jury that they were not being told that Mr Eid was actually in possession of ricin powder and had made it in his home in Las Vegas. 'There is no such evidence before you, and the State reporting Mr Eid was making it does not make it evidence.'

He objected to Robert and Niall Howard's sudden return to the Four Courts to hear the prosecution's closing arguments. The brothers were like 'live exhibits', who had been brought in 'to eyeball' the jury.

He urged the jury to acquit Mr Eid 'with justice and discretion', despite the 'self-serving poetry' of the prosecution's closing speech.

'They [the State] know that the conspiracy to murder charge is a bridge too far. Simple as that and nothing Teresa Engel would say could change that. She says the intention was murder. She hasn't a notion as to how this murder would happen,' Sutton said. 'I say it was a fraud operation from start to finish. It wasn't dial "M" for murder. It was dial "M" for money.'

As Sutton sat back down, Essam Eid rubbed tears of laughter away from his eyes. He had cracked up several times during his barrister's defence.

11

Fool to Cry

Monday, 7 July 2008

By his own admission, Judge Roderick Murphy 'raced' through the final part of his six hours of summing up. The trial had spanned three months, called more than ninety witnesses, and been one of the most expensive criminal trials in recent years.

Having advised the members of the jury to bring overnight bags when they returned after the weekend as they might need to spend the night deliberating in a hotel, he told them, 'You do need time to consider, and I don't want to put any of you under any pressure whatsoever. You will be cut off from the rest of the world until you reach a verdict.' He thanked them for their patience, reminding them they had ten charges to consider. Sharon Collins had been charged on three counts of conspiring to kill PJ, Robert and Niall Howard, and with three counts of soliciting Essam Eid to kill each of them. The four charges against Essam Eid were that he had attempted to extort €100,000 from Robert Howard to cancel the contracts on his life; that he had burgled the office of Downes & Howard; that he had handled stolen goods; and that he had conspired to kill the Howards.

The defendants were not obliged to give evidence, the judge explained. Only Sharon Collins had chosen to take the stand, and he reminded the jury, 'We are dealing with the presumption of innocence.' He described the concept of 'beyond reasonable doubt' as 'not a mathematical certainty or a moral certainty', but something of vital importance to the case the prosecution had made. Where there is a doubt, the benefit must be given to the accused. With that he asked them to begin their deliberations. It was a quarter to four in the afternoon.

At 5.15pm, tension rose when there was a knock on the door, but it was a request for a smoking break. They resumed at 5.40pm. The judge said they were not going to be sitting 'very late' in the evening but he wanted to give them more time for their deliberations. Then just before 7pm he called the jurors back to say he was not going to detain them any longer. He told them he would be recharging them in the morning with some matters that had been raised. In particular, there was one item undated in the email traffic and he asked them to return a number of documents. Then he sequestered them, telling them not to deliberate overnight, to 'relax, have a good evening, have a drink as well. You're entitled to that at this stage.'

Tuesday was a long-drawn-out day of deliberations. The jury looked irritable and angry when escorted on trips outside for smoking breaks. Two had holidays booked for later in the week, and it looked like they were nowhere near a conclusion.

Over the course of their deliberations they requested:

The video of Sharon Collins's interviews with gardaí. She was wearing a plaster cast on her leg, having just returned from a skiing trip.

The results from the UK laboratory that tested the contact lens case found in Mr Eid's cell in Limerick Prison. Copies of lab results were furnished.

The Advent computer stolen from the offices of Downes & Howard, which had been found hidden in bushes at the Two Mile Inn in Limerick, where Mr Eid had stayed with his wife, Teresa Engel. The computer was handed to the jurors.

Photographs of Mr Eid's Las Vegas home. This request was denied as the photos were not formally produced in evidence.

The letter sent to the Director of Public Prosecutions by PJ Howard. This request was denied as, although the jury had heard a reference to part of its contents, it was not formally produced in evidence.

Documents relating to a PayPal account opened in the name of Mr Eid's other wife, Lisa Eid, which had been used to purchase castor beans, a fundamental constituent of ricin, and a castor oil plant. The jury was told that these documents did not exist as evidence in the case.

A recipe for ricin that FBI agents had found on a computer in Mr Eid's house. This request was also denied because the document did not exist as evidence in the case.

The two accused passed the time very differently. Essam Eid dipped in and out of the Koran, occasionally chatting to the prison officers; Sharon Collins chewed gum and drank water, slouched sulkily on benches in the Round Hall, and was accompanied everywhere by her sons. Although her ex-husband, Noel, was there, she didn't spend much time with him. She told journalists they should not have referred to PJ Howard as her ex-partner in coverage of the trial. 'He's not my former partner, he's my partner,' she snapped.

Another night would pass before the jury finally drip-fed their verdicts. Twenty minutes after returning from lunch, they found Sharon Collins guilty on all three counts of soliciting to kill. The only other woman ever found guilty of soliciting to kill was 'Black Widow' Catherine Nevin, who had her husband Tom murdered in their pub, Jack White's, in Brittas Bay, Co. Wicklow. Eid was found guilty of handling stolen goods, and of attempting to extort €100,000 from Robert Howard, but not guilty of the burglary of the family business. The jury retired again to consider the rest of the charges.

Sharon Collins stared stony-faced into the middle distance as the news sank in. When one of her sons began to cry, she broke down. Her ex-husband and his wife, Fiona, quickly moved in front of them to shield them from prying eyes.

More verdicts came through at 3.05pm. Sharon Collins was also found guilty on all three charges of conspiring to murder. Two of the women in the jury were sobbing. After almost eleven hours deliberating, the jury admitted they could not reach a verdict on the conspiracy to murder charges against Essam Eid.

Collins's barrister asked that his client be remanded in Mountjoy Prison rather than Limerick, claiming she wanted to be close to her sons who both live in Dublin.

As he was being led away, Eid stopped in front of Sharon to ask, 'You want to have dinner with me when we get out?'

Outside the court, her solicitor, Eugene O'Kelly, read out a statement. 'I would like to say that the two persons who are most affected other than Sharon as a result of this verdict are her two sons,' he said. 'These are two fine young men that have displayed loyalty and devotion and love for their mother as they have stood by her in this trial, and their lives have now been shattered as a result of the outcome.'

The solicitor also made an appeal on behalf of the men. 'I would ask that they would be afforded the respect and privacy to adjust to the changed circumstances. These circumstances are entirely not of their making and they now have to move on, and I would ask that you would afford them the privacy and space so they can do this with dignity,' O'Kelly said.

He referred to his client's denial of all the charges. 'Sharon Collins has maintained her innocence in this trial. The jury has found her guilty. The judge has adjourned sentencing for the preparation of reports in relation to the verdict. It is inappropriate to comment any further at this stage.'

PJ Howard and his two sons, Niall and Robert, also issued a statement. 'We are relieved that this long trial has come to a conclusion and we would like to express our appreciation to the members of the jury for their patience and attention,' the statement read. 'It is appropriate to record our gratitude to the many people who have assisted us during this difficult period. We now look forward to getting on with our lives and we request the privacy that's necessary to assist us in this respect.'

On 9 July 2008 a red-eyed Sharon Collins was escorted from the Central Criminal Court to Mountjoy in a waiting prison van. Her story was about to take another dramatic twist. Once behind bars, the petite mum of two sought out, then threw her arms around the country's most notorious husband killer, the Black Widow, Catherine Nevin.

Onlookers watched in amazement at discovering that the prim and proper mother of two who had dominated the summer's headlines should be so ready to associate with the notorious Queen of the Joy. Having been shown into the recreation room of Cedar House – where Nevin is serving her sentence – Sharon Collins made a beeline for Nevin. The idle curiosity of other prisoners and staff present was about to turn into jaw-dropping fascination.

The infamous former owner of Jack White's pub, Catherine Nevin, murdered her husband, Tom, in 1996, and climbed to the top of the prison pecking order in exactly the same way she had befriended various influential people – a judge, a garda inspector, paramilitaries – when she ran a bar in Brittas Bay in Wicklow. Nevin had ingeniously managed to wangle a room for herself in the prisoners' favourite house. She'd claimed she'd been exposed to the Aids virus after being pricked by a hypodermic needle that belonged to King Scum Tony Felloni's junkie daughter, Regina.

What gripped the rec-room onlookers was not the fact that diminutive Sharon Collins should have turned up in the best place to acclimatize her to a sudden, dramatic drop in fortunes, it was the realization that Collins had already struck up a friendship with the country's most notorious female prisoner, on her very first night behind bars. They watched open-mouthed as short-haired Sharon, still wearing her black pinstripe suit and expensive perfume, went straight to the 57-year-old who stood up to greet her with outstretched arms.

'We meet at last,' Sharon said, finally beginning to cheer up.

A well-placed prison source revealed: 'It was incredible. They hadn't actually met in person before but it was pretty clear they had been in touch and really liked each other. They were all over each other, asking how the other was and catching up on stuff.' By all accounts it was a strange sight and it was about to get even stranger.

The tip of Collins's nose was red raw and her pale blue eyes bloodshot; her tinted moisturizer and lip-liner had long worn away. She was clearly still reeling from the shock of separation from her two sons and the multi-million-euro lifestyle she wanted to kill three men to keep. She'd gone from riches to rags, hero to zero on a long, wet Dublin afternoon. Her days of jet-setting between her partner PJ Howard's lakeside Ennis mansion and his Malaga penthouse and yacht were well and truly over. Home now was Dublin's North Circular Road.

As if things couldn't get any worse, she'd just learned she was to spend her first night in a room with the prison's most notorious lesbian, Tanya Lamb. It must have seemed like a black joke. Killer Lamb had been placed in the medical unit for her own protection after jealous flings with both Scissor Sisters, Linda and Charlotte Mulhall. Sharon Collins was told she would have to stay there because such was her level of distress, there were genuine fears she might harm herself. The composed, unflappable exterior displayed throughout the trial had finally cracked. The smiling Ennis mum who bounced into the Central Court each day, holding her paperwork flat against her chest like a barrister, had disappeared. In her place was a blotchy, trembling wreck. But the idea that Sharon Collins was about to be eaten alive behind bars vanished into the ether as she and Nevin chattered for hours about their cases.

An inside source said: 'We were like, "Who does this one think she is, coming in here all pally with Catherine Nevin and acting like she's someone?"' As the women's conversation unfolded, it emerged that they had become acquainted through some mystery correspondence. 'We don't know who wrote to the other one first but they have definitely been in contact with each other about their cases,' the source said. During her conversation with Nevin, the stony mask, so impossible to read in court, finally slipped. 'She couldn't believe she'd been found guilty,' the source said. 'That's what she kept going on about, she just could not believe it.' Nevin comforted her with assurances that she had grounds for appeal. And Collins played to Nevin's ego with questions about her own miscarriage of justice case.

In the course of their chat, Sharon also relived the electric moment when the jury first knocked on the door of the Central Criminal Court, signalling the start of their drip-fed decisions. Wife killer Joe O'Reilly had described that moment to a journalist sitting alongside as 'feeling like the sharks are circling'. But Sharon Collins said she just thought she was hearing things.

The source said: 'She was in bits talking about it. Normally you'd feel sorry for someone but people hadn't much sympathy for her. People realized there's more to her than meets the eye.'

Under Nevin's wing in the weeks and months that followed, Collins quickly found her feet. After telling prison brass she was being watched 'inappropriately' when taking showers, she managed to springboard herself into one of only two houses where there is no lock-up. The women's prison – the Dóchas Centre – is split into different houses. Cedar and Elm House are the preserve of prisoners who've earned special privileges through good behaviour, and for those nearing the end of their sentences, who are given a taste of freedom so as not to be overwhelmed upon release. Collins claimed she was being watched by a peeping Tom and got a room in Elm House.

A prison insider said: 'Sharon Collins has always been unpopular with other prisoners because she tells tales. But now the staff is also very wary of her. She's still wearing her high heels, as if she's got someone to dress up for. It's driving the other women prisoners mad, because when they hear her coming, they think it's the governor who is the only other woman wearing heels inside . . . She has convinced herself she's not here for the long haul.'

Amazingly, her prime target, PJ Howard, visited her on 12 August, arriving with her two sons, Gary and David, and spending two hours in close conversation. The property magnate – who had told the jury he didn't believe Sharon was guilty – was clearly still smitten and the couple held hands and kissed. Even PJ's friends, who had come out in force to rubbish Collins's courtroom claims about his private life, admitted they were stunned.

Former mayor of Kilkee in Co. Clare, auctioneer Manuel di Lucia, and Limerick businessman Bob McConkey had slammed Collins's 'pervy' sex allegations about PJ as utterly untrue. McConkey, PJ Howard's friend of twenty years, said: 'When I first heard some of the things which came out during the trial I was absolutely astonished. I have never seen a side like that to him and it is scurrilous what was said and I know it to be scurrilous.' Di Lucia, who has known PJ for thirty years, described the allegations about Mr Howard's private life as 'total fabrication and all lies'.

12

The Auld Triangle

Sharon Collins was sentenced to six years for conspiring to kill PJ Howard and his two sons. She appeared in court in October 2008 for her sentencing looking a million dollars. She sported a glamorous new hairdo and her skin shimmered, courtesy of a spray tan in the prison's beauty salon that resulted in the *Sunday World* headline 'TAN IN THE CAN'.

A prison source explained: 'The women prisoners get their tan done for court hearings, for visits from friends and family, and for parties. They were all thrilled when the prison purchased the spray tan machine, and a mobile tent for the beauty parlour. It's been a huge hit.' The cost of cosmetic products is a thorny issue for the prison authorities. In 2005, some €4,543 of taxpayers' money was spent by Mountjoy on items like make-up, hair dye, wax and body lotions. By 2006, that figure had shot up to €9,520.

Another aspect of her preparation involved getting an angel card reading from her close friend, Catherine Nevin. 'Catherine did Sharon's cards and told her she'd get a suspended sentence. That cheered Collins up no end,' the prison source said.

In any event, all the trouble was for nothing. The sentencing hearing was adjourned pending the completion of psychological reports, and the following month Collins appeared to have observed the *Sunday World*'s coverage.

On 3 November, she showed up without a hint of make-up, looking pale and washed out. She wore a lilac shirt, black trouser suit, and clasped her son David's hand as final representations were made to the judge.

Consultant psychologist Brian Glanville told the court he had interviewed Sharon Collins in Mountjoy, and believed she felt sorry only for herself. Under cross-examination from prosecutor Úna Ní Raifeartaigh, he said, Collins showed concern for her two sons but became most upset when talking about her own situation. He told the court he could not recall Collins ever showing concern for the Howards. 'As I understand it, her position is that she didn't commit the offences so remorse doesn't come into it,' he said about her refusal to take responsibility for her crimes. She had a passive, detached but dependent personality which could lead to conflict within relationships as she craved security but would feel herself to be stifled, he explained. He had visited her on two occasions in prison and she had been suffering from anxiety with major signs of depression, he added.

In a victim impact statement, Robert and Niall Howard said the incident had caused significant changes in their lives. 'The notion that we were made the subject of a contract to kill has affected us socially and emotionally. The degree of planning and the nature of the contract and the person by whom the contract was initiated, particularly in light of her relationship with our father, has exacerbated the situation for us. As the injured parties we have become more self-conscious and are constantly looking over our shoulders and are ill at ease.'

Robert and Niall complained the threat had also damaged their business reputations. 'The crime has impacted on our respective social and business lives. We are not as confident as we were and we feel that the respect that had existed among our peers in our business dealings is not the same as it used to be,' they wrote. 'Furthermore we believe this weakened the quality of our relationship with our father. We can't understand why we were propelled from our normal daily lives into such a national drama and shudder at the realization that had the plan been effected we could have been poisoned to death. It will take a long time, if at all, before we can put the incident behind us.'

In complete contrast, PJ Howard pleaded that Sharon be spared a prison term. He asked Mr Justice Roderick Murphy not to impose a custodial sentence, 'as I do not believe that Sharon poses any threat to my sons. I ask the court to consider how a prison sentence would affect her mother, her two sons and myself.' He added, 'Sharon has a very positive outlook on life and she was very loving and giving of her time to our extended families. Sharon always kept an even keel and I have never known her to do anything drastic over those years. She is a very straightforward and honest person and if she wanted anything she would ask.'

He said Collins had always handled his medication for

a heart complaint and he would always trust her to do this. 'I will not give up on Sharon,' he said. She was, in his opinion, 'one of the nicest people you could ever have been fortunate to know . . . a caring, loving and decent lady'. He would have 'no hesitation whatsoever in living with her again', he stated.

Collins's ex-husband, Noel, broke down in the witness box. He told her barrister, Paul O'Higgins, she had always been a good mother. He said she had never restricted his access to the boys when the couple split after five years of marriage. He said: 'Sharon has been absolutely fabulous – they have been two great boys. She is a great mother to them and has always been very supportive. But this thing has had a dramatic effect – mentally and physically – on both of them.'

He referred to the effect of the ordeal on her elderly mother, Bernadette Coote, who was also present in the court. 'She is a shadow of her former self,' he said, as she now shopped at night 'to avoid the gossips in the town' and had become a 'virtual recluse'. 'She used to be the life and soul but she's not the same woman she was a year ago.'

Justice Murphy also heard character statements on Collins's behalf from the mayor of Ennis, Peter Considine, and the Bishop of Killaloo, Bishop Willie Walsh, and several family friends. Pronouncing a sentence of six years, the judge declared: 'Clearly this is a matter of grave offence to the state, leaving aside the effect it has on the victims.' He said Collins had moved from using the internet as a source of information on inheritance and to gain a proxy marriage certificate into the fantasy of cyber-space where illusion and disillusion took over.

He gave her six years for each of the six counts she was convicted on, all to run concurrently. Collins appeared shocked and whispered in her son's ear. With her auto-matic right to 25 per cent remission and credit for good behaviour, she could be freed in three years' time.

Essam Eid was also given six years in jail for demand-ing €100,000 from Robert Howard as well as a further year for each of the two charges of handling stolen goods, to run concurrently. A plea of *nolle prosequi* (a decision not to pursue the indictment) was entered on the three charges of conspiring to kill PJ Howard and his sons, charges on which the jury had reached no verdict.

Outside the court, Collins's solicitor, Eugene O'Kelly, made a statement in which he said his client took great comfort from the fact that her partner, Mr Howard, had acquitted her. Collins had asked him to apologize to Mr Howard for the embarrassment caused by a letter to the Gerry Ryan radio show read out in court which did not reflect her views of Mr Howard and 'she regrets the use of that incomplete letter taken out of context. Ms Collins believes that the truth has got obscured some place in the elaborate set-up that is cyberspace.' He added, 'She feels she has good grounds of appeal against conviction.'

It was later reported that the DPP planned to appeal the leniency of the sentence.

PJ Howard has continued to maintain Sharon Collins's innocence. In an interview with journalist Mark Tighe, he admitted forking out €200,000 to private investigators to corroborate Sharon's story. He had even commissioned an artist's impression of the elusive Maria Marconi, so convinced was he that she existed, he said.

'America is rife with extortionists. Extortion rackets originate there. They can dream them up quicker than they can whack them out here . . . If I thought she was giving out private information about us, I would have murdered her myself.'

He went on, 'Can you see anyone sending off an email to Tony Luciano saying, "I want two marks killed"?' he asked. 'One in Ennis and another in Fuengirola, to look like suicide? And signing it Sharon Collins? You'd want to be mentally retarded to do something like that. I can assure you Sharon is not. She has a high IQ and could have been in Mensa. I don't believe she sent those emails.'

He also described the plot as being 'too perfect'. 'I have been in business buying property a long time, and I have never seen a deal run through one hundred per cent without any problems,' he said. 'These fellas [the gardaí] had a run like Jesus. They said to me they had never seen so much evidence against a person in their lives, yet they didn't find it unusual.'

He highlighted the ricin found in Eid's jail cell as exactly the type of lucky break that seemed just too lucky, considering it was there for seven months. 'Surely somebody would have noticed this contact lens case before that,' he said, adding, 'If you take the ricin out of this, there is a serious doubt about the whole case. Why do all this investigation over a couple of emails?

'There is something in Ireland that could finish this case,' he said. 'I will continue to look for [evidence] and I will find it eventually. . . . If I believed for one minute that Sharon did what gardaí say she did, I would run a mile from her. But from the moment our offices were broken into, and we heard of the American connection, Sharon told me it might be connected to Maria Marconi. Her story hasn't changed one iota since.' He had 'pushed her hard as to the truth', he said. 'I have spoken to her strongly about this story at various times, and we have had serious words about it, but at no stage has she ever changed her story.

'I don't think I'll be alive by the time Sharon serves her full sentence. I'm past my sell-by date already. I want to set things right before I go. I wouldn't live in Ireland with Sharon but, if she'd have me, we would live somewhere away from everybody.' It was his dying wish for her name to be cleared, he went on.

He has continued to visit Sharon in prison.

Epilogue

I managed to get my hands on a series of photographs of Sharon Collins in prison, some of which were published in the *Sunday World*. They gave the first real insight into how she was coping with her new lot in life. Everything about her – from the clothes she was wearing to the defensive body language – suggested a woman in denial, who did not believe she was there for the long haul.

Sharon was dressed in a scarlet V-neck top, pleated black trousers and trademark high heels. Her clothes contrasted starkly with those of the other prisoners present in the room, dressed in trainers and tracksuit bottoms. Her movements also appeared stilted, and she seemed to make her way into the recreation room like she was trying to avoid touching anything. The room itself resembled a hospital waiting room: various wooden and pink plastic chairs were strewn chaotically around a coffee table. After taking a seat, Collins folded her arms tightly across her chest and stared at the telly, making no effort to chat to the other prisoners. Perhaps her mind drifted to how much she had gambled and how much she had lost – for now.

Her plot to kill PJ and his two sons may have been one

of the most elaborate and far-fetched ever seen but she will probably one day acquire the wealth she craves. PJ has promised to wait for her, and she has without doubt driven a wedge between him and his sons.

Acknowledgements

The *Sunday World True Crime* series was the brainchild of editor Colm MacGinty, managing editor Neil Leslie and managing director Gerry Lennon. Neil Leslie edited the original series, and with art director Finn Gillespie turned the stories around against the clock. Sarah Hamilton tested early proofs for readability, and news editor John Donlon gave expert guidance on the essence of each story. Kieran Kelly covered all matters legal. Huge thanks to all!

To answer the phone afterwards from the legendary Selina Walker in London and hear her say she wanted the book was all a bit surreal. Many thanks for so much time and guidance, Selina. It has been a huge honour, and I've learned so much in the process.

Lauren Hadden edited *Blood Ties* meticulously, but her rigorous approach to the script was in complete contrast to her gentle manner and thoughtfulness – sending good-will messages from Lee Child and David Simon, which kept morale in the stratosphere rather than just up over many late, coffee-fuelled nights!

Even before Transworld Ireland had an office, or the *Sunday World* had a true crime series, Eoin McHugh wanted to know about the next true crime book in the pipeline, and his knowledge of the industry has been blazing a trail ever since. Am I glad we had that coffee in the Morrison, Eoin!

Thanks to Deborah Adams too, for the minute attention to detail.

The effervescent literary agent Sheila Crowley simply makes things happen. Thanks for the original leap of faith, all the work put in ever since, and for imparting so much incredible knowledge about the book world in the process!

'Thank you' falls embarrassingly short for my parents, She and Ea. They stepped in every single Sunday and at the drop of a hat during the week so deadlines could be met. None of it was doable otherwise. You know what I mean. In the same way, how do I thank Brian? For telling me what you really thought and then suffering the consequences, thanks!

Thanks, Al, for making my computer work again; and Siobhan, Mette, Gav and Eamo, Dolly and Sean – always on the other end of a phone.

Thanks, Vanessa O' Laughlin – for the thirty-minutes-from-preparation-to-stomach recipes (there's a book in that, Ginnie), and for offering to step in when things got especially manic.

Thanks to colleagues in the newspaper for their support during the writing, especially to Daragh Keany, the pictures editor, to Dave Dunne, and to Amanda Brunker for one particular piece of good advice.

There are other people who can't be named, who gave

the inside track in relation to each of the stories. You know who you are and what you did: thank you. Thanks especially to Charlotte Mulhall for agreeing to go public, despite being made to pay the price ever since because the authorities do not believe society can learn anything from asking killers to explain what happened.

An Interview with Niamh O'Connor

As a crime reporter, you must have seen some strange and terrible things. What for you personally has been the most bizarre story you've covered?

I'm lucky enough to have Colm MacGinty – one of the most instinctive editors in the newspaper business – as a boss, and Paul Williams as a crime editor, which means I have seen some really incredible stories over the years. It's impossible to single out any one story because when it comes to crime, fact really can be stranger than fiction.

I remember exposing a conman called Oliver Killeen, who claimed to be a psychologist from America. He put a plaque on a wall in Waterford with a string of letters after his name, and set up a practice which specialized in relationship, addiction and abuse counselling. At his peak he was earning £5,000 a week from clients' fees, seminars, relaxation tapes and columns he wrote for newspapers. In reality, Killeen was an unqualified former window cleaner, and a bigamist with fourteen wives, from Castlebar, Co. Mayo. Yet he got away with pretending to have a degree and doctorate from Berkeley, California, and Ontario, Canada.

For weeks after I broke the story, I would get phone calls from victims who would ask me tearfully if it was true and describe how much the breach of trust had affected them. Killeen's latest wife actually turned out to be one of his former patients. The worst part was that he had undermined several court cases because he had given, and was due to give more, expert witness about some of his clients' states of mind as a result of the abuse he had 'analysed'. Juries would have taken his evidence into consideration in deliberating their verdicts, and judges in handing down sentences.

Incredibly, years later, when a Granada TV production company began making a programme about his life and crimes, Killeen faxed newsrooms in Dublin to try to find me, then jauntily offered to give an interview because he said he remembered I had broken the story. In some strange way, he seemed to think he was rewarding me.

I witnessed a similar-sized ego at play on another story, when I doorstepped one of the country's most prolific paedophiles, Derry O'Rourke, shortly after he'd been released from prison. He was living in a remote place, under a pseudonym, and working as an 'artist' – selling religious-themed paintings, and exhibiting them at festivals around the country. He was also producing self-portraits! Just to put this in perspective: Derry O'Rourke was the former national and Olympic swimming coach who raped little girls entrusted to him over three decades. For five years after the revelations broke, he fought tooth and nail to avoid a court case, thus further adding to the victims' trauma. In any event, he got 109 years for his crimes, which he was allowed to serve concurrently over twelve. With remission, he was free after nine years. So it was with a real sense of responsibility to those victims that I knocked that door, knowing he had preyed upon children who'd had no voice, and that the mother of one had committed suicide out of a terrible, misplaced sense of guilt. Yet incredibly, when confronted, he displayed the same arrogance that had made him notorious. He behaved like he was a sports personality giving a media briefing. He coolly and calmly said he had a statement ready, and not to bother taking notes as he had copies he would distribute once he'd read from this typed sheet headed 'Statement of Derry O'Rourke', which amounted to a self-serving apology that claimed he couldn't say much for his victims' sakes. He refused point-blank to answer any questions and finished with a 'God Bless', having conveniently found God behind bars.

Another person who fascinated me because of the extent of

the double life he was leading was Robert Dignam, the former head of the Wicklow County Board. I exposed Dignam as a fraudster, swindling the banks through a bogus mortgage bureau, Abbey Mortgages. To prove the story, I had to go undercover with a hidden camera and tell him I wanted a mortgage. I said I had no job, no home, no savings, three kids and was single. Dignam boasted about his republican and gangland connections during our meetings. He furnished me with counterfeit documents showing false but ample savings in the bank and credit union, and offered to use them to draw down a mortgage worth €350,000. The story showed just how vulnerable the country's banking sector had left itself.

But I got a real sense of just how chilling the face of organized crime was after ending up in the nerve cell of a brothel network being run from an apartment in Limerick. Don't ask how! But what was absolutely astonishing was the efficiency of the people behind this particular sex-for-sale business. On the walls there were wipe boards listing the roster for the prostitutes, a timetable of their hours, the addresses they'd be working from in different towns and cities all around the country, and any pre-booked clients. Another listed flight details and the names and mobile phone numbers of girls to be collected from the airport, who were flying in mostly from Eastern Europe. At the reception there was a meticulous log of internet sites where girls were being sourced from different parts of the world.

So, as you can see, over the years there has been no end of surprises covering crime – from discovering that the female prisoners in Mountjoy were working on phone sex chatlines to having convicted murderer Catherine Nevin trying to call me as a witness in her miscarriage of justice case in the Court of Criminal Appeal because of a secret document published in the *Sunday World*, although I had written a book detailing the full extent of her crimes. But however strange you may think the stories thrown up in crime-writing are, there is nothing weirder than real life. I once interviewed a pawnbroker for a general feature, and when I asked him what was the strangest thing he'd ever been offered, he said, 'A pair of embalmed human feet'!

I believe you're now working on a crime novel. Will your day job as a crime reporter influence your fiction, and if so, how?

I've always been a huge crime fiction fan, and writing crime fiction is a dream come true. And yes, I wanted to merge the gritty, real stuff I see in the day job with something that you don't really get in true crime stories – a plot. With true crime, everybody already knows whodunnit from the outset, so the emphasis has to be on 'why'.

I wanted to take what I know about true crime and blend it with the suspense you get in fiction. My novel is called *If I Never See You Again*, and it's about a series of revenge murders linked to the kidnap of a crime reporter's daughter. I refer to real crime cases in the book, because when Boris Starling mentioned the real killer Colin Ireland in his novel *Messiah* I nearly jumped out of my skin. It gave the story an extra edge of reality that made the book even more terrifying!

The heroine of your novel is a detective attached to Store Street station in Dublin. Can you tell us more about her?

Jo Birmingham is a separated mother of two, who works full time. She is very good at both jobs, but has to battle the pervasive attitude that working women who have children either can't do their jobs as well as their child-free equivalents or must be neglecting their kids, and usually both. This makes her quite spiky. It's true that Jo has absolutely no spare time – her car is in desperate need of a valet, and she hasn't mastered the art of getting clothes out of the washing machine and into the dryer quickly enough before they need another wash. But when it comes to her sons – she's got a one-year-old and a teenager – she's a lioness!

Her situation is extra-complicated because her ex-husband, Dan Mason, is also her boss, and attached to the same station. I'm not sure if they are ever going to get back together properly, but I'm having great fun trying to work it out. I wanted to take some advice on this, so with nothing to lose I emailed Linwood Barclay, who wrote the brilliant *Never Too Late To Say Goodbye* and *Too Close to Home*. I asked him if he sticks rigidly to a plot, or lets the characters take him wherever they have to go. Miraculously, and very generously, he replied. He said he starts out with a plot in mind but sometimes the characters just take over and surprise even him. Once I heard that, I thought I'll just let Jo and Dan work it out between them.

And If I Never See You Again *is going to be the first in a series?*

Yes, and Dublin is as important to the books as any of the characters because it's a city undergoing rapid change. We've gone from the days of mass emigration in the eighties to sipping lattes and sending emails on BlackBerries during the Celtic Tiger and back to recession in the blink of an eye, and I want to record what the characters are witnessing and what crime says about the society we've become.

Weird as it sounds, I feel I owe it to Jo to show that women who work full time can be good mothers while also being brilliant at their jobs, and that sometimes they can be their own biggest critics. So just one book isn't enough to tell her story!

Thank you, Niamh O'Connor, for letting us see into your world as a crime journalist.

If I Never See You Again will be available from Transworld Ireland on 6 May 2010